This book provides research workers with the statistical background needed in order to collect and analyse data in an intelligent and critical manner. Key examples and case studies are used to illustrate commonly encountered research problems and to explain how they may be solved or even avoided altogether. Topics covered include: the differences between observational and experimental studies; the design of sample surveys; multiple regression; interrupted time series; computer intensive statistics; and the ethical considerations of research. This practical and well-structured book will be essential reading for researchers in a wide range of disciplines, including biology, anthropology, medicine and the social sciences.

The design and analysis of research studies

The design and analysis of research studies

BRYAN F. J. MANLY

University of Otago

CAMBRIDGE
UNIVERSITY PRESS

Published by the Press Syndicate of the University of Cambridge
The Pitt Building, Trumpington Street, Cambridge CB2 1RP
40 West 20th Street, New York, NY 10011–4211, USA
10 Stamford Road, Oakleigh, Melbourne 3166, Australia

First published 1992
Reprinted 1993, 1994, 1996

Printed in Great Britain by
Athenaeum Press Ltd, Newcastle upon Tyne

A catalogue record of this book is available from the British Library

Library of Congress cataloguing in publication data
Manly, Bryan F. J., 1944–
The design and analysis of research studies / by Bryan F. J. Manly.
p. cm.
Includes bibliographical references and index.
ISBN 0-521-41453-9. – ISBN 0-521-42580-8 (pbk)
1. Medicine – Research – Statistical methods. I. Title.
R83.S7M36 1992
610′.72 – dc20 91-788 CIP

ISBN 0 521 41453 9   hardback
ISBN 0 521 42580 8   paperback

Transferred to digital reprinting 2001
Printed in the United States of America

KT

'General impressions are never to be trusted. Unfortunately when they are of long standing they become fixed rules of life, and assume a prescriptive right not to be questioned. Consequently those who are not accustomed to original inquiry entertain a hatred and a horror of statistics. They cannot endure the idea of submitting their sacred impressions to cold-blooded verification. But it is the triumph of scientific men to rise superior to their superstitions, to desire tests by which the value of their beliefs may be ascertained, and to feel sufficiently masters of themselves to discard contemptuously whatever may be found untrue.'

Francis Galton
Quoted from *Quotes, Damned Quotes and . . .*
compiled by J. Bibby. Edinburgh: John Bibby
(Books)

To Helen, Nicky and Emma

Contents

CONTENTS

CONTENTS

CONTENTS

Preface

I wrote this book to provide research workers in the biological, health and social sciences with the background that they need in order to collect and analyse data in an intelligent and critical manner. The last thing that I wanted to do was to write yet another text for a first statistics course for undergraduates, since there are many excellent texts already available for that purpose. Instead, I wanted to produce the type of book that will be of value to people who have already mastered the material that is usually presented in courses of that type, and who are ready and willing to know more about the aspects of statistics that are likely to be most useful to the quantitative researcher.

Of course, it is a matter of opinion as to what aspects of statistics are likely to be useful to researchers, and these will not be the same for everyone. However, it is my belief that many books on statistics that are meant for non-statisticians tend to place too much emphasis on mechanical calculations at the expense of emphasizing the important assumptions, the problems that can so easily occur, and the practical application of methods. For example, there are many books that teach how to do a t-test to see if there is any evidence that two sample means are significantly different. I assume that the readers of this book already know this, and are more interested in knowing why a significant sample difference might not be valid evidence of a difference between the populations that are really of interest, or what conclusions they can draw if they know that the samples being compared are not random samples.

This is not to say that the details of statistical calculations are not important. If the calculations are not straightforward in the examples that I have used then in many cases I have provided all the details, including the original data, so that everything can be checked.

The particular aspects of statistics that I have chosen to concentrate on are the differences between observational and experimental studies, the design of sample surveys (including the control

xv

of non-sampling errors), encounter sampling methods, the many uses of the multiple regression model, the design of experiments both with and without the randomization of the experimental units to control and treated groups, methods for the analysis of count and frequency data, computer intensive methods of statistical inference, the question of what makes a study ethical or unethical, and the synthesis of the different components of a study.

Within chapters, I have used examples to illustrate the application of methods and concepts at the time when they are discussed. Also, at the end of Chapters 2 to 10, I have provided some case studies that are intended to demonstrate the value of the material discussed in these chapters in the context of important real-life research studies.

A number of people have helped me in writing this book. I would particularly like to thank Raechel Laing for allowing me to use her experiment on lockstitch seams for Case Study 7 and commenting on my description of the design and analysis of the experiment, David Harte for providing me with the 'Roadshow' data in Exercise (1) of Chapter 6, and Liliana Gonzalez for reading and commenting on parts of the manuscript.

Bryan F. J. Manly
Dunedin

1

Preview

1.1 Introduction

This book is intended to provide research workers with a guide to statistical issues involved with the design and analysis of research studies. The topics that are addressed are the potential for bias and misleading conclusions with observational studies, sample surveys, encounter sampling methods, experimental and quasi-experimental designs, methods of analysis with random and non-random samples, and ethical concerns. This first chapter is a preview to put the topics into perspective. To begin with it is useful to consider the different types of research study that can be carried out.

1.2 Different types of research study

An important distinction is between what can be called *observational* and *experimental* studies. In the first case the data are collected by observing some process which may not be well-understood. For example, hospital records might be studied to see if they indicate that the incidence of a disease is related to blood groups, or accident records might be used to assess the effects of changing traffic laws. A sample survey that is used to elicit peoples' attitudes to political questions or consumer goods is also a type of observational study from this point of view.

On the other hand, experimental studies are usually thought of as involving the collection of data on a process when there is some manipulation of variables that are assumed to affect the outcome of a process, keeping other variables constant as far as possible. For example, a psychology experiment might involve seeing how the reaction times of subjects changes after they have been given different amounts of a drug, keeping the temperature, time of day, etc. constant.

In many cases the same statistical analysis can be used with either observational or experimental data. However, as will be emphasized many times in the pages that follow, the validity of any inferences that result from the analysis depends very much on the nature of the data. An effect that is seen consistently in replications of a well-designed experiment can only reasonably be explained as being caused by the manipulation of the experimental variables. With an observational study the same consistency of results might be obtained because all the data are affected in the same way by some unknown and unmeasured variable. Therefore the 'obvious' explanation for an effect that is seen in the results of an observational study may be quite wrong.

This argument suggests that our understanding of the world should be based entirely on experiments rather than observational studies, but this is obviously not possible. Some experiments cannot be performed either because the variables involved are not controllable, or because the experiment is unethical. For example, suppose that a medical researcher wants to study the relationship between the levels of certain air pollutants and the incidence of cancer in cities. Changing the levels of pollutants in cities would then probably be beyond the ability of the researcher, and, even if it could be done, increasing levels on purpose would be unethical. Hence, the only study possible may be one involving analysing the prevailing levels of air pollution and cancer rates, with an attempt being made to allow for the possible effects of some other factors that are thought to influence cancer rates.

Although the broad distinction that has been made between observational and experimental studies is useful, a little thought will show that both these categories can be further subdivided in meaningful ways. There are various subdivisions that can be made, with one approach being the one shown in Figure 1.1 that was proposed recently by Eberhardt and Thomas (1991).

Eberhardt and Thomas were mainly concerned with environmental field studies but their classification is applicable to research studies generally. They begin (on the left-hand side of Figure 1.1) by dividing studies into those where the times and places at which events occur ('treatments') are controlled by the investigator, and those where events are uncontrolled. This is essentially the difference between experimental and observational studies.

Studies where events are controlled are further divided in Figure 1.1 into those where an experiment is replicated, those where an experiment is only carried out once, and those where the purpose of an experiment is to estimate the parameters of a model that is assumed to describe the process being investigated.

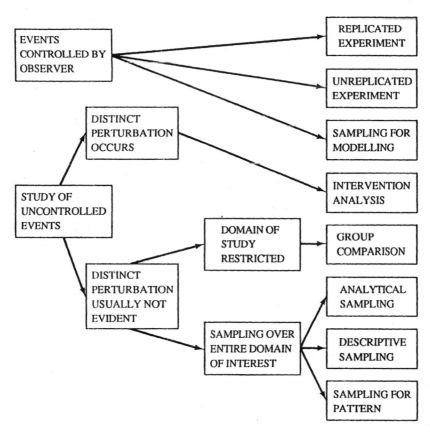

Figure 1.1. A classification of types of research study that has been proposed by Eberhardt and Thomas (1991).

When events are uncontrolled, Eberhardt and Thomas make a distinction between situations where some definite perturbation of the system occurs and situations where this is not the case. The first of these two classes of situation lead to an intervention analysis to determine whether the perturbation seems to have had any effect on measured variables. Since the data often take the form of a time series of observations, with the perturbation occurring at some point in the series, this type of study is also sometimes called an *interrupted time series*.

Four situations are recognized when there is no clear perturbation to the process being investigated. The first of these is where a comparison is made between different groups in a population as an alternative to a controlled experiment. Eberhardt and Thomas call this an observational study, but this seems too general a term for a rather special type of non-experimental study. Here, therefore, the term group comparison is used.

Three situations are recognized when a study encompasses the entire domain (population) of interest. These can be thought of as types of sample survey where the data obtained are used in different ways. With analytical sampling, comparisons are made between different subgroups to estimate the magnitude of differences and test for significant differences. This is like the group comparison, but without sampling being restricted only to the groups of interest. With descriptive sampling, all that is required is the estimation of certain population parameters. Sampling for pattern, refers to certain types of study where the interest is in the spatial distribution of a variable. For example, a botanist might be interested in whether a certain species of plant occurs in what appear to be random locations in a field, or a geologist might be interested in studying the distribution of an ore in an area.

The classification shown in Figure 1.1 may well seem rather complicated at first sight since the principles that are being used to classify different types of study have not yet been fully discussed. However, for the moment the main point to understand is that there are a variety of different types of research study that can be carried out, and that inferences that can be made depend on which type of study is used.

1.3 Bias and confounding in observational studies

As noted earlier, there are a number of potential problems with observational studies. Perhaps the most important of these problems is that a prima facie conclusion may be invalid because of the *confounding* effects of uncontrolled variables. That is to say, there may be no way of knowing whether an effect observed in the data is due to a change in the variable of interest, or is instead due to changes that happen to also occur in other variables at the same time.

Another problem is that estimates may be biased because of non-random sampling. Truly random sampling is often difficult to carry out, and there is a temptation to assume that a sample that is obtained in some convenient way is equivalent to a random sample. Unfortunately, however, it is then very easy for a systematic bias in the sampling procedure to distort estimates of key parameters to such an extent that a study becomes quite worthless.

A third problem applies in cases where observations have to be taken on groups of individuals, rather than on the individuals themselves. For example, dietary risk factors might be assessed by comparing a number of communities in terms of their rates of heart disease and the average amounts of different types of food consumed. If high rates of heart disease occur in those communities that have a high intake of certain types of food, then it might be assumed that eating these foods increases the risk of the disease. However, this is not necessarily a valid conclusion, and might be an example of what has been called an *ecological fallacy* (Robinson, 1950; Piantadosi *et al.*, 1988).

The terminology here follows from the practice of calling variables that describe groups of individuals 'ecological' variables. The potential fallacy comes about because it is easy to show that the relationships that apply to individuals within groups can be very different or even the reverse of the relationships that apply to the corresponding ecological variables. Therefore, it is possible for a community to have a high level of heart disease and a high average intake of a certain type of food, while at the same time the individuals that suffer from heart disease have a low consumption of the food in question.

The examples that follow illustrate the nature of these problems with observational studies. The first example, which is artificial, demonstrates how confounding can make valid inferences difficult even when comparing simple proportions. The second example, which is real, gives a stark illustration of how the 'obvious' effect of a treatment can be quite misleading. The third example shows that taking a large sample gives no guarantee that satisfactory results will be obtained. The fourth example demonstrates the nature of ecological fallacies.

Example 1.1: A sex difference in the recovery rate from a disease

Apart from confounding, this example also illustrates what is sometimes called *Simpson's paradox*, whereby a difference between two proportions disappears or even reverses when the proportions are considered separately for different groups of observations.

Suppose that hospital records from a certain city show there were 100 cases of a disease for men and also 100 cases of the disease for women over a certain period of time. The records also show that 46 men and 24 women recovered after one month of treatment. Thus it seems that there is evidence that men generally recover from this disease faster than women.

However, the 100 cases of the disease were treated in two hospitals, and the results for each hospital separately are as shown in Table 1.1. In both hospitals the men and women recovered about as well, so that there is now no reason to argue for a sex difference, although overall the proportion of women recovering in one month is much less than the proportion for men. The explanation for the overall difference is that the recovery rate is much lower in hospital B, where most of the women were treated, than in hospital A where most of the men were treated. In other words, if only the total results for both hospitals are considered then the difference between the two sexes is *confounded* with the difference between the two hospitals.

Even this may not be the full story since it does not explain why the recovery rates are so different in the two hospitals. It could be that the treatment is not as good in hospital B, but it is also possible that hospital B tends to take the more serious cases of the disease, or tends to take the oldest patients. Of course, if hospital B has more patients that are harder to treat, then it must now be noted that these are mainly women, so that the evidence for a difference in recovery rates that is related to sex returns again.

It is a sobering thought that Simpson's paradox may be involved whenever two or more proportions are being compared but in some cases there is no way of knowing how the data have to be separated in order to understand properly the situation.

Table 1.1. *Disease recovery by men and women in two hospitals*

	Hospital A		Hospital B	
	Men	Women	Men	Women
Patients	80	15	20	85
Recovered in one month	42 (53%)	8 (53%)	4 (20%)	16 (19%)

Quite apart from the problem of separating the effects of the sex of the patient and the hospital where the patient is treated, this type of study may also suffer from other difficulties if it is a retrospective study. For example, the methods for the diagnosis of the disease may have been different in the two hospitals during the period to which the data relate, and definitions of 'recovery' may also have varied. Generally with retrospective studies it is difficult to be sure that factors of this nature are not important.

Example 1.2: Fluoridation and cancer

A study by Yiamouyiannis and Burk (1977) has caused a good deal of controversy, since it purports to show that there is evidence that adding fluoride to drinking water is responsible for large numbers of people dying from cancer each year in the United States. However, this study has not been well-received by the medical and dental professions, with most physicians and dentists agreeing that there is no evidence that fluoride at low doses is carcinogenic. Furthermore, it is argued that the adding of fluoride to water has a greatly beneficial effect on the dental health of the population and should therefore be continued.

Part of the evidence presented in favour of the hypothesis that fluoridation causes cancer is the striking figures that are shown in Table 1.2, which compares overall cancer death rates in ten United States cities where fluoridation was started in the period 1952–1956, and ten 'comparable' non-fluoridated US cities. The fluoridated cities (Chicago, Philadelphia, Baltimore, Cleveland, Washington, Milwaukee, St Louis, San Francisco, Pittsburg and Buffalo) were the 10 largest in this category and the non-fluoridated cities (Los Angeles, Boston, New Orleans, Seattle, Cincinnati, Atlanta,

Table 1.2. *Cancer deaths per 100 000 population in fluoridated and non-fluoridated cities in the United States (Yiamouyiannis and Burk, 1977)*

	Fluoridated cities	Non-fluoridated cities
1950	181	179
1970	217	197
Change	+36	+18

Kansas City, Columbus, Newark and Portland) were the 10 largest with comparable cancer rates in 1950. The increase in the cancer death rate over the period from 1950 to 1970 was 36 per 100 000 of population in the fluoridated cities, compared to 18 per 100 000 of population in the other cities. Therefore, at face value the data indicate that fluoridation was responsible for 'excess deaths' at the rate of 18 per 100 000 of population per year.

An even more disturbing picture appears if results are considered on a year by year basis from 1940 to 1969, as shown in Figure 1.2. It seems that the two groups of cities had comparable increasing cancer death rates until the period during which fluoridation was introduced. From that point on the rate continued increasing for the fluoridated cities, but levelled out somewhat for the non-fluoridated cities.

Faced with the evidence in Table 1.2 and Figure 1.2, the average citizen may well feel concern about the continuing fluoridation of water supplies, and oppose the introduction of this measure in new areas. Yet the Royal College of Physicians, the United States National Cancer Institute and the Royal Statistical Society have all

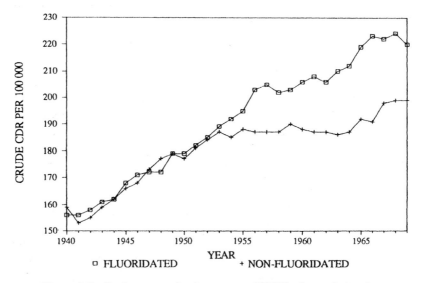

Figure 1.2. Crude cancer death rates per 100 000 of population for ten fluoridated and ten non-fluoridated cities in the United States, 1940–69. Fluoridation of cities took place over the period 1952–56.

concluded that there is no evidence that fluoride increases the incidence or mortality of cancer in any organ on the grounds that the apparent effect of fluoridation is confounded with systematic changes in the demographic structures of the cities (Oldham and Newell, 1977).

A hint of the problem comes from finding that the population in the 10 fluoridated cities dropped from 11.9 million in 1950 to 10.8 million in 1970, but during the same period the population in the non-fluoridated cities increased from 6.3 million to 7.3 million in 1970. This alone suggests that some trends in differences between mortality rates for the two groups may not be surprising since growing cities are likely to attract young people with low mortality rates. When in addition it is learned that yearly cancer death rates vary from about 4 per 100 000 for non-white females aged 5–14 years to about 1733 per 100 000 for white males aged 85 or more, it becomes quite obvious that comparisons between cities may be quite misleading if they do not take into account the age, sex and race composition of those cities.

In fact, if national United States cancer death rates by age, sex and race are used to calculate how many deaths are expected to have occurred in fluoridated and non-fluoridated cities in 1950 and 1970 then the increasing difference in cancer death rates between the two groups is easily explained by changing age, sex and race compositions (Oldham and Newell, 1977).

Another consideration that should not be ignored is the location of the fluoridated and non-fluoridated cities. This can be expected to be related to some of the variation in cancer mortality rates since, for example, pollution levels are not uniform over the United States. In fact, as Figure 1.3 shows, the fluoridated cities are mainly concentrated in the industrial northwest but this is not so much the case with the non-fluoridated cities. This raises the question of how comparable are the two groups of cities in terms of environmental changes over the period 1950 to 1970.

It seems on the basis of demographic considerations only that there is no need to introduce the idea of an adverse effect of fluoride in order to explain the increasing difference in cancer death rates between fluoridated and non-fluoridated cities. This does not prove that fluoride has no effect, since there is no way to do this with data of the type being considered. Fluoridation could have a small beneficial or adverse effect on cancer death rates that is completely swamped by other effects. However, there is nothing in the data to justify the claim that fluoride causes cancer.

9

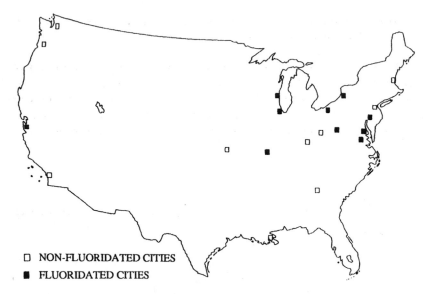

□ NON-FLUORIDATED CITIES
■ FLUORIDATED CITIES

Figure 1.3. Location of the fluoridated and non-fluoridated cities involved in the study of fluoridation and cancer rates.

Example 1.3: The *Literary Digest* poll of 1936

The *Literary Digest* poll of 1936 was carried out in the United States to determine in advance what was to be the outcome of the presidential election to choose between the Republican Landon and the Democrat Roosevelt. It is a classic example of a sample survey that went wrong.

A total of 10 million survey forms were sent out to people on lists of telephone subscribers, car owners, etc. About two and a third million responded and they were strongly in favour of Landon for President rather than Roosevelt, with a ratio of three supporting Landon for every two supporting Roosevelt. The election result was quite the reverse, with Roosevelt winning 62% of the popular vote and carrying 46 out of 48 states.

There have been various explanations of why this survey gave a result so far from the truth. Two obvious possibilities are:

    (a) That economic status was strongly associated with voting preferences, and also with being on the lists that were used for mailing

(b) That the voting preferences were different for respondents and non-respondents

One thing to note from this example is that an unrepresentative sample cannot necessarily be improved by making it bigger. The *Literary Digest* sample of over two million got a very precise estimate of the percentage support for Landon, but this was a percentage relating only to a small and apparently unrepresentative part of the entire body of voters.

Example 1.4: The correlation between income and education in the United States

In their discussion of the ecological fallacy, Piantadosi *et al*. (1988) gave a number of examples based on data from the Second National Health and Nutrition Examination Survey, which involved a 24-hour dietary recall questionnaire for 13 820 adults in the United States. From the survey results, it is possible to calculate correlations and regressions between many different variables, at a number of different grouping levels. Piantadosi *et al*. chose to do this at four levels: for individuals, for 64 primary sampling units (counties or county aggregates), for 34 states, and for six national regions. In this way, they demonstrated how results can vary considerably according to the level of grouping that is used.

As an example, consider the Pearson correlation coefficient between income and education level. For all 13 820 adults in the survey, this was 0.29. A similar degree of correlation was also found for individuals within primary sampling units, individuals within states, or individuals within regions. However, if average incomes and average education levels are calculated for each of the 64 primary sampling units and the correlation between these averages is calculated then it is found to be 0.60, which is about twice the value for individuals. For averages for the 34 states, the correlation is 0.67. For averages for the six regions, the correlation is 0.99.

This example shows quite clearly that correlations for group averages may be a poor indication of the correlations that apply for individuals. The same lack of consistency for values calculated with different levels of grouping also holds true for regression coefficients.

Piantadosi *et al.* found that, for some pairs of variables, correlations and regression coefficients for grouped data were lower than those for individuals and they note that in general there is no way of knowing which way the difference will be. They suggest for this reason that the proper role of ecological analyses (i.e. analyses on variables describing groups of individuals) should be only to generate new hypotheses that can be tested using more appropriate observational or experimental methods.

1.4 The sample survey

The potential problems with observational studies are greatest when the data that are available were collected for some other purpose at some time in the past. However, the problems can be minimized if a sample survey is carried out with the sole aim of collecting the required data, using a well-designed sampling scheme.

Because of its importance, the design of sample surveys is a specialized area of statistics. Important aspects are the most efficient use of resources through using such tools as stratified sampling and ratio estimation, and ways to keep non-sampling errors (the errors that will not necessarily be close to zero for large samples) as small as possible. Both these aspects are reviewed in Chapter 2 of this book.

There are times when a different type of sample survey is required because it is not possible to know in advance where or when the individuals in a population will be encountered. For example, the size of an insect population can be estimated by marking, releasing, and recapturing insects, and the number of polar bears in a region of the arctic can be estimated by flying in straight lines over the area and recording the positions of the bears that are seen. It is also possible to determine the density of trees in a forest by measuring the distances between trees and their nearest neighbours. There are many special sampling and estimation methods of this type, of which some are covered in Chapter 3.

1.5 Data analysis

It is inevitable that much of the discussion in the pages that follow is about the appropriate analysis of data gathered in different ways. In many cases the proposed approach involves using linear regression, and Chapter 4 is devoted, therefore, to a review of the theory and applications for this important method. Further general discussions on data analysis are in Chapter 8, which covers some special types of data that researchers will inevitably sometimes be faced with.

Research workers are often unable to take truly random samples from the populations that they wish to make inferences about. However, strictly speaking, the standard methods for statistical inference only apply with random samples. A typical response to this problem is to argue that the method of sample selection was effectively random and that therefore the standard methods can still be used. An alternative is to use a method of inference based on a randomization argument, as discussed in Chapter 9. This approach is also available if the data collected represent the whole population of interest so that the concept of a random sample is not even relevant.

Randomization methods are a subset of methods that can be described as computer intensive since they rely on the researcher being able to carry out large numbers of calculations in order to carry out an analysis. Chapter 9 also reviews jackknifing, bootstrapping and Monte Carlo methods, which are three other techniques within this general category.

1.6 Experiments and quasi-experiments

In practice, the distinction between experimental and observational studies that is shown in Figure 1.1 is often blurred because a study has only some of the characteristics of what can be called a 'true' experiment. To see why this is so, it is necessary to consider how the subject of experimental design developed with Sir Ronald Fisher's work in the 1920s and 1930s (see Fisher 1925, 1935, 1936) at Rothamstead Experimental Station.

Fisher was concerned mainly with agricultural experiments, where the researcher generally has the ability to control conditions to a very large extent. From his experience in this area, Fisher emphasized the need for (i) the randomization of experimental units to treatments, (ii) a control group, and (iii) replication, as being crucial to a proper experiment. Unfortunately, it often happens that a 'proper' experiment in this sense cannot be performed because the investigator is not completely free to manipulate the system being studied. It might be, for example, that certain conditions are predetermined, or that certain treatments cannot be applied, since this would be unethical. Nevertheless, a *quasi-experiment* may be feasible, where this means a study that has some but not all the properties of a 'true' experiment in the Fisherian tradition. The inferences from such an experiment may then be stronger than those from a purely observational study, but not as strong as what would be possible with a true experiment.

For example, suppose that there is some interest in determining whether a low salt diet helps to reduce heart disease. An observational study might then involve collecting data on the salt intake of a large number of individuals, and determining their record of heart problems over the next five years. This is a weak study, since it is always possible that any apparent effect of salt is really due to something else. For example, incipient heart problems may lead to a desire for salt. In that case the heart problems cause the diet rather than vice versa.

A much stronger study would involve randomly assigning some subjects to a high salt diet and some to a low salt diet and comparing the subsequent experiences of the two groups. However, this is not possible, since it is not ethical to give a treatment that is thought to be potentially detrimental to health (a high salt diet) to human subjects. Also, of course, subjects will tend to eat what they want, irrespective of what diet they are assigned in the experiment.

Given this situation, the experimenter might decide that a quasi-experiment is better than no experiment. It might, for instance, be possible to persuade some people that are initially on a high salt diet to change to a low salt diet for the duration of the study. Their subsequent experiences with heart disease can then be compared with the experiences of those who remained on a high salt diet, and those who remained on a low salt diet by their own choice. What is missing from this experiment is then the randomization of subjects to treatments. Still, any differences in experiences with heart disease between those who stayed on a high salt diet and those who changed to a low salt diet might be considered to be most likely caused by the change in diet.

The price that is paid for not randomizing subjects to treatments is the possibility of alternative explanations for treatment effects, due to some systematic initial differences between the subjects in different groups. For example, the subjects that could most easily be convinced to change from a high salt to a low salt diet might be those who were more health conscious to begin with. In that case the experimental group of individuals (those with a changed diet) may differ from the control group (those with the unchanged high salt diet) in many ways, any one of which might be the true cause of differences in rates of heart disease.

There are many standard designs for quasi-experiments, just as there are for 'true' experiments, and some quasi-experiments are better than others. The issues concerning strengths and weaknesses of different designs are conveniently discussed in terms of the simplest possible situation where the effect of a treatment is to be assessed by comparing the results for an experimental group receiving the treatment with the result for an untreated control group. This is done in Chapter 5, while Chapter 6 considers situations where the data come in the form of successive values in time series. Chapter 7 covers some more complicated designs for experiments to assess the effects of manipulating several factors at the same time.

1.7 Ethical considerations

Ethical considerations are of prime importance to the design of experiments involving human subjects, and are becoming increasingly important with animal experiments. Often research can only be carried out after it has been approved by the Ethics Committee of some institution.

A difficulty is that to a certain extent the meaning of 'ethical' is debatable, particularly with experiments on animals. Supporters of the animal rights movement will insist that no experiment that involves animal suffering should be permitted, but ethical committees may only insist that unnecessary suffering is avoided.

When using human or animal subjects, there must always be a balance between the importance of the experiment and the effect on subjects. For example, some psychology experiments may involve putting subjects in situations where they are under emotional stress. Then the experiment may or may not be justifiable, depending on the circumstances. When an experiment is considered to be justifiable, a common requirement is that the number of subjects used is large enough so that an experiment will have a high probability of detecting an effect of practical importance, but is not larger than is necessary.

Ethical issues, and the statistical problems that they pose, are discussed at greater length in Chapter 10.

1.8 Planning and carrying out a research study

A research study can be thought of as consisting of five related parts: deciding on the objectives of the study, choosing an appropriate study design with adequate sample sizes, collecting the data accurately and consistently, analysing the data with appropriate methods, and producing a final report that includes all the important details about the study. Each of these parts must be carried out properly to ensure that a study is successful, and therefore Chapter 11 addresses them in turn.

2

The sample survey

2.1 Introduction

A sample survey involves estimating some parameters of a population using a sample of items from the population. There are therefore three key elements in a sample survey: the *population* being sampled, the *sampling scheme* and the *parameters* being estimated.

The *population* is the collection of all the items that are of interest. For example, this might be all the hospitals in a country, all the patients with a disease now and in the future, all the wild cats in an area, or all the invoices processed by a company in a one-year period. Some populations, such as the hospitals in a country, are of a finite size that can be determined if necessary. Others, such as all the patients with a disease now and in the future are finite, but with an indeterminate size. In some cases a population is infinite, an example being the results that can be obtained by repeatedly tossing a coin and seeing whether the result is heads or tails (assuming that the coin does not wear out).

A *simple random sample* is one that is drawn from a population in such a way that all items are given the same chance of selection. This can be *with replacement* (so that an item can be included more than once) or *without replacement* (so that repeats are not allowed). For finite populations, sampling without replacement is preferable, since this gives slightly better accuracy than sampling with replacement. Therefore, for the remainder of this chapter sampling without replacement can be assumed unless something is said to the contrary.

As will be seen later, the sampling schemes used with sample surveys are frequently more complicated than simple random sampling. However, an element of random selection of items must be maintained if valid statistical inferences are to be made. The alternatives to random sampling may be easier to use, but they may give quite misleading results. Thus for a survey on a social question a sample of volunteers will consist of people who tend to be most interested in the question considered. As a result they may have rather unusual opinions. More generally, using a sample that is convenient can introduce severe biases in any survey.

The most satisfactory situation for designing a sample is where there is a *sampling frame*, which is a list of all the items in the population of interest. Such a list makes it straightforward to choose a random sample, and a good deal of effort in obtaining one will often be worthwhile. Nowadays, the selection from a sampling frame is often made using computer generated random numbers but physical devices such as drawing numbers from a bin are also possible.

The parameters of a population are numerical quantities that summarize information about the items in the population. Often they are means or total values of certain variables measured on the items, or proportions of items in the population that possess certain characteristics. These parameters can then be estimated using sample data in an obvious way. For example, a sample mean can be used to estimate the corresponding population mean.

Defining clearly the population to be studied is an essential first step in planning a sample survey. In doing this a distinction must often be made between the *sampled population* and the *target population*, since some parts of the target population may be almost impossible to reach. For example, the 'street people' in big cities are on no lists and have no permanent residences. Nevertheless, they are still part of the population of the city. Similarly, in considering the population of potential patients with a disease, there is no way to sample those not yet born. Studies should be designed so that the correspondence between the target and the sampled population is as close as possible.

There are three main reasons why a population may be sampled rather than a full census being taken:

(1) A full census may be impractical because of the cost and effort involved. For example, a botanist may just not have enough time to survey every plant in an area, and it would cost too much for a market research company to question every potential consumer of a new product

(2) Sampling is faster than a full count. For example, a government may decide to take a 10% sample of the population because the results of a full census would be partly out of date by the time they are processed

(3) Samples may be more accurate than full censuses

The third reason may be surprising. It comes about because often the largest errors in a survey are not the *sampling errors* (due to the chance effects of choosing units to sample). Rather, they are the *non-sampling errors* that are due to such things as biased sampling, mispunching data, questions not being understood, records being lost, etc. A relatively small but well-organized sample will often give better results than a full survey or a large sample that cannot be properly administered because of the lack of adequate resources. A classic case of a very large sample giving very poor results because of non-sampling errors was the *Literary Digest* poll that was described in Example 1.3.

In many surveys there will be some choice about the *sample unit*. For example a market research survey can sample individual consumers, households, streets, etc. Similarly, in a survey of the numbers of an insect that subsist on leaves the sample unit might be one leaf, one branch, one tree, etc. Often the choice of an appropriate sample unit is crucial for a good survey, particularly in terms of what units can be randomly sampled most easily.

2.2 Simple random sampling

A simple random sample of size n items has been defined as one that is drawn from a population in such a way that every item in the population has the same probability of being included. What is important here is the process of selection rather than the outcome. Therefore, a sample may be random even though it appears to be non-random because by chance all its items happen to come from a small part of the population. For example, if a random sample is taken of the women working in a company then it might be noticed that it seems to contain too many young women. This does not invalidate the sample since most small random samples have some appearance of not being representative.

If the individuals in a population can be numbered from 1 to N then one way to draw a random sample involves selecting n of these numbers using a random number table such as the one that is provided in Table 2.1. This table was constructed so that each of the digits 0 to 9 was equally likely to occur in any position, independent of what digit occurs in any other position.

As an example of the use of the table, suppose that a random sample of 10 of the 650 employees of a company is required. To obtain this, the employees can be numbered from 1 to 650. Next,

Table 2.1. *Random numbers*

684	036	858	674	550	784	109	915	489	457	170	748	222	005	778
183	826	530	932	474	120	875	604	283	701	217	987	237	967	760
658	136	145	905	976	713	298	793	922	354	044	447	660	696	687
890	048	222	906	750	752	076	675	350	739	361	994	853	047	130
364	084	991	135	345	426	248	324	539	797	142	249	871	928	252
141	488	347	426	345	844	709	017	427	560	276	463	073	169	755
470	368	217	575	914	919	249	586	361	994	088	087	149	216	462
344	221	084	477	592	113	300	177	806	799	102	181	902	348	474
799	625	643	135	354	522	733	168	936	218	756	249	938	783	968
621	900	624	423	080	879	647	244	866	635	183	773	755	267	005
512	150	490	898	462	590	580	802	565	999	593	237	046	708	863
204	472	639	692	424	184	863	351	087	818	890	268	770	540	344
087	760	154	382	053	655	282	661	853	222	108	526	768	510	595
107	936	419	609	667	471	881	348	835	707	489	619	711	893	598
502	008	458	817	788	517	810	623	762	203	739	380	545	348	452
800	785	499	978	739	394	234	491	165	852	256	230	804	711	055
599	031	361	246	230	341	047	168	542	887	225	717	697	263	973
896	356	830	896	658	166	639	498	040	873	183	022	152	178	688
908	487	130	719	985	268	321	703	320	777	601	963	534	423	006
591	969	684	998	953	607	474	264	353	139	105	025	957	498	736

starting at some arbitrary row in Table 2.1, successive three digit numbers can be chosen until ten different numbers between 1 and 650 have been found (treating 001 as 1, for example). The employees with the ten chosen numbers then provide the sample.

The pseudo-random number generators that are provided on computers and some calculators provide numbers within the range 0 to 1. However, if R is such a number then the formula $INT(N \cdot R) + 1$ will convert this to a random integer between 1 and N, where $INT(X)$ is the function that produces the integer part of the number X. In this way the random number generator can be used to choose a random sample of n items from a list of N items.

2.3 The distribution of sample means

If several random samples of size n are taken independently from a population then generally they will have different sample means,

$\bar{X}_1$, $\bar{X}_2$, $\bar{X}_3$, and so on. These differences are due to sampling errors, and an important question concerns how large this variation is likely to be. If the level of variation is 'small' then most random samples will give more or less the same result. If it is 'large' then the result obtained will depend heavily on luck. This means that whenever a sample mean is used to estimate a population mean it is important to know the level of sampling errors in order to assess the likely accuracy of the estimate.

There are three important facts to remember concerning the use of the mean of a random sample of size n units to estimate the population mean:

(a) The sample mean $\bar{X}$ is an unbiased estimator of the population mean in the sense that if a very large number of random samples of size n is taken from a population then the average of the $\bar{X}$ values obtained will be equal to the population mean

(b) For samples taken without replacement the standard deviation of $\bar{X}$ that would be obtained from repeated sampling, which is usually called the *standard error of the mean*, is

$$\text{SE}(\bar{X}) = (\sigma/\sqrt{n})\sqrt{\{1 - (n/N)\}}. \qquad (2.1)$$

Here, σ is the population standard deviation and N is the population size. The factor $1 - n/N$ in this equation is the *finite population correction*, which is sometimes written as $1 - f$, where $f = n/N$ is the *sampling fraction*. For samples taken with replacement the finite sampling correction does not apply so that the standard error becomes $\text{SE}(\bar{X}) = \sigma/\sqrt{n}$

(c) The *central limit theorem* tells us that for samples from most distributions the sample mean will tend to be normally distributed if the population and sample size are large enough

In most sampling situations the population standard deviation σ is not known, so that it has to be estimated from the available data. This can be done using the usual formula for the sample standard deviation,

$$s = \sqrt{\left\{\sum (X_i - \bar{X})^2/(n - 1)\right\}}. \qquad (2.2)$$

The estimated standard error of $\bar{X}$ is then given by

$$\hat{SE}(\bar{X}) = (s/\sqrt{n})\sqrt{\{1 - n/N)\}}. \qquad (2.3)$$

The 'cap' on SE is used here to indicate that it is an estimate of the standard error, rather than the true standard error. This convention of using a 'cap' to indicate an estimate is standard in statistics and will be used in a number of places in the pages that follow.

From result (c) it follows that if the sample size n is reasonably large (say 25 or more) and the population size N is 100 or more, then the sample mean will be approximately normally distributed for samples from most distributions, taken either with or without replacement. For this reason, it is common to regard

$$\bar{X} - 2 \cdot \hat{SE}(\bar{X}) < \mu < \bar{X} + 2 \cdot \hat{SE}(\bar{X})$$

as an approximate 95% confidence interval for the true population mean μ. It can be shown that for about 95% of random samples the interval calculated this way will include the true mean. In sample surveys, $2 \cdot \hat{SE}(\bar{X})$ is sometimes called the *margin of error*.

Some people use 1.96 instead of 2 as the multiplier of the standard error for a 95% confidence interval since this is the correct value for a normal distribution with $SE(\bar{X})$ known exactly. Using the factor 2 gives slightly wider limits to compensate for non-normality and the fact that the standard error is usually only estimated.

Alternatively, for a small sample from an approximately normal distribution, where the population standard deviation has to be estimated from the data, the multiplication factor can be taken as $t_{5\%,n-1}$ the 5% critical value from the t-distribution with $n - 1$ degrees of freedom (i.e. the absolute t-value that is exceeded with probability 0.05). The 95% confidence limits for the population mean are then

$$\bar{X} - t_{5\%,n-1}\hat{SE}(\bar{X}) < \mu < \bar{X} + t_{5\%,n-1}\hat{SE}(\bar{X}).$$

As an example of the calculation of a confidence interval, suppose that there are 200 people employed by a company, and a random sample of 50 people is taken without replacement to estimate the mean number of years that employees have been with the company. The sample mean is 2.7 years and the sample standard deviation is 3.5 years. The estimated standard error of the mean is then

$$\hat{SE}(\bar{X}) = (3.5/\sqrt{50})\sqrt{\{1 - (50/200)\}} = 0.43,$$

and an approximate 95% confidence interval for the company mean is $2.7 \pm 2(0.43)$, or 1.8 to 3.6 years. The 5% critical value from the t-table with $n - 1 = 49$ degrees of freedom is $t_{5\%,49} = 2.01$. Hence the 95% confidence interval based on the t-distribution is $2.7 \pm 2.01 \, (0.43)$. This gives essentially the same result as was obtained using the factor 2 to multiply the estimated error.

The 95% confidence limit is the one that is most commonly used. However, other levels of confidence can easily be obtained by changing the multiplier of the standard error appropriately. Thus the interval $\bar{X} \pm 2.58 \cdot \text{SÊ}(\bar{X})$ gives approximately 99% confidence, and the interval $\bar{X} \pm 3.29 \cdot \text{SÊ}(\bar{X})$ gives approximately 99.9% confidence.

2.4 Estimation of totals and proportions

Many surveys are more concerned with population totals than they are with means. For example, if the sample units are households then interest may be in the total yearly expenditure of all the households in a city on a particular category of consumer goods.

The population total of a variable X is $T = N\mu$, where N is the population size and μ is the population mean for X. This total can be estimated by

$$\hat{T} = N \cdot \bar{X}. \tag{2.4}$$

Since N is a constant, the standard error of $\hat{T}$ is simply

$$\text{SE}(\hat{T}) = N \cdot \text{SE}(\bar{X}), \tag{2.5}$$

and an approximate 95% confidence interval for T is

$$\hat{T} - 2 \cdot \text{SE}(\hat{T}) < T < \hat{T} + 2 \cdot \text{SE}(\hat{T}).$$

In practice $\text{SE}(\hat{T})$ will usually have to be estimated by $\text{SÊ}(\hat{T}) = N \cdot \text{SÊ}(\bar{X})$, so that the approximate 95% confidence interval for T becomes

$$\hat{T} - 2 \cdot \text{SÊ}(\hat{T}) < T < \hat{T} + 2 \cdot \text{SÊ}(\hat{T}).$$

Another possibility is that it is a population proportion π that is of interest. An example of this would be where the sampling units are individual animals and π is the proportion of females. In that case if a random sample of n from the population gives r females then the sample proportion

$$p = r/n \qquad (2.6)$$

is an unbiased estimator of π with standard error

$$SE(p) = \sqrt{[\{\pi(1 - \pi)/n\}\{1 - f\}]}. \qquad (2.7)$$

Since π is unknown this standard error must be estimated by

$$\hat{SE}(p) = \sqrt{[\{p(1 - p)/n\}\{1 - f\}]}, \qquad (2.8)$$

with the estimate p replacing π. An approximate 95% confidence interval is then

$$p - 2 \cdot \hat{SE}(p) < \pi < p+2 \cdot \hat{SE}(p).$$

These equations for estimating a proportion apply only if p really is a proportion of sampling units. If each sampling unit has a proportion measured on it (for example, the measurement is the proportion of a sample plot covered with grass) then this variable should just be treated as a measured or counted variable and analysed using the methods that have been described in the previous section.

Example 2.1: Survey of book purchases and exercise

For a numerical illustration of the use of the above equations, suppose that the adults in a town are surveyed to estimate the total number of magazines or books purchased per month and the proportion of people who regularly take part in an exercise programme. The town has 6000 inhabitants over 18, from which a simple random sample of 40 are chosen to be interviewed. The number of books and magazines purchased is recorded for each of the sampled adults, as well as an indication of whether or not they have a regular exercise programme, with the results that are shown in Table 2.2.

Consider first the estimation of the total number of magazines purchased. As shown in Table 2.2, the number of purchases has a sample mean of 0.90, and a sample standard deviation of 0.67. The standard error of $\bar{X}$ is therefore estimated as

$$\hat{SE}(\bar{X}) = \sqrt{[(0.67^2/40)\{1 - (40/6000)\}]} = 0.106.$$

Hence, the total number of magazines purchased by all adults is estimated to be $\hat{T} = N \cdot \bar{X} = 6000 \times 0.90 = 5400$, with standard error $\hat{SE}(\hat{T}) = 6000 \times 0.106 = 633.5$. Approximate 95% confidence

24

Table 2.2. *Results of a survey of 40 adults chosen at random from the 6000 adults in a town*

The data shown are the number of books and magazines purchased in the last month; and an indication of whether the respondents take part in an exercise programme (1 for 'yes', 0 for 'no').

Person	Number of books/ magazines	Exercise Programme	Person	Number of books/ magazines	Exercise Programme
1	0	1	21	1	0
2	2	0	22	2	0
3	0	1	23	1	0
4	1	1	24	1	1
5	1	0	25	2	0
6	1	0	26	0	0
7	1	0	27	0	1
8	2	1	28	2	0
9	1	0	29	1	0
10	1	0	30	1	0
11	0	0	31	0	0
12	1	1	32	1	1
13	1	0	33	1	0
14	0	0	34	2	1
15	1	1	35	1	0
16	1	1	36	1	1
17	1	1	37	2	0
18	0	0	38	0	1
19	1	0	39	1	0
20	0	0	40	0	0
			Total	36	14
			Mean	0.90	0.35
			SD[a]	0.67	

[a] SD is standard deviation.

limits for the true total are then given by

$$5400 - (2 \times 633.5) < T < 5400 + (2 \times 633.5),$$

or

$$4132 < T < 6668.$$

Fourteen out of the 40 sampled individuals took part in an exercise programme. The estimate of the proportion of all adults with this characteristic is therefore $p = 14/40 = 0.35$. Notice that this is also the mean value of the 0–1 variable indicating participation in an exercise programme. The estimated standard error is $\hat{SE}(p) = \sqrt{[\{0.35(1 - 0.35)/40\}\{1 - (40/6000)\}]} = 0.075$, and the approximate 95% confidence limits for the population proportion are

$$0.35 - (2 \times 0.075) < \pi < 0.35 + (2 \times 0.075),$$

or

$$0.20 < \pi < 0.50.$$

The large range here reflects the rather small sample size for estimating a proportion.

2.5 Determining sample sizes with simple random sampling

An important question for the design of samples is the sample size required to achieve a particular level of precision. This can be determined by setting the confidence bounds to reflect the required level of accuracy. Therefore, to get an approximately 95% confidence interval for a population mean of $\bar{X} \pm \delta$, with δ specified, requires that the margin of error is

$$\delta = 2(\sigma/\sqrt{n})\sqrt{\{1 - (n/N)\}}.$$

Rearranging this equation gives

$$n = N\sigma^2/(N\delta^2/4 + \sigma^2), \qquad (2.9)$$

which shows the sample size that is required in order to achieve the desired margin of error as a function of the population size, the population standard deviation and the desired margin of error. For a large population size N equation (2.9) becomes

$$n \approx 4\sigma^2/\delta^2. \qquad (2.10)$$

This is the appropriate equation to use if N is unknown since it gives an upper limit to the sample size that is required for all population sizes.

As an example, suppose that the population size is $N = 500$, the population standard deviation is $\sigma = 2$, and the required margin of error is $\delta = 0.5$. Then this implies that the sample size should be $n = 500(2)^2/[\{500(0.5)^2/4\} + 2^2] = 56.7$, say 57.

26

These sample size equations require σ to be known. Sometimes an approximate value is available from a previous study. Alternatively, if the range of possible values of X is guessed to be R then $R/4$ will give an approximate value for σ, the idea being that for many distributions the effective range is the mean plus and minus about two standard deviations. This type of approximation is often sufficient in practice since it is only necessary to get the sample size roughly right.

To get specified bounds on a population total, these can be expressed as bounds on the mean, and the above equation can then be used. Therefore, if the required 95% confidence interval for T is $\hat{T} \pm d$, then this can be written as $N\bar{x} \pm N\delta$. The required interval for the population mean is then $\bar{x} \pm \delta$, where $\delta = d/N$.

Returning to the last example with $N = 500$ and $\sigma = 2$, suppose that the estimated population total is to have a margin of error of 100. Then the margin of error on the mean must be $\delta = 100/500 = 0.2$, and the sample size requirement is for $n = 500(2^2)/\{500(0.2)^2/4 + 2^2\} = 222.2$, say 222.

To get an approximate 95% confidence interval of $p \pm \delta$ for a population proportion requires that the margin of error should be

$$2 \cdot \text{SE}(p) = \delta = 2\sqrt{[\{\pi(1 - \pi)/n\}\{1 - (n/N)\}]}.$$

Solving for n then gives

$$n = N\pi(1 - \pi)/\{N\delta^2/4 + \pi(1 - \pi)\}. \tag{2.11}$$

To use this equation the value for π can be guessed, or a conservative value can be used. The conservative approach involves noting that the largest possible sample size is needed when $n = \frac{1}{2}$, in which case the required sample size becomes

$$n = N/(N\delta^2 + 1). \tag{2.12}$$

For large populations this becomes

$$n \approx 1/\delta^2, \tag{2.13}$$

which is useful as a general guide for sample sizes needed for surveys. Whenever samples are going to be used to estimate proportions the last equation indicates that to get an accuracy of about ± 0.1 ($\pm 10\%$) needs a sample of $n = 1/0.1^2 = 100$, an accuracy of ± 0.05 ($\pm 5\%$) needs $n = 1/0.05^2 = 400$, an accuracy of ± 0.01 ($\pm 1\%$) needs $n = 1/0.01^2 = 10\,000$, and so on.

Example 2.2: Sampling trees in a forest

Suppose that a forest is arranged in a grid of 6000 plots, and that there is interest in estimating (i) the total number of trees in the forest, and (ii) the proportion of plots where a certain species of tree is present. Assume that it is desirable to determine the total number of trees with a 95% confidence interval of $\hat{T} \pm 1000$, and the proportion of plots with the species of interest with a 95% confidence interval of ± 0.05.

Before sampling it is known that the minimum and maximum numbers of trees per plot are probably 1 and 7, suggesting a standard deviation of about $(7 - 1)/4 = 1.5$. The limits on the estimated mean corresponding to limits of ± 1000 on the total are $\pm 1000/6000$, or ± 0.167. Equation (2.9) then suggests that a sample size of

$$n = 6000 \times 1.5^2/\{(6000 \times 0.167^2/4) + 1.5^2\} \approx 306$$

is required.

Next, suppose that an initial guess is that 30% of plots will contain the species of interest. Then the sample size requirement for estimating the population proportion is obtained from equation (2.11) to be

$$n = 6000 \times 0.3 \times 0.7/\{(6000 \times 0.05^2/4) + (0.3 \times 0.7)\} \approx 318.$$

It seems that a sample size of about 318 will satisfy both the requirements of this survey. It is common to have several objectives for a survey. The sample size required is the minimum needed to achieve all of these.

2.6 Stratified sampling

A problem with simple random sampling is that there is no control over how sampled items are spread through the population. Therefore, in sampling streets in a town the sampled streets may mostly be concentrated in a small area, rather than being well spread out. This does not matter if the variable being studied has a fairly uniform distribution over the town. It is important if streets with similar values tend to be clustered together.

One way of ensuring that a population is well covered by sampling involves using *stratification*. This means dividing the sampling units into non-overlapping strata, and selecting a simple random sample from each of these strata. In general there is nothing to lose by using this more complicated type of sampling but there are some potential gains. First, if the individuals within strata are rather more similar than individuals in general then the estimate of the overall population mean will have a smaller standard error than can be obtained with a simple random sample of the same size. Second, there may be value in having separate estimates of population parameters for the different strata. Third, stratification makes it possible to sample different parts of a population in different ways, which may make some cost savings possible.

Generally, the types of stratification that should be considered are those based on spatial location, regions within which the population is expected to be uniform, and the size of sampling units. For example, in sampling a plant population over a large area it is natural to take a map and partition the area into a few apparently homogeneous strata based on factors such as altitude and vegetation type. In sampling insects on trees it may make sense to stratify on the basis of small, medium and large tree diameters. In sampling households a town can be divided into regions within which the age and class characteristics are relatively uniform. Usually the choice of what to stratify on is just a question of common sense for the survey in question.

Assume that K strata have been chosen, with the ith of these having size N_i and the total population size being $\sum N_i = N$. Then if a random sample of size n_i is taken from the ith stratum the sample mean $\bar{X}_i$ will be an unbiased estimate of the true stratum mean μ_i with estimated standard error

$$\text{S}\hat{\text{E}}(\bar{X}_i) = \sqrt{[(s_i^2/n_i)\{1 - (n_i/N_i)\}]},$$

where s_i is the sample standard deviation of X for the ith stratum. In terms of the true strata means, the overall population mean is the weighted average

$$\mu = \sum_{i=1}^{K} N_i\mu_i/N. \tag{2.14}$$

The corresponding sample estimate is therefore

$$\bar{X}_S = \sum_{i=1}^{K} N_i\bar{X}_i/N, \tag{2.15}$$

with estimated variance

$$\text{Vâr}(\bar{X}_S) = \sum_{i=1}^{K} \{N_i \text{SÊ}(\bar{X}_i)/N\}^2$$

$$= \sum_{i=1}^{K} \{(N_i/N)^2 s_i^2/n_i\}\{1 - (n_i/N_i)\}. \qquad (2.16)$$

An approximate 95% confidence interval is then given by $\bar{X}_S \pm 2 \cdot \text{SÊ}(\bar{X}_S)$, where $\text{SÊ}(\bar{X}_S) = \sqrt{\text{Vâr}(\bar{X}_S)}$ is the estimated standard error of $\bar{X}_S$.

If the population total is of interest then this can be estimated by $\hat{T} = N \cdot \bar{X}_S$, with estimated standard error $\text{SÊ}(\hat{T}) = N \cdot \text{SÊ}(\bar{X}_S)$. Again, adding and subtracting two standard errors gives an approximate 95% confidence interval.

Example 2.3: Stratified sampling of trees in a forest

Suppose that a forest is laid out in four blocks, with each block being divided into 400 plots in a 20 by 20 grid. To estimate the total number of trees in the forest, a random sample of ten plots is taken from each of the blocks (strata) by choosing a random row number between 1 and 20 and a random column number between 1 and 20 using the random number generator on a computer. This results in the sample counts for the number of trees per plot that are shown in Table 2.3.

From these data, the estimated population mean is found using equation (2.15) to be $\bar{X}_S = 5.075$, with a standard error that is estimated from equation (2.16) to be $\text{SÊ}(\bar{X}_S) = 0.238$. The estimated population total number of trees is therefore $5.075 \times 1600 = 8120$, with estimated standard error $0.238 \times 1600 = 380.8$. Hence, the approximate 95% confidence interval for the population total is $8120 \pm 2 \times 380.8$, or 7359 to 8882.

2.7 Sample size allocation for stratified samples

In designing a stratified sample, the sample sizes in different strata must be chosen. A common approach is to use *proportional allocation*, which means that n_i, the sample size for stratum i, is made proportional to N_i, the number of units in that stratum. However, this is not necessarily the best use of the resources available. In general, it is best to concentrate sampling in the strata that are largest, most variable, and have the lowest sampling cost.

For many surveys it will be reasonable to assume that the total

Table 2.3. *The numbers of trees found in u stratified sample of the blocks in a forest*

Sample Unit	Stratum			
	1	2	3	4
1	8	3	8	0
2	6	5	3	4
3	8	5	5	3
4	6	6	8	4
5	7	2	2	5
6	7	4	4	4
7	7	6	7	6
8	6	4	6	3
9	8	5	5	3
10	8	3	7	4
Mean	7.1	4.3	5.5	3.4
SD	0.88	1.34	2.07	1.65

cost C of sampling consists of a fixed cost F plus variable costs that are proportional to sample sizes in strata. That is, the total cost has the form

$$C = F + \sum_{i=1}^{K} c_i n_i,$$

where c_i is the cost of sampling one unit from stratum i. In that case, it can be shown that to gain the maximum precision at least cost, the sample size in the ith stratum should be made proportional to $N_i \sigma_i / \sqrt{c_i}$, where σ_i is the within-stratum standard deviation for stratum i. Note that if σ_i and c_i are the same in all strata then proportional allocation is optimal. In practice the within-strata standard deviations often have to be guessed in order to determine an approximately optimum allocation.

If, as is usually the case, a sample survey is being carried out to estimate the means of several different variables then the optimum sample allocations to strata will almost certainly be different for the different variables. One possibility is then to use proportional allocation. Alternatively, optimum allocations can be worked out for every variable, and these can be averaged to obtain a 'compromise' sample allocation. The choice between proportional allocation and the compromise allocation can then be based on seeing how they both perform for estimation with each of the variables.

Example 2.4: Designing a survey

Suppose that a population is divided into four strata, for which the information shown in the first four columns of Table 2.4 is available. Assume that it is desired to take a stratified random sample with a total sampling cost, $\sum c_i n_i$, of \$500. Then for the minimum variance at this cost the sample sizes in the different strata should be proportional to $N_i \sigma_i / \sqrt{c_i}$, with the sizes chosen to get the correct cost. One way to achieve this involves setting the sample sizes equal to $N_i \sigma_i / \sqrt{c_i}$, calculating the resulting sampling cost, and then scaling the sample sizes up or down to get the desired cost. These calculations are shown in the last three columns of Table 2.4. The column headed 'Trial n' gives the values of $N_i \sigma_i / \sqrt{c_i}$, which give a total sampling cost of \$13 480 instead of \$500. Multiplying these trial sample sizes by 500/13 480 gives the column headed 'Scaled n'. Converting to integers then gives the sample sizes shown in the last column of the table, which have the required sampling cost of \$500.

If it is required that the variance of the estimated population mean has a certain maximum value, and this variance is to be obtained at the least cost, then the calculations are very similar to those shown in Table 2.4, except that the trial sample sizes need to be scaled to give the required variance instead of the required cost.

2.8 Stratified sampling for proportions

Stratified sampling can also be used with the estimation of proportions. If p_i is the sample proportion in stratum i then this is an

Table 2.4. *Determining optimum sample sizes in strata when the total sampling cost should be \$500*

Stratum	Size	Sampling cost \$	SD	Trial n	Scaled n	Integer n
1	400	10	1	126.4	4.7	5
2	1000	5	2	894.4	33.2	32
3	200	20	3	134.1	5.0	5
4	400	10	4	505.9	18.8	19
Total	2000				61.7	
Cost (\$)				13 480		500

unbiased estimator of the stratum proportion π_i with variance

$$\text{Var}(p_i) = \{\pi_i(1 - \pi_i)/n_i\}\{1 - (n_i/N_i)\}.$$

An unbiased estimator of the overall population proportion π is therefore

$$p_S = \sum_{i-1}^{K} (N_i/N)p_i, \tag{2.17}$$

with variance

$$\text{Var}(p_S) = \sum_{i=1}^{K} (N_i/N)^2 \text{Var}(p_i)$$

$$= \sum_{i=1}^{K} (N_i/N)^2 \{\pi_i(1 - \pi_i)/n_i\}\{1 - (n_i/N_i)\}. \tag{2.18}$$

A 95% confidence interval for π is given by $p_S \pm 2.\text{SE}(p_S)$, where $\text{SE}(p_S) = \sqrt{\text{Var}(p_S)}$ is the standard error of p_S. It is usually necessary to approximate π_i by p_i in the variance equation, to obtain

$$\text{Vâr}(p_S) = \sum_{i=1}^{K} (N_i/N)^2 \{p_i(1 - p_i)/n_i\}\{1 - (n_i/N_i)\}. \tag{2.19}$$

The equations discussed in Section 2.7 for optimum stratified sampling apply just as well to the estimation of proportions if the population variance is taken as $\sigma_i^2 = \pi_i(1 - \pi_i)$ in the ith stratum. However, two important results apply in this case (Cochran, 1977, p. 109). First, if the cost to sample a unit is the same for all strata then the gain from stratified random sampling over simple random sampling is small unless the proportions π_i vary greatly with the strata. Second, optimum allocation is little better than proportional allocation unless some strata proportions are outside the range 0.1 to 0.9.

2.9 Poststratification

With some variables that are suitable for stratification it is difficult to know the strata to which units belong until a survey has been conducted, although the strata sizes are known accurately for the population. For example, in sampling a human population the numbers in different age and sex classes may be known, although there is no easy way to take a simple random sample from each class.

One possible procedure in this case is to use *poststratification*, whereby a simple random sample of n is taken from the entire population and the sampled units are classified into K strata. Instead of the sample mean $\bar{X}$ the stratified sampling estimator $\bar{X}_S = \sum N_i \bar{X}_i / N$ is then used to estimate the population mean.

Poststratification is almost as precise as stratified sampling with proportional allocation providing that the sample size is larger than about 20 in each of the strata. Furthermore, equation (2.16), which gives the variance of $\bar{X}_S$, is still approximately correct.

2.10 Quota sampling

Another method of stratification that is used in opinion surveys involves determining how many units need to be sampled in each stratum, and instructing the sampler to continue until the 'quota' is filled for all the strata. Typical stratification variables are age, sex, race, area and economic level. Random sampling is not used because it is difficult or impossible to determine which population to sample from in each stratum, although it is easy to recognize members. In effect availability sampling is used.

It seems that quota sampling produces samples that are biased on some characteristics (income, education, occupation, etc.), but may give reasonable results for questions on opinions and attitudes. However, it is not valid to apply random sampling variance formulae to quota surveys.

2.11 Ratio and regression estimation

Occasions arise where the estimation of the population mean or total for a variable X is assisted by information on a subsidiary variable U. Two ways to do this are by *ratio estimation* and by *regression estimation*. In both cases, what is required is that the items in a random sample of size n have values $X_1, X_2, \ldots, X_n$ for X, and corresponding values $U_1, U_2, \ldots, U_n$ for U, and that μ_U, the population mean for U, and $T_U = N\mu_U$, the population total for U, are known values.

With ratio estimation it is assumed that X and U are approximately proportional, so that $X \approx R \cdot U$, where R is some constant. The value of R can then be estimated from the sample data by

$$r = X/U, \qquad (2.20)$$

and hence the population mean of X can be estimated by multiplying r by the population mean of U, to get

$$\bar{X}_r = r\mu_U. \qquad (2.21)$$

Multiplying both sides of this equation by the population size N, the ratio estimate of the population total for X is found to be

$$\hat{T}_X = rT_U. \qquad (2.22)$$

As an example, suppose that an estimate is required of the total number of inhabitants in all the $N = 100$ towns in a developing country. A previous full census was made in 1970, so that population sizes at that time (U) are known for all N towns, with a total of $T_U = 30\,000\,000$. Assume that a random sample of 20 towns gives a mean current population of $\bar{X} = 350\,000$, with a mean for the 1970 sizes of 270 000. Then the estimated ratio relating the current populations to the 1970 populations is $r = 350\,000/270\,000 = 1.296$, and the ratio estimate of the current population for all towns is $\hat{T}_X = rT_U = 1.296 \times 30\,000\,000 = 38\,888\,889$.

In this example, and other cases where the ratio of X to U should be relatively constant, the ratio estimators of the population mean and population total for X can be expected to have lower standard errors than the estimators $\bar{X}$ and $N \cdot \bar{X}$. This is because the ratio estimators allow for the fact that the observed sample may, by chance alone, consist of items with rather low or high values for X. Even if the random sample does not reflect the population very well the estimate of r may still be reasonable, which is all that is required for a good estimate of the population total.

The variance of $\bar{X}_r$ is given approximately by the equation

$$\mathrm{Var}\,(\bar{X}_r) \approx \{\mathrm{Var}\,(X - RU)/n\}\{1 - (n/N)\}, \qquad (2.23)$$

where $R = T_X/T_U$ is the ratio of the X total to the U total for the population, and $\mathrm{Var}\,(X - RU)$ is the variance of the variable $X - RU$ in the population. An estimate of $\mathrm{Var}\,(\bar{X}_r)$ can be obtained by replacing $\mathrm{Var}\,(X - RU)$ with the sample variance of $X - rU$, with r being estimated from equation (2.20). An approximate 95% confidence interval for the population mean of X is then given by

$$\bar{X}_r \pm 2 \cdot \text{SÊ}(\bar{X}_r),$$

where $\text{SÊ}(\bar{X}_r) = \sqrt{\text{Vâr}(\bar{X}_r)}$, with $\text{Vâr}(\bar{X}_r)$ being the estimated value for $\text{Var}(\bar{X}_r)$.

Since the ratio estimator of the population total of X is $N\bar{X}_r$, it follows that

$$\text{Var}(\hat{T}_X) \approx N^2 \text{Var}(\bar{X}_r) = N^2\{\text{Var}(X - RU)/n\}\{1 - (n/N)\}.$$

$$(2.24)$$

Again, this can be estimated if necessary by replacing $\text{Var}(X - RU)$ with the sample variance of $X - rU$, and an approximately 95% confidence interval is given by

$$\hat{T}_X \pm 2 \cdot \text{SÊ}(\hat{T}_X).$$

The equations for variances, standard errors and confidence intervals should give reasonable results providing that the sample size n is large, which in practice means 30 or more, and the coefficients of variation of $\bar{X}$ and $\bar{U}$ (their standard deviations over their means) are less than 0.1 (Cochran, 1977, p. 153).

Ratio estimation assumes that the ratio of the variable of interest X to the subsidiary variable U is approximately constant for the items in the population. A less restrictive assumption is that X and U are approximately related by an equation of the form $X = \alpha + \beta U$, in which case regression estimation can be used.

Regression methods are discussed in Chapter 4. Here it can merely be noted that the standard regression estimators of the values α and β are a and b, respectively, where these are calculated from the equations

$$b = \sum_{i=1}^{n} (X_i - \bar{X})(U_i - \bar{U}) / \sum_{i=1}^{n} (U_i - \bar{U})^2, \qquad (2.25)$$

and

$$a = \bar{X} - b\bar{U}. \qquad (2.26)$$

The estimated relationship between X and U is then

$$X = a + bU,$$

and the regression estimator of the mean of X is

$$\bar{X}_l = a + b\mu_U = \bar{X} + b(\mu_U - \bar{U}).\qquad(2.27)$$

This can be interpreted as $\bar{X}$ corrected by $b(\mu_U - \bar{U})$ to allow for a low or high mean of the U values for the sampled items.

The variance of $\bar{X}_l$ can be estimated by

$$\text{Vâr}(\bar{X}_l) = \sum_{i=1}^{n} (X_i - a - bU_i)^2/\{(n-2)n\}\{1 - (n/N)\},\qquad(2.28)$$

and an approximate 95% confidence interval for μ_X is $\bar{X}_l \pm 2\cdot\text{SÊ}(\bar{X}_l)$, where $\text{SÊ}(\bar{X}_l) = \sqrt{\text{Var}(\bar{X}_l)}$.

Multiplying $\bar{X}_l$ by the population size N gives the regression estimator of the population total of X, T_X, to be

$$\hat{T}_X = N\bar{X} + b(T_U - N\bar{U}).\qquad(2.29)$$

The estimated standard error is $\text{SÊ}(\hat{T}_X) = N\cdot\text{SÊ}(\bar{X}_i)$ and approximate confidence limits for T_X are $\hat{T}_X \pm 2\cdot\text{SÊ}(\hat{T}_X)$.

More details about ratio and regression methods of estimation, including ways to combine these methods with stratified sampling, will be found in Chapter 6 of Scheaffer *et al.* (1990).

2.12 Cluster sampling

Cluster sampling involves sampling clusters of items rather than single items. The usual reason for doing this is cost reduction, since it costs much less to sample several close items than the same number of items some distance apart. For example, rather than choose a random sample of households in a town it may be convenient to sample all the houses in some streets.

Generally, cluster sampling cannot be expected to give the same precision as a simple random sample with the same total number of items, since close items tend to be more similar than items in general. Therefore, a cluster sample is equivalent to a random sample of independent units with a somewhat smaller size. However, cost savings may allow a cluster sample to be considerably larger than a simple random sample can be. Hence a cluster sample may give better precision than a simple random sample for the same sampling cost.

If cluster sizes are constant at m then the simplest way to estimate the mean of the variable of interest from a random sample of n clusters involves defining X, the variable being studied, as the total of the observations in the clusters so that $\bar{X}$ is an unbiased estimator of the population mean for cluster totals. The usual simple random sampling results can then be used to estimate the standard error of the sample mean and put 95% confidence limits on the population mean. The population mean for individual items is then estimated by $\overline{X}/m$, with 95% confidence limits for this parameter being obtained by dividing the limits $\overline{X} \pm 2 \cdot SE(\overline{X})$ by m.

If cluster sizes vary then a cluster total X can be expected to be approximately proportional to the cluster size. This size can therefore be used as the value for the subsidiary variable U for ratio estimation providing that the mean cluster size is known for the population sampled.

Cluster sampling can be combined with stratified sampling. See Scheaffer *et al.* (1990, Chapter 8) for more details.

2.13 Systematic sampling

Systematic sampling can be carried out whenever a population can be listed in order or it covers a well-defined spatial area. In the former case, every kth item in the list can be sampled, starting at an item chosen at random from the first k. In the second case sampling points can be set out on a grid at equally spaced intervals.

There are two reasons why systematic sampling is sometimes used. First, systematic sampling is often easier than random sampling. Second, it seems likely that a systematic sample will be more 'representative' than a random sample, and hence more precise.

In effect, systematic sampling puts the population into strata consisting of the first k units, the second k units, etc., and takes a sample of one from each of these strata. This suggests that systematic sampling should be about as precise as stratified random sampling with one unit per stratum, although the two schemes differ because with systematic sampling the unit taken is from the same relative position in each of the strata.

Systematic sampling may give a better coverage of a population than a simple random sample. However, it suffers from the disadvantage of not allowing any determination of the level of sampling errors unless it is assumed that the units in the population are in a random order. Of course, if the units are in a random order then a systematic sample can be treated as being effectively a simple random sample and all the various results given earlier for this type of sampling can be used.

Another possibility involves the estimation of a sampling variance by replicating a systematic sample. For example, suppose that a 10% sample of a population of size 20 000 is required. Rather than taking every tenth unit starting with one of the first ten units, it might be possible to take 20 systematic samples, each starting at a different randomly chosen unit in the first 200, and sampling every 200th unit from then on. Thus if the first randomly chosen unit is 65 then the systematic sample would consist of units 65, 265, ..., 19 865. The population can then be thought of as consisting of $N = 200$ 'clusters' of potential systematic sets of observations, from which 20 are randomly sampled. Inferences concerning the population mean and total can then be made in the manner indicated in the previous section for situations where clusters are all of the same size.

Systematic sampling may not work well when the population has some periodicity. To take an extreme case, suppose that a population has values that are listed as follows:

1 2 3 4 5 6 5 4 3 2 1 2 3 4 5 6 5 4 3 2 1 2 3 4 5 6 5 4 3 2
1 2 3 4 5 6 5 4 3 2 1 2 3 4 5 6 5 4 3 2 1 2 3 4 5 6 5 4 3 2
$\vdots$

1 2 3 4 5 6 5 4 3 2 1 2 3 4 5 6 5 4 3 2 1 2 3 4 5 6 5 4 3 2
1 2 3 4 5 6 5 4 3 2 1 2 3 4 5 6 5 4 3 2 1 2 3 4 5 6 5 4 3 2

A 1 in 10 sample starting from the second unit gives 2, 2, 2, etc. It appears that the population mean can be estimated at 2 with no error, although the real mean is 3.5. If the population is divided into 5 by 5 blocks and the central value of each block is chosen as 'representative' then the sample values are 3, 4, 3, 4, etc. and the mean is exactly right. If the top left-hand corner of each block is sampled then the values obtained are 1, 6, 1, 6, etc. Again this is exact. However, if blocks of another size are used then quite misleading results can occur. Clearly periodicity in a population can cause problems, although not usually to the extent indicated here.

2.14 Multi-stage sampling

Sometimes sampling has to be conducted at several levels of the classification of a population This is called *multi-stage sampling*, or *subsampling*. For example, consider the estimation of the number of plants of a certain type in a large area. The area might be stratified into several regions and random samples taken of 1 km square blocks (the primary units) in each of these regions. It may then not be practical to count all the plants in each block. Hence each block can be divided into 100 m square plots (secondary units) from which a certain number are chosen at random to be surveyed. It might still be necessary to choose some smaller subplots at random from within each plot (third stage units) in order to get small enough areas on which all plants can be counted.

Quite apart from practical considerations, common sense might suggest that the secondary units within one primary unit will often tend to be rather similar so that it is a waste of effort to sample many of these units, effort being better spent in sampling more primary units. Similarly, third stage units are likely to give rather similar results so that here again the effective allocation of sampling effort needs to be considered carefully.

A proper analysis of a multi-stage sample requires taking into account the sampling variation at each stage and can get quite complicated. A specialist text such as that of Cochran (1977) should be consulted for more details about the design and analysis of this type of sample.

2.15 Non-sampling errors

An estimate of a population parameter that is determined from a random sample will generally differ from the true value to some extent. The difference is a *sampling error*, the properties of which can be well understood by statistical theory. The other errors in a survey are the *non-sampling errors*, about which statistical theory has little to say. However, it is likely that in many surveys it is the non-sampling errors that are most important. Therefore, anyone contemplating carrying out a survey should be aware of the likely causes of non-sampling errors and do everything possible to ensure that they are minimized.

The possible causes of non-sampling errors can be divided into three classes: those due to inadequate procedures during preparing and carrying out of a survey; those occurring during data collection; and those occurring during data processing. These will now be considered in turn.

2.16 Biased procedures

A biased procedure is one involving problems with the selection of the sample, the estimation of population parameters, the variables being measured or the general operation of the survey. One thing to avoid is the assumption that a random sample is obtained just because there is an element of randomness used in the selection. For example, a random sample from the items in only a part of a population may lead to very biased results. Also, if the procedure for determining sampled units favours those with certain characteristics (such as the most visible ones) then biases can be expected.

If a questionnaire is used in a social survey then this is a prime source of biases, some of which can be quite subtle. Some possibilities are as follows:

(a) Misinterpretations may exist because questions are not specific and respondents do not want to show their ignorance. Studies have shown that subjects will often respond to nonsense questions. For example, they may claim to have heard of things that do not really exist

(b) Incomplete alternatives for questions requiring a choice may result in respondents choosing one of the wrong answers

(c) The use of technical terms and jargon will result in some subjects not understanding questions

(d) Leading and loaded questions will cause some subjects answering in what they perceive to be the 'correct' way. In some cases, the loading will be the result of earlier questions so that subjects must answer one way in order to be consistent, although they would have answered in the opposite way if the last question was given first

(e) It has been found that respondents pay more attention to items at the start and end of a list. Therefore, if they have to choose an item from a list then they will tend to choose one from the top or bottom

(f) Many questions involve asking people to recall past events. They may do this very badly, depending on the time lapse and the importance of the event. 'Recall loss' can occur even with major events. 'Telescoping' occurs when people recall an incident as taking place within a certain period when in fact it occurred at an earlier time. This may be common, for example, when subjects are asked to recall the purchase of large and expensive items

(g) Instructions and the training of interviewers may be of considerable importance for the quality of data. Studies have shown that more care in this direction, including practice interviews, can have an important effect in cutting error rates

2.17 Bias introduced during data collection

Undoubtedly, missing data are one important source of bias in surveys. There is plenty of evidence to show that non-respondents are different from respondents in many surveys so that non-response should not just be ignored. Missing data occur for several reasons such as difficulties in contacting subjects, refusals to respond, language difficulties, illness in the family, etc. There is considerable value in following up non-respondents so that it is possible to see how, if at all, they differ from respondents. Adjustments can then sometimes be made to survey results to take this into account. For example, the initial non-respondents can be thought of as being one of the strata in a stratified population, and the formulae given earlier for stratified sampling can be used for estimation.

When a respondent starts to answer a series of questions a number of complicated psychological processes may begin. For various reasons wrong answers may be given even when questions are understood and the correct answer is known. In other cases a 'reasonable' answer may be given as a guess to save the work of finding the correct one, results may be rounded, and prestige and conditioning errors may occur. Prestige errors are the result of respondents trying to impress. People become younger, medical assistants become doctors, expenditure on tobacco and alcohol goes down, and so on. Conditioning can be a problem in longitudinal and panel surveys. This refers to the changes in response to particular questions as a result of hearing them before and thinking about the answers. For example, in labour force surveys in some countries the same respondents are used for a number of surveys. Typically the unemployment rate is found to be higher in the first survey than in the following ones and it is suspected that this is due to people preparing their answers.

A number of studies have shown that the personal characteristics of the interviewer can influence the answers obtained, either because of their general behaviour, or the way that questions are asked. However, it seems that cheating is rare. Problems are more likely to occur because of the expectations of interviewers about the views and behaviour of respondents. Questions occurring early in the interview may bring about these expectations which then cloud the interpretation of answers later in the interview. A useful check on interviewers involves asking a sample of those interviewed to comment on how the interview went. If the interviewers know that this is being done then they will tend to be more careful to ensure that no problems arise.

Carelessness in recording is another potential source of error. Interviewers have to be reminded often to be careful, and forms should be designed so that recording is as simple as possible.

2.18 Processing errors

In many ways, processing errors are the easiest to control. Nevertheless, they can occur, particularly when data are being transferred from field records to the computer. The need to transcribe data from survey to punching forms should be avoided at all costs, and the survey forms should be designed to make entry into the computer as easy as possible.

Once input to the computer careful checking is important to make sure that data are within reasonable bounds. This often leads to the discovery of anomalous values and inconsistencies.

Even when the data are completely correct on a computer there are still many ways that errors can occur. Variables can get mixed up, methods of analysis may not be appropriate, and people may forget the details of how the data are stored.

2.19 Methods of data collection

There are several standard methods for collecting the data for surveys of human populations, each with advantages and disadvantages.

The *personal interview* requires the interviewer to ask prepared questions. The main advantage is that people will usually respond when asked a question by someone else. In addition, a good interviewer can note specific reactions and eliminate misunderstandings. The main disadvantage is cost. Also, there is the potential for the interviewers to bias the results. Well-trained, high quality interviewers are of crucial importance.

Telephone interviews are possibly a cost effective alternative to personal interviews. In some places a fixed fee will allow any number of calls to be made in an area. Travel expenses are minimized and the interviewer can do a lot to ensure that questions are understood. A major problem is establishing the appropriate sampling frame. Telephone directories contain many numbers that are not appropriate (e.g. business numbers for a household survey). Some households have no telephone, and some numbers are unlisted. A technique with some promise involves avoiding a telephone directory altogether by randomly dialling the last four digits of numbers until a certain number of acceptable numbers have been obtained. Generally telephone interviews must be kept short. People get impatient more quickly than they do with personal interviews.

Self-administered questionnaires are usually mailed to potential respondents, to fill in at a convenient time. The questionnaire must be carefully constructed to encourage participation. Costs are relatively low, but this is usually at the expense of a low response rate. The potential bias that may result from this can be reduced by following up respondents using the telephone, another letter, or a personal interview.

It should not be forgotten that much important information can be gathered by *direct observation*. Rather than asking a farmer what area he has planted for a certain crop, someone can go to the farm and measure it at an appropriate time. Instead of asking people about illness, hospital records can be used etc. This may or may not be more expensive than surveying the people involved. Also, standard records might not provide precisely the information needed.

2.20 Designing a questionnaire

The above review of non-sampling errors shows that questionnaire design is not as easy as it might appear at first sight. Some general points in this area will now be reviewed.

It may be helpful to ask a few general questions about a subject before the one of major interest so as to give respondents a chance to think about the whole area. Care must be taken in this case to avoid leading them towards particular responses on the key question.

When subjects are asked a series of questions involving ratings the first question often has more extreme results than others because there are initially no standards for good and bad. Therefore, the first question tends to be the one that fixes standards for the rest.

The ordering of alternatives for the possible answers to a question has already been noted as important, with respondents tending to choose ones that are at the top or bottom of a list. Ways for avoiding questionnaire-induced biases are: printing questionnaires with different orders for some key questions, using show cards or repeating questions as often as necessary to ensure that they are understood, and carefully explaining the context of questions when discussing survey results.

Most questions will be *closed* because this makes the analysis by computer more straightforward. Each question will have either a simple numerical answer like age, or a set number of alternatives to choose from. On the other hand, *open* questions allow respondents to freely state what they think, which will be of considerable value if some potential opinions have been overlooked. In some cases none of the closed alternatives may be sensible for a respondent, and this is important to know. Allowing 'none of the above' is one way to handle this, with a space for an explanation.

One approach is to use an open question for a pretest of a questionnaire and then using the results obtained to design a closed question. For example the initial question might be:

What drink do you consume most of?

The closed question could then be:

The drink I consume most of is (choose one)
(a) Tea, (b) Coffee etc.

Typical survey practice attempts to avoid allowing people to say that they 'don't know' because some will opt for this as an easy way out. It may make sense to have screening questions to make sure that people are not asked about things of which they have no experience. It may be useful to force a decision by using questions like:

> Do you think that the enforcement of laws on drugs
> is too strict or too lenient?

This does not allow the choice that the present situation is satisfactory. The interviewer must explain that it is a matter of choosing which side is most favoured. Of course, often more than two choices are allowed.

Even with questions where the possible responses are clear it is important that the phrasing is balanced. Thus: 'Do you favour or oppose longer prison sentences for drug offenders?' is better than 'Do you favour longer prison sentences for drug offenders?'

Questions should be clearly defined so that the question

> How much water do you drink?

is better replaced by

> Here is an eight ounce glass. How many eight ounce
> glasses of water do you drink each day?

2.21 Summary and further reading

The sample survey is an important basic tool for researchers, particularly those interested in social questions. The aspects of this subject that have been covered in this chapter include the importance of random sampling, the estimation of population means, totals and proportions, complex sampling designs including those involving stratified and cluster sampling. For further information on these and related topics the specialized texts of Cochran (1977) and Scheaffer et al. (1990) can be consulted. Another useful reference for environmental biologists is that of Gilbert (1987). The other main topics that have been considered are the avoidance of non-sampling errors and the design of questionnaires. Lemeshow (1985) and Tortora (1985) provides references for further reading in the area of non-sampling errors, while the design of questionnaires is considered at length by Schuman and Presser (1981) and Sudman and Bradburn (1982).

Designing a survey for the accurate, unbiased estimation of the parameters of a population is usually not a simple matter, and it is suggested that anyone embarking on this process should carefully study the checklist that is provided in the Appendix to this chapter before they begin.

Exercises

1. Consider a large grass-covered area such as a local park and design a survey to estimate the total number of blades of grass present and the mean length of these blades on a specific day. Is it appropriate to use stratified sampling to take into account different densities of grass in different parts of the area? Should multi-stage sampling be used in order to count and measure only some of the blades of grass in each sampling unit? What are the definitions of a 'blade of grass' and the 'length' of a blade of grass? What accuracy do you expect to get from the survey?

2. Design a survey to assess the opinion of the general public in your local area on some controversial topic such as the amount of money that the government spends on welfare benefits for the unemployed. Are the target and sampled populations well-defined? Are the procedures and the questionnaire as free as possible from biases? What accuracy do you expect to obtain from the survey?

3. Table 2.5 shows the results (percentage support for nine candidates for the position of Mayor of Dunedin) of the first of the two surveys that are described in Case Study 1. Using the methods described in the case study, show that estimated levels of support for the different candidates, for voters who were prepared to make a choice, are as shown in Table 2.6.

CASE STUDY 1

The 1989 Mayoral election in Dunedin

This case study is about two surveys that were carried out in 1989 to estimate the level of support for each of the nine candidates for the position of the Mayor of the city of Dunedin in New Zealand. The election was unusual in three respects:

(a) A local government reorganization meant that the size of the town was substantially larger than for earlier elections through the inclusion of several satellite towns and areas within the new boundaries.

Table 2.5. *Percentage support for mayoral candidates from the first survey in clusters (streets) within voting wards*

The number of respondents in each street is shown in the final column of the table. In this and the following tables the candidates shown in Figure 2.1 are referred to by their initials so that, for example, S. E. Alexandra is shown as SEA. See Case Study 1 for a description of the sample design.

Ward	Street	None	SEA	DB-P	PWB	GBC	WJG	MHNH	EAH	IWMc	RW	Don't know	n
(A) Results for central city wards													
North	1	41.7	5.0	15.0	0.0	0.0	5.0	1.7	8.3	5.0	8.3	10.0	60
	2	32.0	4.0	12.0	4.0	0.0	0.0	12.0	12.0	8.0	4.0	12.0	25
	3	7.7	15.4	0.0	0.0	0.0	0.0	3.8	15.4	23.1	15.4	19.2	26
	4	15.6	9.4	3.1	0.0	0.0	0.0	6.3	3.1	6.3	3.1	53.1	32
	Mean	24.2	8.4	7.5	1.0	0.0	1.3	5.9	9.7	10.6	7.7	23.6	
	SD	15.4	5.2	7.1	2.0	0.0	2.5	4.5	5.3	8.4	5.6	20.1	
East	1	16.7	0.0	22.2	0.0	0.0	0.0	16.7	0.0	11.1	16.7	16.7	18
	2	0.0	4.3	13.0	0.0	0.0	0.0	17.4	4.3	13.0	17.4	30.4	23
	3	5.0	10.0	15.0	0.0	0.0	0.0	0.0	10.0	10.0	5.0	45.0	20
	4	25.0	8.3	8.3	0.0	0.0	0.0	16.7	0.0	0.0	16.7	25.0	12
	Mean	11.7	5.7	14.6	0.0	0.0	0.0	12.7	3.6	8.5	13.9	29.3	
	SD	11.3	4.5	5.8	0.0	0.0	0.0	8.5	4.7	5.8	6.0	11.9	

Percentage of voters

Central	1	22.7	4.5	18.2	0.0	0.0	0.0	9.1	0.0	4.5	4.5	36.4	22
	2	46.9	3.1	6.3	0.0	0.0	6.3	0.0	3.1	12.5	3.1	18.8	32
	3	13.5	5.4	8.1	0.0	0.0	0.0	5.4	8.1	10.8	2.7	45.9	37
	4	22.6	0.0	6.5	0.0	0.0	0.0	0.0	0.0	3.2	25.8	41.9	31
	Mean	26.4	3.3	9.7	0.0	0.0	1.6	3.6	2.8	7.8	9.0	35.7	
	SD	14.3	2.4	5.7	0.0	0.0	3.1	4.4	3.8	4.6	11.2	12.0	
West	1	33.3	11.1	0.0	0.0	0.0	0.0	0.0	0.0	0.0	11.1	44.4	9
	2	0.0	4.0	4.0	0.0	0.0	0.0	0.0	4.0	12.0	24.0	52.0	25
	3	4.5	0.0	18.2	4.5	0.0	0.0	13.6	0.0	0.0	13.6	45.5	22
	4	19.4	0.0	16.1	0.0	0.0	0.0	6.5	0.0	3.2	3.2	51.6	31
	Mean	14.3	3.8	9.6	1.1	0.0	0.0	5.0	1.0	3.8	13.0	48.4	
	SD	15.1	5.2	8.9	2.3	0.0	0.0	6.5	2.0	5.7	8.6	4.0	

(B) Results for Other Wards

Mosgiel	1	11.1	0.0	0.0	0.0	0.0	0.0	11.1	0.0	0.0	22.2	55.6	9
	2	6.7	6.7	13.3	0.0	0.0	0.0	0.0	13.3	6.7	20.0	33.3	15
	Mean	8.9	3.3	6.7	0.0	0.0	0.0	5.6	6.7	3.3	21.1	44.4	
	SD	3.1	4.7	9.4	0.0	0.0	0.0	7.9	9.4	4.7	1.6	15.7	
Saddle Hill		14.3	0.0	14.3	4.8	0.0	0.0	0.0	4.8	14.3	19.0	28.6	21
St Kilda		13.5	2.7	8.1	0.0	0.0	0.0	5.4	13.5	16.2	2.7	37.8	37
Green Island		25.0	2.5	7.5	0.0	0.0	0.0	2.5	0.0	20.0	5.0	37.5	40
Port Chalmers		10.0	0.0	5.0	10.0	0.0	0.0	5.0	10.0	5.0	15.0	40.0	20
Outlying areas		27.6	0.0	0.0	0.0	0.0	0.0	13.8	3.4	6.9	3.4	44.8	29

Table 2.6. *Estimates of support for candidates from committed voters in the first survey of mayoral candidates*

	SEA	DB-P	PWB	GBC	WJG	MHNG	EAH	IWMc	RW
Support (%)	9	20	2	0	1	14	11	19	24
SE	2	3	1	0	1	3	2	3	4

(b) A postal ballot was being held for the first time ever
(c) The number of candidates standing was higher than normal, with several 'labour' and several 'conservative' candidates, so that even long-standing residents of the town were completely unsure of the likely election result

To add some interest to the campaign, a local newspaper commissioned a survey soon after the candidates were announced in order to assess the initial level of support that each attracted. This survey indicated that several leading candidates had about the same support, but that most potential voters were unsure about how they would vote. A second opinion poll was therefore commissioned to take place a few days before the end of the voting period, at which time most voters were expected to have already posted off their voting form. In this way, the newspaper planned to give an accurate estimate of the final election result before this was officially announced. In the event, the second opinion poll correctly predicted the successful candidate and the ordering of the unsuccessful candidates.

It was initially suggested by the newspaper that a telephone survey should be carried out. The main merit of this approach was that it appeared that it would cost less than visiting households, and therefore allow a larger sample size. However, this idea was rejected on the grounds that many voters would not know the names of all the candidates, and it was considered that it would be difficult to provide the names of nine candidates, with their party affiliations, over a telephone and then expect people to say which one they were intending to vote for. Also, much of the savings from telephone interviewing rather than visiting households would be offset by the cost of preparing a list of random voters, particularly if the sample was to be stratified by areas of the town.

The final design chosen was a stratified cluster sample with proportional allocation. The strata were the voting wards in Dunedin City and the clusters were streets in these wards, as indicated in Table 2.7. The choice of this design was based on two considerations. First, stratification was employed because it was considered highly likely that support for different candidates varied in different parts of the city. Second, cluster sampling of streets was used because the street was the easiest unit to use for random sampling.

The sample size of 23 that is shown in this Table 2.7 was determined by the human resources available, which were 16 interviewers for one evening, and a calculation that indicated that these interviewers would be able to collect enough data to enable the percentage support for each mayoral candidate to be determined with a margin of error (95% confidence interval) of about ± 2%. Each pair of interviewers was required to sample two or three streets during the evening, for 45 to 60 minutes per street. They were instructed to question as many eligible voters as possible in the time allowed, by moving systematically from house to house down the streets. If a street was finished early then they were to move on to an adjacent street, which was then regarded as being in the same cluster.

Very detailed instructions were provided for the interviewers. They were told to choose their starting point in each street exactly as specified, and to use certain particular phrases when introducing themselves and conducting the survey. When asked to indicate their choice for mayor, respondents were shown a photocopy of the ballot paper, which took the form shown in Figure 2.1. In that way, any biases due to ordering of names on the ballot paper were reproduced in the survey. Up to three voters were accepted from each household.

To analyse results, the percentage support for each candidate was calculated for each cluster. For the wards with only one cluster, these percentages were taken as the estimates for the ward. For those wards with more than one cluster the percentages were averaged over clusters to obtain ward averages, and the differences between clusters within wards were used to estimate within-strata variances. The overall support for a candidate in the whole city was then estimated as

$$p = \sum w_i p_i, \tag{2.30}$$

where w_i is the fraction of voters in the ith ward, and p_i is the estimated percentage support for the candidate in that ward, the sum being over all the wards. This is essentially a slightly modified form of equation (2.15).

Table 2.7. *Voting wards in Dunedin city, with number of voters and the sample sizes allocated to each ward*

Ward	Number of voters	Sample size (streets)
North City	14364	4
East City	13823	4
Central City	13808	4
West City	12278	4
Mosgiel	6879	2
Saddle Hill	3173	1
St Kilda	4598	1
Green Island	4516	1
Port Chalmers	2400	1
Other outlying areas	5309	1
Total		23

Independent Labour	ALEXANDER, Stephen Elwyn
Labour	BENSON-POPE, David
Independent	BROOKS, Paul William
Campbell Progressive Party	CAMPBELL, Gregor Bruce
McGillicuddy Serious Party	GUMBLEY, Warren John
Citizens	HAGGITT, Michael Hunter Norman
Independent	HANAN, Elizabeth Ann
Community Independent	McMEEKING, Ian William
	WALLS, Richard

Figure 2.1. List of candidates for the Mayoral ballot in Dunedin in 1989, in the format given on the postal voting forms.

Since p is just a linear combination of the percentages of support for a candidate in different wards, which are estimated from independent samples, the standard error of p is given by

$$\text{SE}(p) = \sqrt{\left\{\sum w_i^2 \text{Var}(p_i)\right\}},$$

where Var (p_i) is the variance of p_i. Since the variance of p_i can be estimated by s^2/n_i, where s^2 is the pooled estimate of within-strata variance of the percentage support for the candidate, and n_i is the number of clusters in the ith ward, this leads to the estimated standard error

$$S\hat{E}(p_i) = \sqrt{\left(\sum w_i^2 s^2/n_i\right)}. \qquad (2.31)$$

Only about 1% of eligible voters were sampled, which means that a finite population correction is unnecessary here. Pooling of the within-strata variances assumes that the level of variation between streets is about the same in all wards. This is essential in order to calculate a standard error for the overall estimate because it was not possible to directly estimate variances for the wards that had only one sampled cluster.

Information on age, sex, and party support was collected for each respondent and used to estimate the support for the candidates from those in different categories on these variables. However, these breakdowns will not be considered in any detail here.

Table 2.8 shows the full results for the second survey, which was carried out a few days before postal votes were counted. The second-to-last row in the table, headed 'Overall mean', shows the estimated overall percentages of voters supporting none of the candidates, each of the candidates, and the 'don't knows', obtained using equation (2.30). The final row in the table shows estimated standard errors from equation (2.31).

The agreement between the predicted results and the final results was quite good, as can be seen from the comparison shown in Table 2.9 between the percentages of votes cast in the official postal ballot and the percentages from the survey, when the 'don't knows' and non-responders are excluded. Here the estimated percentages and their standard errors are obtained by multiplying the last two rows in Table 2.8 by 100.0/76.1 (1.316), since the sample result was that 76.1% of voters were estimated to have chosen a candidate.

When the second survey was being analysed it was discovered that there was a potential problem with the results provided by one of the interviewers used in the West Ward, who, on the evening of the survey, had to replace another interviewer who was unable to work. The number of survey forms returned was suspiciously high, and indicated an unusually low level of support for Richard Walls

Table 2.8. *Percentage support for mayoral candidates from the second survey in clusters (streets) within voting wards. The number of respondents in each street is shown in the final column of the table*

Ward	Street	Percentage of voters											n
		None	SEA	DB-P	PWB	GBC	WJG	MHNH	EAH	IWMc	RW	Don't know	
(A) Results for central city wards													
North	1	13.9	2.8	5.6	0.0	0.0	0.0	16.7	19.4	8.3	25.0	8.3	36
	2	25.8	0.0	25.8	0.0	0.0	3.2	3.2	6.5	0.0	16.1	19.4	31
	3	14.3	3.6	10.7	10.7	0.0	0.0	7.1	0.0	7.1	39.3	7.1	28
	4	26.1	4.3	17.4	0.0	0.0	0.0	4.3	4.3	4.3	21.7	17.4	23
	Mean	20.0	2.7	14.9	2.7	0.0	0.8	7.8	7.6	5.0	25.5	13.1	
	SD	6.8	1.9	8.8	5.4	0.0	1.6	6.1	8.4	3.7	9.9	6.2	
East	1	13.3	3.3	6.7	0.0	0.0	0.0	16.7	13.3	10.0	13.3	23.3	30
	2	9.4	0.0	0.0	0.0	0.0	0.0	21.9	12.5	21.9	28.1	6.3	32
	3	7.9	0.0	23.7	0.0	0.0	0.0	10.5	2.6	13.2	21.1	21.1	38
	4	15.0	0.0	12.5	0.0	0.0	0.0	10.0	5.0	15.0	27.5	15.0	40
	Mean	11.4	0.8	10.7	0.0	0.0	0.0	14.8	8.4	15.0	22.5	16.4	
	SD	3.3	1.7	10.0	0.0	0.0	0.0	5.6	5.4	5.0	6.9	7.6	
Central	1	13.3	10.0	3.3	0.0	0.0	3.3	13.3	10.0	23.3	23.3	0.0	30
	2	0.0	4.0	12.0	0.0	0.0	0.0	8.0	4.0	24.0	44.0	4.0	25
	3	10.7	10.7	3.6	0.0	0.0	0.0	28.6	7.4	14.3	21.4	3.6	28
	4	12.5	4.2	4.2	0.0	0.0	0.0	12.5	4.2	25.0	16.7	20.8	24
	Mean	9.1	7.2	5.8	0.0	0.0	0.8	15.6	6.3	21.7	26.4	7.1	
	SD	6.2	3.6	4.2	0.0	0.0	1.7	9.0	2.8	5.0	12.1	9.3	

West												
1	10.2	0.0	30.5	0.0	0.0	0.0	8.5	10.2	23.7	3.4	13.6	55
2	7.1	0.0	30.4	0.0	0.0	0.0	25.0	0.0	33.9	1.8	1.8	56
3	22.0	0.0	4.0	0.0	0.0	0.0	14.0	4.0	52.0	2.0	2.0	50
4	12.5	0.0	12.5	0.0	0.0	0.0	12.5	37.5	12.5	0.0	12.5	8
Mean	13.0	0.0	14.3	0.0	0.0	0.0	15.0	12.9	25.5	11.8	7.5	
SD	6.4	0.0	13.3	0.0	0.0	0.0	7.1	16.9	16.8	1.4	6.4	
(B) Results for Other Wards												
Mosgiel 1	5.4	2.7	5.4	2.7	0.0	2.7	18.9	16.2	13.5	21.6	10.8	37
2	6.7	13.3	13.3	0.0	6.7	0.0	20.0	6.7	20.0	0.0	13.3	15
Mean	6.0	8.0	9.4	1.4	3.3	1.4	19.5	11.4	16.8	10.8	12.1	
SD	0.9	7.5	5.6	1.9	4.7	1.9	0.8	6.8	4.6	15.3	1.8	
Saddle Hill	6.5	0.0	13.0	4.3	0.0	2.2	2.2	6.5	6.5	56.5	2.2	46
St Kilda	20.6	0.0	2.9	5.9	0.0	0.0	5.9	5.9	26.5	20.6	11.8	34
Green Island	5.3	0.0	2.6	0.0	0.0	0.0	5.3	10.5	28.9	42.1	5.3	38
Port Chalmers	37.5	0.0	25.0	0.0	0.0	0.0	0.0	12.5	6.3	12.5	6.3	16
Outlying areas	22.9	2.9	8.6	0.0	0.0	0.0	2.9	5.7	11.4	40.0	5.7	35
Overall mean	13.9	2.7	10.6	1.1	0.3	0.5	11.3	8.7	16.7	24.2	10.1	
SE	1.2	0.6	2.0	0.6	0.3	0.3	1.4	2.1	1.9	2.0	1.5	

Table 2.9. *Estimated percentage support for candidates for respondents in the second mayoral survey who made a choice, compared with the percentages obtained in the official ballot*

	SEA	DB-P	PWB	GBC	WJG	MHNH	EAH	IWMc	RW
Survey support(%)	4	15	1	0	1	15	11	23	30
SE	2	3	1	1	1	2	3	2	3
Official result	5	12	1	0	1	16	10	20	34

compared to the results from the other interviewers. It was conceivable that there was low support for Walls in the West Ward compared to the other wards, and a few calculations indicated that the overall percentage estimates would not be too seriously affected by errors in the results for the interviewer in question. Therefore, it was decided to include the interviewer's results as they stood. However, it seems very likely that the somewhat low estimate of the support for Walls and the somewhat high estimate of the support for McMeeking, compared to the final poll results, were at least to some extent due to the suspect results.

This problem is an example of how easy it is for biases to be introduced into a survey in unexpected ways, and for reasons that are largely outside the control of the organizer of the survey. It also highlights the need to examine the survey results carefully to see whether there are any obvious anomalous records.

Appendix: Checklist for planning a sample survey

(1) Objectives should be clear and concise. Refer to them regularly during the design and implementation of the survey

(2) The target population and sampling units should be clearly defined

(3) The sampling frame should be chosen to ensure that the sampled and target populations are close. Difficulties in this respect may be overcome by changing the sampling unit, for example by sampling the streets in a town instead of the households

(4) Choose the sampling design (e.g. stratified cluster sampling). Make trial calculations to ensure that the sample sizes chosen will give sufficient accuracy for population estimates

(5) If relevant, consider the merits of alternative methods of measurement (personal interviews, telephone interviews, mail survey, etc.), taking into account costs, possible levels of non-response, and the accuracy of the data that can be obtained

(6) Take care to avoid bias in the measurement instruments that are used, particularly with a questionnaire

(7) Ensure that the selection and training of field workers is done well, and that these workers are of high quality

(8) When possible do a pilot survey to test the questionnaire and survey procedures. Make appropriate changes to procedures

(9) Plan the organization of fieldwork in detail. Make sure the field workers know their duties and responsibilities by giving them clear written statements of these

(10) Plan the organization of data management, covering all aspects of recording and processing. Have a quality control scheme to check for data entry errors and unacceptable data values. Make sure that the proposed data analysis meets the objectives of the survey

3

Other sampling designs

3.1 Introduction

The previous chapter was concerned with what can be described as the classical theory of sampling finite populations. This theory covers many of the sampling problems that are likely to arise in a research study, but there are situations where different approaches are required. In particular, cases sometimes arise where it is not possible to decide in advance where and when the items in a population will be sampled. Instead a sampling scheme must be devised which allows items to be encountered with a certain probability. The analysis of data must then take into account the nature of this sampling scheme.

A number of different types of encounter sampling are reviewed in this chapter. First, some methods for estimating the number of individuals in a population are discussed. These are mainly of value in a biological setting, for example for estimating the number of mice living in a certain region. Next, size-biased sampling is considered, where the probability of sampling a unit in the population of interest depends on a measure of the size of that unit.

This chapter also provides an introduction to the handling of spatial data. This includes distance-based methods, involving the measurement of distances between the items in a population or between random points in space and the nearest items, and also methods for analysing quadrat counts. With these types of data there are two questions that are often of interest:

> Are the items of interest distributed at random positions within the study area?
> What is the density of the items over the study area?

3.2 Mark–recapture sampling

Mark–recapture sampling methods have been developed mainly for the estimation of the number of individuals in a mobile animal population. Early uses of the principles involved were by Laplace in 1786 to estimate the human population in France, by Petersen in 1896 to estimate the size of a fish population, and by Lincoln in 1930 to estimate the wildfowl population in North America (see Cormack, 1968).

The basic principle is based on a simple argument of proportions. For example, suppose that it is desired to estimate N, the number of fish in a lake. This can be done as follows. First, take a sample of n_1 fish from the lake, tag each of them, and release them back into the lake. Next, wait long enough for the tagged fish to mix freely with the untagged fish and then take another sample, of size n_2, which contains m tagged fish. It can then be argued that the proportion of tagged fish in the lake should be approximately the same as the proportion in the second sample, which is m/n_2. Thus $n_1/N \approx m/n_2$ and the mark–recapture estimator of the population total is

$$\hat{N} = n_1 n_2 / m. \qquad (3.1)$$

For example, if the first and second sample sizes are 100, and the second sample contains 50 tagged fish then $\hat{N} = 100 \times 100/50 = 200$.

An approximate equation for the standard error of $\hat{N}$ is

$$\mathrm{SE}(\hat{N}) \approx \sqrt{\{n_1^2 n_2 (n_2 - m)/m^3\}} \qquad (3.2)$$

and approximate 95% confidence limits for the true population size are $\hat{N} \pm 2 \cdot \mathrm{SE}(\hat{N})$. An approximate equation for the bias in $\hat{N}$ (the mean that would be obtained from repeated sampling minus the true size) is also available, this being

$$\mathrm{Bias}(\hat{N}) \approx N(N - n_1)/(n_1 n_2). \qquad (3.3)$$

Since in principle it is possible to get no marked animals in the second sample, an infinite estimate of N can occur. Therefore the above formulae for the standard error and bias are 'large sample' results that assume a negligible probability of obtaining $m = 0$. For this reason, the modified estimate

$$\hat{N}^* = (n_1 + 1)(n_2 + 1)/(m + 1) - 1, \qquad (3.4)$$

is better (Seber, 1982a). This is unbiased when $n_1 + n_2 \geqslant N$ and approximately unbiased otherwise. The estimate of the standard error is

$$\mathrm{S\hat{E}}(\hat{N}^*) = \sqrt{[(n_1 + 1)(n_2 + 1)(n_1 - m)(n_2 - m)/\{(m + 1)^2(m + 2)\}]}. \qquad (3.5)$$

As an example, suppose that before the start of the hunting season, a wildlife organization wants to estimate the size of a deer population. A sample of 300 deer is taken, and the deer are tagged and released. A second sample of 200 deer is taken two weeks later and found to contain 62 tagged deer. Then the nearly unbiased estimate is $\hat{N}^* = 301 \times 201/63 - 1 = 959.3$, with $\hat{SE}(\hat{N}^*) = \sqrt{\{301 \times 201 \times (300 - 62) \times (200 - 62)/(63^2 \times 64)\}} = 88.4$. This suggests that the population size is probably within the range 959 ± 177.

The assumptions that are required for mark–recapture estimations using the above formulae are:

(a) The population is 'closed' so that the size N does not change during the sampling period
(b) The second sample is a simple random sample from the population
(c) Individuals do not lose their marks between samples
(d) All marks are recognized in the second sample

These assumptions may be difficult to ensure with natural populations.

The uses of mark–recapture are not restricted to the estimation of animal population sizes. For example, suppose that an author goes through a book and finds 25 misprints. Independently, an editor goes through and finds 30 misprints, of which 20 are the same as the authors and 10 are not. Here the total number of misprints is N, of which $n_1 = 25$ are 'marked' by the author. The second sample of size $n_2 = 30$ finds $m = 20$ marked misprints. The estimate of N is therefore $\hat{N}^* = 26 \times 31/21 - 1 = 37.3$, say 37, with $\hat{SE}(\hat{N}^*) = \sqrt{\{26 \times 31 \times 5 \times 10/(21^2 \times 22)\}} = 2.0$. It seems that the number of misprints is probably within the range 37 ± 4.

As another example, suppose that a medical researcher wants to determine the number of cases of a rare disease that have occurred in the last 10 years in a city. There are two types of record that can be used, neither of which can be expected to cover all cases. According to the first type of record there were 10 cases. According to the second type of record there were also 10 cases, but only 7 of these are the same as those found in the first records. Here $n_1 = 10$, $n_2 = 10$ and $m = 7$. Hence $\hat{N}^* = 11 \times 11/8 - 1 = 14.1$, say 14 cases, with estimated standard error 1.4. A reasonable assessment is that the number of cases was between 11 and 17. Notice that in this case the lower 95% confidence limit is not very sensible because 13 different cases were actually seen during sampling. This indicates that the sample sizes are too small for the limits $\hat{N}^* \pm 2 \cdot \text{S}\hat{\text{E}}(\hat{N}^*)$ to be reliable.

In both these non-biological examples the key assumption is that the two samples are independent in the sense that all cases are equally likely to occur in the second sample, irrespective of their occurrence or not in the first sample.

The mark–recapture method can be used with several samples. For instance, returning to the example of estimating the number of misprints in a book, suppose that four readers go through the book and find 12 misprints between them, as shown in Table 3.1. For example, the first of the 12 misprints was missed by reader 1 but picked out by the other three readers.

There are various ways of handling data of this type. One simple approach along lines suggested by Menkins and Anderson (1988) is to use readers 1 and 2 as giving a 'marking sample', and readers 3 and 4 as the 'second sample'. Then $n_1 = 10$ misprints were marked, of which $m = 7$ were seen in the second sample, of size $n_2 = 9$. Hence the total number of misprints can be estimated as $\hat{N}^* = (10 + 1)(9 + 1)/(7 + 1) - 1 = 13.8$, say 14, with estimated standard error 0.8. This compares with the 12 misprints found by the four readers between them.

Many of the developments in mark–recapture sampling have been designed for open animal populations, where new animals are entering through births and immigration, and animals are leaving through deaths and emigration. With such populations it is common for researchers to want to estimate survival rates and the numbers of new entries between sample times, as well as population sizes. This can be done if a series of samples are taken from the population, for example at daily intervals, and the animals captured are marked before being released. The marking has to make it possible to know when each animal is recaptured, which means that either each animal is given a unique mark or a new date-specific mark is added at each recapture. Although this sounds complicated, marking of this type has been used successfully even with small insects.

Mark–recapture sampling can be used to estimate survival rates since the fall-off in the number of recaptures of marked animals with time can be attributed to deaths and permanent emigration. Numbers of new entries can be estimated, since in their absence the proportion of marked animals in the population (and in samples) should steadily increase with time. If the rate of increase is less than expected on this basis then new entries are indicated.

A major milestone in the development of methods for estimating population parameters for open populations was the publication of the *Jolly–Seber model* (Jolly, 1965; Seber, 1965), which provides explicit estimators with variances. This does require rather good data since the survival rates and the numbers of entries to the population are estimated with separate parameters for each interval between two samples. For this reason some more recent work has been directed towards models with fewer parameters.

There is a large literature on mark–recapture sampling and estimation methods. Those interested in relatively non-mathematical accounts will find the books by Begon (1979) and Blower *et al*. (1981) and Chapter 3 of Southwood (1978) to be useful. A more comprehensive review is provided by Seber's (1982*b*) book, updated by Seber (1986). For closed populations, Otis *et al*. (1978) and White *et al*. (1982) are useful references for models where capture probabilities are allowed to vary with time or individual or capture history, as well as some combinations of these. The recent monograph by Pollock *et al*. (1990) serves the same role for open populations.

3.3 Removal sampling

The removal method is an alternative to mark–recapture sampling that is sometimes used to estimate the size of a closed animal population. Instead of marking animals, they are completely removed from the population. Then, as more and more samples are taken the numbers caught in each sample goes down because of the reducing population size.

For example, suppose that a party of anglers discover a lake and start fishing, with the results shown in Table 3.2. It is a reasonable assumption that the reduction in numbers is due to fishing, and that most fish were taken by day 5. On this basis, the total number of fish that were originally in the lake can be estimated by extrapolating the number caught beyond day 5, to get a total that is somewhat higher than 172.

In the simplest of cases, estimation from removal sampling relies on the following assumptions, which ensure that when a sample is taken the expected number of captures is proportional to the number of individuals that have not yet been removed:

  (a) Whenever a sample is taken, each available individual in a population has the same chance of being captured

Table 3.1. *Misprints found by four readers of a book, where 0 indicates that a misprint was missed by the reader and 1 indicates that the misprint was noticed*

Misprint	Reader			
	1	2	3	4
1	0	1	1	1
2	1	0	1	0
3	1	1	1	1
4	0	0	0	1
5	1	1	1	1
6	0	1	1	0
7	0	1	1	0
8	1	1	1	1
9	0	1	0	0
10	0	0	0	1
11	1	1	0	0
12	1	0	0	0

Table 3.2. *Results of fishing a lake for five days*

Day	Fish caught
1	65
2	43
3	34
4	18
5	12
Total	172

(b) The population is closed so that the size remains constant over the sampling period, apart from the removal losses

(c) The catching of one individual does not change the probability of catching other individuals

On this basis, there are several possible methods of estimation. One simple approach (Hayne, 1949) is based on the fact that whenever a sample is taken a proportion p of the available individuals are expected to be captured, and that when no further captures can be made the sum of all previous captures is the initial population size.

To make this clearer, let X_i be the total catch before the ith sample, Y_i be the catch in the ith sample, N be the population size, and p be the expected proportion of the available population captured in a sample. Then the approximate relationship

$$Y_i \approx p(N - X_i) = pN - pX_i,$$

should apply since $N - X_i$ is the number available for capture in the ith sample. This shows that there is an approximately linear relationship between Y_i and X_i, and that $Y_i = 0$ when $X_i = N$.

Given data values of X and Y, the linear relationship can be estimated by fitting a regression line. Regression methods have been mentioned already in Section 2.11, and are discussed further in Chapter 4. Here it can merely be noted that this is one way to estimate the relationship between Y and X values, although the usual assumptions that justify the use of regression are not applicable with data from removal sampling.

To take a numerical example, consider again the fishing data given in Table 3.2, which can be used to produce X and Y values shown in Table 3.3. Figure 3.1 shows Y plotted against X, with the fitted regression line

$$Y = 65.42 - 0.327X.$$

From this line, $Y = 0$ when $0.327X = 65.42$. That is, $Y = 0$ when $X = 65.42/0.327 = 200.1$. The initial number of fish in the lake therefore appears to have been about 200.

It is not actually necessary to remove individuals physically from a population in order to use the principle behind removal sampling. If individuals are marked on first capture then they can simply be ignored if they are captured again. Using 'removal sampling' in this way may give a better population estimate than one of the more sophisticated mark–recapture methods that use information from multiple recaptures if the first capture of an individual tends to change that individual's behaviour.

The simplicity of the regression method for estimating the population size from removal sampling is appealing. However, it does suffer two disadvantages in comparison with an alternative method that was suggested by Zippin (1956). First, there is no simple way to calculate a standard error for the regression estimator. Second, Zippin's method, which uses maximum likelihood

Table 3.3. *The data in Table 3.2 arranged in a form suitable for estimating the population size by removal sampling*

Day	Number previously caught (X)	Latest catch (Y)
1	0	65
2	65	43
3	108	34
4	142	18
5	160	12

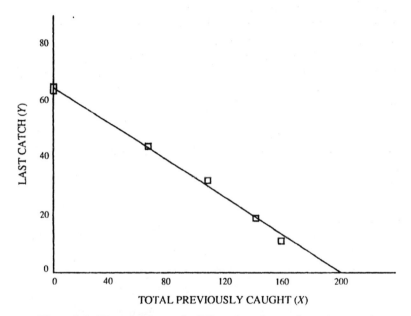

Figure 3.1. Plot of fish caught (Y) against the total previous catch (X), with the regression line $Y = 65.42 - 0.327X$. The estimated population size by removal sampling is given by the point where the regression line crosses the X axis, i.e. 200.1.

estimation, should produce an estimator with a smaller standard error than the regression estimator.

More information about the removal method, including generalizations that allow the sampling effort to vary for different samples, can be found in Seber's (1982*b*) book, updated by Seber

(1986). Other useful sources of information about the method are provided by Otis *et al*. (1978) and White *et al*. (1982), and Southwood (1978, p. 230).

3.4 Transect sampling

Following Eberhardt (1978), transect sampling methods can be classified into three types:

(a) With *line intercept sampling*, a line is taken through a sampling region and what is recorded is the number of units that are crossed by the line. This method is most appropriate for sampling large immobile objects that are easily seen, such as clumps of vegetation

(b) With *strip transect sampling* objects are counted in a strip running through the region. This is appropriate with smaller objects that can be thought of as being located at points, such as bird nests

(c) With *line transect sampling* an observer moves along a straight line through the area covered by a population, and counts how many members of the population are seen. Sometimes individuals will be flushed out by the observer while at other times they can be sighted whilst stationary. Generally, the probability of a sighting will depend on the distance of an individual from the transect line and the data have to be used to estimate the detection probability as a function of distance

The analysis of data obtained by transect sampling methods can be quite complicated, particularly for line transect sampling when the detection probability function must be estimated. For more information, see Seber (1982*b*, 1986) and Burnham *et al*. (1980).

3.5 Size-biased sampling

Size-biased sampling occurs when the objects in a population are encountered with probabilities that are proportional to a measure of their size. For example, suppose that medical records are kept on file cards, with a variable number of cards per patient, and that a sample of records is chosen by picking random cards and then extracting the records that they are part of. In that case the probability of choosing a particular record will be proportional to the number of cards for that record. As a result, longer records will tend to be over-represented, and short records will tend to be under-represented.

The effect of size-biased sampling is to give a biased distribution for any variable that is correlated with the size of the sampling units. The obvious case is, of course, the size variable itself since the sampled units may have a mean size that is considerably larger than the population mean.

Size-biased sampling is sometimes either more convenient than simple random sampling, or is inevitable because of the nature of the sampling process. However, its use should not cause any great concern since it is straightforward to adjust estimates of population means and totals for the size-bias, providing that the relationship between the size of a unit and its probability of being sampled is known (Cox, 1969).

Therefore, suppose that a population consisting of N items, is sampled in such a way that the probability of choosing the ith item is kX_i, where X_i is the size of the item and k is a positive constant. Then it can be shown that an unbiased estimator of the population total of X is

$$\hat{T}_X = n/k, \tag{3.6}$$

where n is the number of items sampled. Also, an unbiased estimate of the population mean is

$$\hat{\mu}_X = n \Big/ \sum (1/X_i), \tag{3.7}$$

where X_i is the size of the ith unit sampled, and the summation is over the n sampled units.

If all the units in the sample have a second variable Y measured on them an unbiased estimator of the population total of Y is

$$\hat{T}_Y = (1/k) \sum (Y_i/X_i), \tag{3.8}$$

where Y_i is the value of Y for the ith sampled unit and the summation is over the sampled units. Furthermore, an unbiased estimator of the population mean of Y is

$$\hat{\mu}_Y = \sum (Y_i/X_i) \Big/ \sum (1/X_i). \tag{3.9}$$

As an example of the use of these equations, consider again the example of sampling medical records by selecting individual cards. Suppose that 10 records are extracted by selecting cards at random and removing the records that they are part of, and that these provide the data shown in Table 3.4 on the number of cards per record and the age of the patient.

The means shown in Table 3.4 are arithmetic means, calculated in the normal way. However, allowing for the size-biased sampling the estimate of the mean of X is $\hat{\mu}_X = n/\sum(1/X_i) = 10/6.92 = 1.4$ cards per record, and the estimate of the mean age of patients is $\hat{\mu}_Y = \sum(Y_i/X_i)/\sum(1/X_i) = 25.2$ years. Therefore, the estimated population means, 'corrected' for size-biased sampling, are both slightly smaller than the arithmetic means.

These equations for estimation with size-biased sampling are discussed further by McDonald and Manly (1989) within the general framework of methods for adjusting estimates to take into account biased sampling schemes, where size-biased sampling is only a special case. As McDonald and Manly note, it will sometimes by necessary to estimate the relationship between the probability of selection and variables that are measured on the units in a population, possibly by resampling a biased sample. Formulae for variances of bias corrected estimators are provided by McDonald and Manly, but in practice it may be better to determine variances either by doing several complete replications of the sampling process or by using bootstrapping, as discussed in Section 9.7.

3.6 Sampling positions of objects in space

With many studies the main interest is in the location of objects in space rather than on variables measured on those objects. This is obviously often true in geography, but sometimes is also the case in other areas such as botany, zoology and medicine. For example, spatial considerations are of prime importance with the following questions:

(1) What is the density of a rare plant over a large study area, and is the distribution of plants random in the sense that it appears that plants are equally likely to occur anywhere in the area?

Table 3.4. *The result of sampling 10 medical records*

	Patient no.										
	1	2	3	4	5	6	7	8	9	10	Mean
Cards	1	2	1	3	1	1	2	4	1	3	1.9
Age	20	25	18	31	25	28	34	38	22	35	27.6

(2) Are the nests of a bird species distributed randomly over an area?

(3) Do cases of childhood leukaemia tend to occur close to nuclear installations?

(4) What is the density of trees in a forest?

(5) How are supermarkets distributed in the urban area?

(6) Are galaxies randomly located in space?

What these questions have in common is that there are certain 'objects' being studied, where these can be considered to occur at points in space. There is interest in whether the objects appear to be at random positions within the study area and, in some cases, the density of points (number per unit area) needs to be estimated.

The alternatives to a random distribution are *clustering*, and *regularity*. In the first of these cases the objects tend to occur in clusters that might themselves be randomly or non-randomly located, while in the second case objects tend to be about the same distance apart.

There are a range of approaches to the sampling of points in space, and the analysis of the data obtained from such sampling. One important distinction is between (a) methods based on measuring distances between objects, or between random points and objects, and (b) methods based on counting the number of points occurring within quadrats laid out over the area of interest. Generally, distance-based methods are appropriate when only a sample from a large population of points can be considered, or where the whole population contains a small enough number of points so that it is practical to determine the precise location of each one. On the other hand, quadrat methods are appropriate when it is easy to count the number of points in small areas, but not easy to determine their precise positions. In practice a study may consider both distance and quadrat data.

3.7 Distance-based methods

Distance-based methods for sampling points in space are sometimes called *nearest neighbour* methods. They are widely used in forestry, for example, to estimate the density of trees in a region when quadrat methods are difficult to use. Various types of distances have been used in this context, such as distances from random points to the nearest (or nth nearest) trees, distances from trees to their nearest neighbours (or nth nearest neighbours), or distances from random points to their nearest trees and then to the nearest neighbouring trees. Of course, all these types of distance can also be used for sampling other objects.

One approach to the estimation of the density of points requires the assumption that objects occur at random positions, and that the distances from m random points to their nearest objects have been measured as $X_1, X_2, \ldots, X_m$. This means that the area searched from the ith random point before an object was found is the area within a circle with radius X_i, say $A_i = \pi X_i^2$. Hence, an unbiased estimate of the area in the population that is occupied by one object is

$$\bar{A} = \sum_{i=1}^{m} A_i/m = \pi \sum_{i=1}^{m} X_i^2/m,$$

where the summations are over the m random points. It follows that an estimate of the density of objects per unit area is

$$\hat{D} = 1/\bar{A} = m/\left\{\pi \sum_{i=1}^{m} X_i^2\right\}. \tag{3.10}$$

It can be shown that $\hat{D}$ has the approximate standard error

$$\mathrm{SE}(\hat{D}) = \sigma_A D^2/\sqrt{m}, \tag{3.11}$$

where σ_A is the population standard deviation of A_i values. The standard error can therefore be estimated by

$$\mathrm{S\hat{E}}(\hat{D}) = s_A \hat{D}^2/\sqrt{m}, \tag{3.12}$$

where s_A is the sample standard deviation of A_i values.

For a regular pattern of objects the distance from random points to objects will tend to be smaller than with a random pattern, while the distances from each object to its nearest neighbour will tend to be larger than with a random pattern. The reverse is true with a clustered pattern, so that distances from random points to their nearest objects will tend to be large and the distances between neighbouring objects will tend to be small. For this reason, one recommendation is to combine estimates based on both types of distance if the assumption of randomness seems questionable.

One useful way to obtain both point to object and object to object distances involves the use of *T-square sampling*. Here, the distance is measured from a random point to the nearest object, and then from that object to the nearest neighbour in the direction away from the initial point, as shown in Figure 3.2. Therefore, the area searched for the first object is omitted in the search for the second object. Hence, if objects are located at random then the search area for the first object and the search area for the second object will be independent random variables.

Suppose that a T-square sample of size m is taken, so that the distances $X_1, X_2, \ldots, X_m$ from m random points to the nearest objects are determined, and also the distances $Y_1, Y_2, \ldots, Y_m$, from each of the m objects to their nearest neighbours in the directions away from the random points. The search area from the ith random point to the nearest object is then $A_{Xi} = \pi X_i^2$, so that an estimate of density based on the X distances is

$$\hat{D}_X = m \bigg/ \sum_{i=1}^{m} A_{Xi}.$$

(3.13)

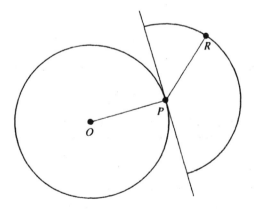

Figure 3.2. T-square sampling. The point O is randomly chosen, and the nearest object is found at P. The nearest neighbour to P is then found by searching only in the area above the T which is formed by the line OP and the line through P that is perpendicular to OP.

On the other hand, the half circle search area from the ith object to its nearest neighbour is $A_{Yi} = \frac{1}{2}\pi Y_i^2$, so that an estimate of density based on the Y distances is

$$\hat{D}_Y = m \Bigg/ \sum_{i=1}^{m} A_{Yi}. \qquad (3.14)$$

A combined estimate of density that may be somewhat robust to a non-random pattern is then

$$\hat{D}^* = \sqrt{(\hat{D}_X \hat{D}_Y)}. \qquad (3.15)$$

The standard errors of $\hat{D}_X$ and $\hat{D}_Y$ can be estimated using equation (3.12), and an approximate standard error for $\hat{D}^*$ can then be determined from the equation

$$\mathrm{S\hat{E}}(\hat{D}^*) = (\hat{D}^*/2)\sqrt{\{\mathrm{S\hat{E}}(\hat{D}_X)^2/\hat{D}_X^2 + \mathrm{S\hat{E}}(\hat{D}_Y)^2/\hat{D}_X^2\}}. \qquad (3.16)$$

A test for randomness can be carried out using the same data since for randomly located objects, the statistic

$$U = \sum_{i=1}^{m} \{A_{Xi}/(A_{Xi} + A_{Yi})\}/m, \qquad (3.17)$$

has an approximately normal distribution with mean $\frac{1}{2}$ and standard error $\mathrm{SE}(U) = 1/\sqrt{(12m)}$. Hence the statistic

$$Z_U = (U - \tfrac{1}{2})/\sqrt{\{1/(12m)\}} \qquad (3.18)$$

will approximately have a standard normal distribution. Significantly low values of Z_U indicate regularity in the point pattern, non-significant values indicate randomness, and significantly large values indicate clustering (Ripley, 1981, p. 136). This test, and the density estimates, assume that the area being sampled is large enough, and contains enough objects, for the m sample points to be effectively independent.

For further information about the use of distance-based methods for estimating densities and testing for randomness the books by Diggle (1983) and Ripley (1981) will be found to be useful.

Example 3.1: T-square sampling of bramble canes

As an example of the use of T-square sampling to estimate density and to test for randomness, consider the locations of 368 bramble canes in an area of size 9 m by 4.5 m that is shown in Figure 3.3. This figure is redrawn from Figure 1 of Diggle and Milne (1983),

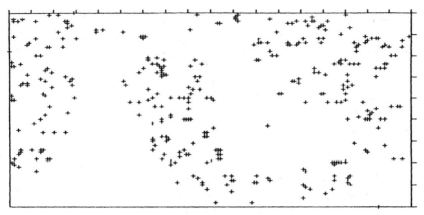

Figure 3.3. Positions of 368 bramble canes in an area 9 m by 4.5 m. (Diggle and Milne, 1983; Hutchings, 1978.)

and comes from an original study by Hutchings (1978). The actual density is $368/(9 \times 4.5) = 9.09$ bramble canes/m^2, with a clear indication of clustering shown in the figure.

A T-square of size 20 was taken from the region, with the results shown in Table 3.5. To avoid meeting the boundary of the region when searching for canes, the random points were chosen from within a rectangle with horizontal coordinates in the range 0.5 to 8.5 m and vertical coordinates in the range 0.5 to 4.0 m.

From the table it can be seen that the estimated density calculated from point to cane distances using equation (3.13) is $\hat{D}_X = 2.053$ canes/m^2, with estimated standard error $\hat{SE}(\hat{D}_X) = 1.018$. However, the estimated density calculated from the cane to cane distances using equation (3.14) is $\hat{D}_Y = 25.00$ canes/m^2, with estimated standard error $\hat{SE}(\hat{D}_Y) = 9.92$. The combined estimate from equation (3.15) is therefore $\hat{D}^* = \sqrt{(2.053 \times 25.00)} = 7.16$, with estimated standard error $\hat{SE}(\hat{D}^*) = (7.16/2)\sqrt{\{(1.018^2/2.053^2) + (9.92^2/25.00^2)\}} = 2.273$, suggesting that the true density is probably within the range $7.16 \pm (2 \times 2.273)$, or 2.61 to 11.71. This is satisfactory because the true density of canes is 9.09 canes/m^2, and the combined estimate $\hat{D}^*$ is much better than either of the direct estimates $\hat{D}_X$ or $\hat{D}_Y$.

For the test of randomness, the statistic of equation (3.17) is $U = 0.77$, where this is the sum of the values in the last column of Table 3.5. For randomly located objects, this statistic is a random value from a normal distribution with mean $\frac{1}{2}$ and standard

Table 3.5. *The result of taking 20 T-square samples of bramble canes. (Diggle and Milne, 1983; Huchings, 1978)*

H, horizontal location of random point; V, vertical location of random point; X, distance from random point to nearest cane; Y, distance from cane to the nearest neighbour in the opposite direction to the random point; A_X and A_Y, search areas.

Point	H	V	X	Y	A_X	A_Y	$A_X/(A_X + A_Y)$
1	1.41	0.96	0.17	0.10	0.09	0.02	0.85
2	5.99	0.81	0.21	0.05	0.13	0.00	0.97
3	6.83	1.89	0.47	0.11	0.69	0.02	0.97
4	4.62	2.97	0.07	0.10	0.02	0.02	0.51
5	7.66	1.36	0.17	0.14	0.09	0.03	0.73
6	1.33	3.38	0.18	0.05	0.11	0.00	0.96
7	3.10	0.67	0.15	0.15	0.07	0.04	0.68
8	4.11	3.24	0.19	0.05	0.12	0.00	0.97
9	6.02	3.94	0.68	0.11	1.47	0.02	0.99
10	3.38	3.75	0.13	0.15	0.05	0.04	0.60
11	6.89	3.76	1.23	0.11	4.72	0.02	1.00
12	6.29	1.70	0.11	0.11	0.04	0.02	0.66
13	7.27	2.52	0.46	0.43	0.67	0.29	0.70
14	0.81	2.07	0.18	0.14	0.10	0.03	0.76
15	5.02	2.34	0.09	0.00	0.03	0.00	1.00
16	8.16	1.75	0.11	0.35	0.04	0.19	0.16
17	3.27	0.97	0.10	0.11	0.03	0.02	0.61
18	6.48	1.63	0.04	0.11	0.01	0.02	0.22
19	6.34	2.22	0.13	0.00	0.05	0.00	1.00
20	6.40	3.35	0.62	0.11	1.20	0.02	0.98
Mean					0.487	0.040	0.77
SD					1.080	0.071	
$\hat{D}$					2.053	25.000	
$\hat{SE}(\hat{D})$					1.018	9.920	

deviation $\sqrt{\{1/(12m)\}} = 0.0645$. The test statistic of equation (3.18) is therefore $Z_U = (0.77 - 0.5)/0.0645 = 4.19$, which is significantly different from zero at the 0.1% level. There is clear evidence of a non-random distribution. In fact, since Z_U is greater than zero there is evidence of clustering, as is obvious from Figure 3.3.

3.8 Quadrat counts

Another way of looking at spatial data is by using quadrat counts. With this approach, the area of interest is divided into quadrats and a count is made of the number of objects in some or all of these quadrats. The quadrats are usually square, but that is not essential. A key theoretical result is that if objects occur at random positions then the quadrat counts will be random values from a Poisson distribution. That is to say, the probability of observing r objects in a quadrat will be

$$P(r) = \exp(-\mu)\mu^r/r!, \qquad r = 0, 1, 2, \ldots$$

for some value of μ, which is the mean of the distribution.

The variance of the Poisson distribution is also μ. Hence, if the observed variance exceeds the observed mean then this suggests a clustered distribution, with a tendency for some cells to be empty while others hold many objects. On the other hand, if the observed variance is less than the observed mean then this indicates a tendency for regularity, with the quadrat count being more constant than expected from randomness. Therefore, the sample variance to mean ratio, $s^2/\bar{x}$, is a simple measure of non-randomness. A test statistic for randomness based on this ratio is

$$t = \{(s^2/\bar{x}) - 1\}/\sqrt{\{2/(n-1)\}}, \qquad (3.19)$$

which can be compared with the t distribution with $n - 1$ degrees of freedom, where n is the number of quadrats being considered (Rogers, 1974, p. 6).

Example 3.2: Quadrat counts for Swedish pine saplings

As an example, consider the positions of 71 Swedish pine saplings in a 10 m by 10 m area, as shown in Figure 3.4 which is redrawn from Figure 8.7(a) of Ripley (1981) and is based on original data of Strand (1972). If the area is divided into 64 quadrats of size

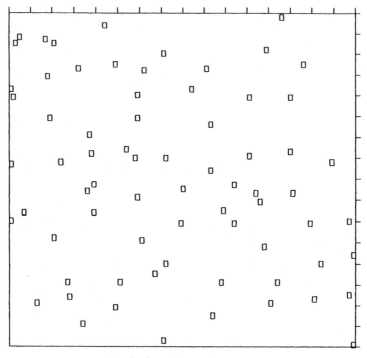

Figure 3.4. The positions of 71 Swedish pine saplings in a 10 m by 10 m square.

1.25 m by 1.25 m, then the counts in these quadrats are as shown in Table 3.6.

The mean count is $\bar{x} = 1.109$ and the variance is $s^2 = 0.702$. The variance to mean ratio is therefore 0.63 which suggests some regularity in the distribution. From equation (3.19) it is found that

$$t = (0.63 - 1)/\sqrt{(2/63)} = -2.07$$

which is significantly different from zero on a two-tailed test at the 5% level. Therefore, there is clear evidence of non-randomness, and, since the test statistic is negative, there is a suggestion of regularity in the location of the Swedish pine saplings.

Example 3.3: The location of non-food stores in Ljubljana

As a second example involving quadrat counts, consider the locations of the 239 non-food stores in Ljubljana, Yugoslavia, as

Table 3.6. *Quadrat counts obtained from Figure 3.4 showing the location of Swedish pine saplings. (Ripley, 1981; Strand, 1972)*

1	0	0	1	1	1	1	0
3	2	0	1	2	1	1	2
2	1	2	0	2	0	1	0
0	1	3	1	1	1	3	2
1	1	1	1	1	2	2	1
0	1	1	1	0	2	1	2
0	1	0	2	2	1	1	2
0	1	1	0	0	1	1	3

recorded by Rogers (1974, p. 91). If the city is divided into 16 quadrats then the counts in these quadrats are as shown in Table 3.7. The mean is $\bar{x} = 14.94$ and the variance is $s^2 = 1632.2$. The variance to mean ratio is 109.25, with a corresponding t-value from equation (3.19) of 296.5, with 15 degrees of freedom. The evidence for clustering is very clear.

3.9 Sampling of quadrats

In the two examples just considered the total area was systematically covered with quadrats. However, sometimes this will involve too much work so that sample quadrats have to be used. This makes no difference to the test for randomness, since if objects occur at random positions then the counts in systematic quadrats are just as random as the counts in random quadrats.

With a complete coverage of the area of interest the density of objects is exactly the number of objects divided by the total area. This can also be thought of as the mean quadrat count divided by the quadrat area, again determined without error. On the other hand, if a simple random sample of n quadrats is taken, then the sample mean quadrat count $\bar{x}$ is an estimate of the population mean count, with estimated standard error

$$\hat{SE}(\bar{x}) = \surd\{(s^2/n)(1 - n/N)\} \qquad (3.20)$$

where N is the total number of quadrats in the population. The estimated density is then $\hat{D} = \bar{x}/A$, where A is the area of a quadrat, with estimated standard error $\hat{SE}(\hat{D}) = \hat{SE}(\bar{x})/A$.

Table 3.7. *Quadrat counts for non-food stores in Ljubljana, Yugoslavia. (Rogers, 1974)*

5	3	1	0
4	20	5	0
0	164	10	1
2	24	0	0

For further information about methods for the analysis of quadrat counts the books by Ripley (1981) and Rogers (1974) will be found to be useful.

3.10 Summary and further reading

This chapter has reviewed a number of special sampling methods that do not fall within the scope of the classical theory for sampling finite populations. First, a number of encounter sampling procedures were covered, where the main interest is usually in the estimation of the number of items in the population. This was followed by some discussion of approaches for the analysis of spatial data. Although it has been possible only to refer briefly to the large literature on these topics, readers will now at least have some idea of what can be done when simple random sampling is not possible. Most applications of these methods to date have been in ecology and a useful reference in this area is the text by Southwood (1978).

The analysis of spatial data is an area where there is great potential for computer intensive methods because of the difficulty in handling some of the distribution problems that arise in any other way. For example, bootstrapping can be used to estimate standard errors for density estimates while Monte Carlo methods can be used for tests of randomness (Manly, 1991). A full discussion of computer intensive methods is reserved for Chapter 9, but the opportunity is taken in Case Study 3 to show how Monte Carlo methods can be used to assess whether prehistoric sites were randomly located in an area of Thailand.

There are many interesting applications of spatial data analysis in archaeology. Those interested in reading further in this area will find the book by Hodder and Orton (1976) to be a useful source of information.

Exercises

1. A number of studies have been conducted to see how well methods for estimating the size of an animal population work with populations of known size. One such study was carried out by Mahon (1980) and is used as an example by White *et al.* (1982). This involved taking seven removal samples of the fantail darter (*Etheostoma flabellare*) that were longer than 35 mm from a stream and then collecting the remaining fish by using rotenone. The numbers caught in the seven removal samples were as follows:

Day

	1	2	3	4	5	6	7	Total
Captures	180	115	94	84	75	58	60	666

Estimate the total number of fish present using the regression method that is described in Section 3.3. After taking these samples, the use of rotenone produced another 485 fish, to give a total actual population size of 1151. From analysing these data White *et al.* concluded that the capture probability was not constant for each sampling occasion. Using the seven removal samples, and a method of estimation that allows for unequal capture probabilities, they obtained an estimated population size of $\hat{N} = 1025$, with a standard error of 105.

2. An albatross colony on the Otago Peninsular in New Zealand includes a 42 m by 60 m rectangular area on which 22 nests are located. If this area is divided up into 25 quadrats of size 12 m by 8.4 m, then the numbers of nests in each quadrat are as shown in Table 3.8. Calculate the variance to mean ratio and test for a random location of the nests over the area. (These data on the location of albatross nests are considered again in Example 9.2.)

CASE STUDY 2

Estimating the size of a population of mice

This case study is based on an example of population estimation that is considered by Otis *et al.* (1978, p. 87) in their monograph

Table 3.8. *Counts of number of albatross nests in 25 quadrats on the Otago Peninsular, New Zealand*

0	4	0	0	0
2	2	2	0	1
1	1	4	0	0
0	1	1	0	0
0	3	0	0	0

on the estimation of the sizes of closed animal populations using mark–recapture and removal methods. The data come from an original study by V. Reid. They were obtained from a six-day trapping study of the deer mouse *Peromyscus maniculatus* that was carried out near Wet Swizer Creek in Colorado in August, 1975. A rectangular grid of 9 by 11 traps was used with 15.2 m spacing. A small mammal trap was placed at each grid point, so that 99 traps were used altogether. Traps were checked on mornings and afternoons, but only the morning captures are considered here. It is reasonable to regard the population as closed (not changing because of ingress or egress) over the relatively short study period.

Table 3.9 gives a summary of the recapture data. The estimates of the population sizes and their standard errors that are shown in the final two columns of the table come from the equations (3.4) and (3.5), treating M, the total number of marks to date as the first sample size n_1, the sample size on the day in question as n_2, and the number of marked animals seen on the day in question m. In other words, all the samples prior to day i are regarded as providing the marked animals that can be captured on day i.

If the assumptions required to use the estimator $\hat{N}^*$ were valid for this study it would be expected that the series of estimated population sizes shown in Table 3.9 would differ just because of sampling errors. However, what can be seen is an upward trend with the estimates increasing from 33.0 on day 2 to 52.1 on day 6. The standard errors indicate that sampling errors are fairly small and it is considered unlikely that immigration was causing the trend. It seems, therefore, that the assumptions involved in using the estimator $\hat{N}^*$ are suspect for this example.

Otis *et al*. (1978) fitted several different models to the recapture data using their computer program CAPTURE, and concluded that the trapping of mice was leading to them becoming 'trap-happy', possibly because the bait in traps was a source of food.

Table 3.9. *Summary of the recapture data from a six day study of the deer mouse. (Otis et al., 1978)*

M = number of mice marked before the day in question; n = the sample size on the day; u = the unmarked mice captured on the day; m = the marked mice captured on the day; $\hat{N}^*$ = estimated population size; $\hat{SE}$ = the estimated standard error of $\hat{N}^*$.

Day	Marked to date M	Sample size n	Unmarked mice u	Marked mice m	Estimated population size $\hat{N}^*$	$\hat{SE}$
1	0	16	16	0	—	—
2	16	29	15	14	33.0	2.1
3	31	27	7	20	41.7	2.7
4	38	29	6	23	47.8	2.7
5	44	32	4	28	50.2	1.9
6	48	38	3	35	52.1	1.2

That is, the probability of recapture was higher than the probability of first capture. This type of trap response is not uncommon, and animals also sometimes become 'trap-shy'.

A simple way to estimate a population size when there is a trap response involves using the equations for removal estimation that have been discussed in Section 3.3, with marked animals being thought of as being removed from the population. This leads to summarizing the data as shown in Table 3.10 with the notation used in that section. Thus X corresponds to M and Y corresponds to u in Table 3.9.

A plot of Y against X indicates an approximately linear relationship (Figure 3.5), with the fitted linear regression line

$$Y = 17.27 - 0.297X.$$

This suggests that there would be no mice left to recapture when $0.297X = 17.27$, so that $X = 17.27/0.297 = 58.1$. In other words, the estimated population size is about 58, which can be compared with the 51 individual mice that were trapped during the six-day study. The removal sampling estimate is very close to Otis *et al.*'s estimate of 56 obtained from their program CAPTURE, illustrating the value of using the removal method with mark–recapture data when there is trap response.

CASE STUDY 3
Site location in prehistoric Thailand

This case study concerns part of an investigation into the factors governing the positions and sizes of prehistoric settlement sites in north-east Thailand that is described by Higham *et al.* (1982). Here the question addressed is whether the sites in the Khorat Basin appear to be located at random positions within the region. The Khorat Basin is bounded by the Mekong River to the east and north, and the Petchabun and Dang Raek mountains to the west and south, respectively. However, this case study only refers to moated sites within an area of about 225 km by 225 km bounded by longitudes 102°30' and 104°30', and latitudes 14°30' and 16°30'. The area was apparently first occupied about 400 BC, with increasing site size and social stratification through to about AD 1100, at which time the sites were abandoned (Higham *et al.*, 1982, p. 22).

Table 3.10. *The data on recaptures of deer mice set out to enable estimation of the population size by the removal method*

Day	1	2	3	4	5	6
Number previously trapped (X)	0	16	31	38	44	48
Trapped for the first time (Y)	16	15	7	6	4	3

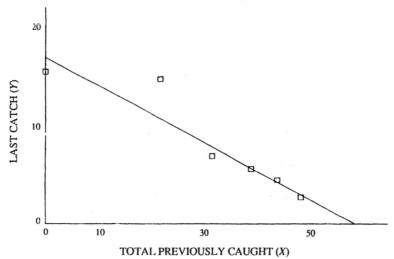

Figure 3.5. Plot of numbers of unmarked mice captured (Y) against the total number of mice previously marked (X) for a six-day study at Wet Swizer Creek, Colorado. The fitted regression line $Y = 17.27 - 0.297X$ is also shown.

Figure 3.6 shows the positions of 95 sites within the area of interest, with an indication of whether the site is 'small' (under 35 ha) or 'large' (over 35 ha). The size of the sites is important here since the largest sites may well have been social centres around which smaller sites tended to cluster.

A very simple analysis of the distribution of the sites can be based on quadrat counts. For example, if the study region is divided into 16 equal size squares, then the counts of all sites within these squares are as shown in Table 3.11. Here, the mean number of sites per square is $\bar{x} = 5.94$, and the variance is $s^2 = 46.32$. The variance to mean ratio is therefore $s^2/\bar{x} = 7.80$, and the test statistic for randomness given by equation (3.19) is

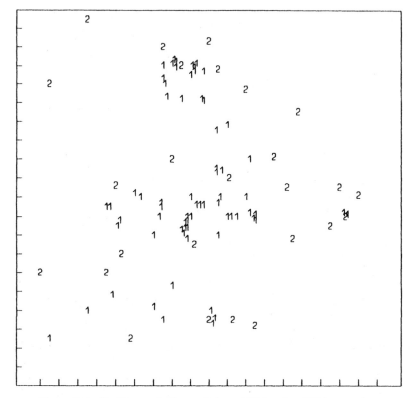

Figure 3.6. Positions of sites within a 225 km by 225 km region within the Khorat basin of Thailand, with sites of less than 35 ha indicated by '1' and larger sites by '2'.

$t = (s^2/\bar{x} - 1)/\sqrt{\{2/(n - 1)\}} = 18.63$. This statistic can be assessed for significance in comparison with the t-distribution with $n - 1 = 15$ degrees of freedom, where n is the number of quadrats. Clearly the result is very highly significant, indicating clustering of sites.

Consider next the quadrat counts for the 26 large sites only, as shown in Table 3.12. Here the mean is $\bar{x} = 1.63$ and the variance is $s^2 = 1.32$. The variance to mean ratio is $s^2/\bar{x} = 0.81$, and the test statistic for randomness is $t = -0.51$, with 15 degrees of freedom. In this case there is no evidence of non-randomness.

It seems from this analysis of quadrat counts that the large sites could well have been in random positions, but when all sites are considered there is clustering. In fact Figure 3.6 indicates that the

Table 3.11. *Quadrat counts for 95 sites in an area in north-east Thailand*

2	20	2	0
0	4	12	2
4	22	11	4
3	4	5	0

Table 3.12. *Quadrat counts for the 26 large sites in an area in north-east Thailand*

2	3	2	0
0	2	4	2
2	2	1	2
0	2	2	0

small sites are indeed clustered together and tend to be close to the large sites.

Another way to approach the question of the clustering of sites is through nearest neighbour distances. For example, it can be noted that if the distance from each of the 95 sites to its nearest neighbour is determined, then the average of these distances is 7.7 km. The question can then be asked whether this is the magnitude of average distance that can be expected if sites were placed in random positions.

Since the nearest neighbours are being considered for all 95 sites, and these sites are in a bounded region, the distribution of the mean nearest neighbour distance that is obtained for randomly placed sites is not straightforward to determine, although some theoretical results are available (Ripley, 1981, p. 152). However, it is fairly straightforward to carry out a computer simulation of the placing of sites at random positions within the study area using, for example, a FORTRAN computer program that is provided by Manly (1991, Chapter 8). If a large number of random allocations are made then the distribution of the mean nearest neighbour distance can be determined empirically, and it can be determined whether the statistic observed with the real data is a typical value from this distribution.

When the process of randomly allocating 95 sites to random positions in the study region was repeated 5000 times on a computer it was found that on no occasion was the mean nearest neighbour distance as small as the 7.7 km found for the actual sites. On this basis it is clear that a mean distance as small as 7.7 km is extremely unlikely to occur by chance, so that there is clear evidence that sites are not in random positions with respect to each other. Instead, it appears that there is some tendency for sites to be clustered together.

Consider next the 26 large sites only. For these the average distance from each site to its nearest neighbour is 23.0 km. When 5000 random allocations of sites to the study region were made by computer it was found that on about 45% of occasions the mean nearest neighbour distance was less than 23.0 km. Hence, the observed mean nearest neighbour distance is well within the range of values that are likely to occur from randomly placed sites and there is no reason to reject the hypothesis of random positioning for the real sites.

The conclusion from the nearest neighbour analysis is therefore the same as was obtained from the analysis of quadrat counts: large sites could well have been located in random positions but small sites are clustered to some extent.

Of course, common sense suggests that settlement sites are not generally randomly located since factors such as the type of soil and the distance to water must have been of some importance. Indeed, sites are always fairly close to water. For this reason, the analysis of Higham *et al*. (1982) was more concerned with determining the characteristics of a region that gave a high probability of a site being present than with the question of whether the positions of sites appeared to be random. Logistic regression models, as discussed in Chapter 8, were used to this end. The approach is exemplified by Case Study 8 at the end of that chapter, which is concerned with the factors which determined the locations of prehistoric Maya sites in the Corozal district of Belize in Central America.

4

The linear regression model

4.1 Introduction

Regression analysis is undoubtedly one of the most important and most used tools available for data analysis. Before computers became readily available these uses were mainly restricted to *simple linear regression*, which is a method for relating the values of a dependent variable Y to a single other variable X. However, nowadays *multiple linear regression*, where a Y variable is related to several X variables, is straightforward using one of the many available computer programs for this purpose.

The utility of regression methods has meant that it has been necessary to mention them in earlier chapters: regression estimation with sample surveys was discussed in Section 2.11, and in Section 3.3 linear regression was suggested for relating the number of new captures to the number previously captured when estimating a population size by removal sampling. However, in the chapters that follow regression methods will be used much more extensively. It is, therefore, appropriate to devote this chapter to a review of the theory and applications of these methods.

4.2 The simple linear regression model

As just mentioned, with the simple linear regression model there is a relationship between two variables X and Y, where X is thought of as in some sense determining Y. The assumption made is that the relationship between the variables takes the form

$$Y = \alpha + \beta X + \varepsilon,$$

where α and β are constants and ε is a random 'error' with mean 0 and standard deviation σ. Regression methods can be used to estimate α, β and σ, and hence quantify the relationship between X and Y.

Example 4.1 Gene frequencies related to altitude

Consider Table 4.1 which shows some data on environmental variables and estimated frequencies of Hk 1.00 genes in colonies of the butterfly *Euphydryas editha* at different altitudes in California and Oregon. The data come from the study by McKechnie *et al.* (1975), with some close colonies combined to ensure independent data for the 18 cases. Only the relationship between the Hk 1.00 gene frequencies and altitude will be considered for the present example.

The plot of the Hk 1.00 gene frequency against altitude shown in Figure 4.1(a) indicates a non-linear relationship between the Hk 1.00 gene frequency and altitude. However, taking $X = 1/\text{al-}$ titude gives the plot that is shown in Figure 4.1(b), which looks far more like a linear relationship. The fitted regression line

$$\text{Gene frequency} = 10.74 + 29.05 \ (1/\text{altitude})$$

that is shown in part (b) of the figure gives a reasonable approximation to the relationship between the two variables, although the deviations from this line are quite large for some colonies. It is not uncommon for some transformation to be needed before an approximately linear relationship between two variables is obtained.

4.3 Estimation and tests with simple linear regression

In the standard linear regression situation, the two variables X and Y are both measured on n individuals. The data have the form (x_1, y_1), (x_2, y_2), ..., (x_n, y_n), and estimators of α and β are given by a and b, respectively, where

$$a = \left(\sum y_i - b \sum x_i \right) \Big/ n \tag{4.1}$$

and

$$b = \left\{ \sum y_i x_i - \sum y_i \sum x_i / n \right\} \Big/ \left\{ \sum x_i^2 - \left(\sum x_i \right)^2 \Big/ n \right\}, \tag{4.2}$$

the summations being over the n data values. These are *least-squares* estimators in the sense that they give the equation for which the sum of squares for errors, $\text{SSE} = \sum (y_i - a - bx_i)^2$, is as

Table 4.1. *Environmental variables and percentage frequencies of the hexokinase 1.00 (Hk 1.00) gene as determined by electrophoresis for colonies of the butterfly* Euphydryas editha *in California and Oregon. (Mckechnie et al., 1975)*

Colony	Altitude (thousands of feet)	1/altitude X_1	Annual precipitation (inches) X_2	Maximum temp. (°F) X_3	Minimum temp. (°F) X_4	Hk 1.00 freq. (%) Y
PD+SS	0.50	2.00	58	97	16	98
SB	0.80	1.25	20	92	32	36
WSB	0.57	1.75	28	98	26	72
JRC+JRH	0.55	1.82	28	98	26	67
SJ	0.38	2.63	15	99	28	82
CR	0.93	1.08	21	99	28	72
MI	0.48	2.08	24	101	27	65
UO+LO	0.63	1.59	10	101	27	1
DP	1.50	0.67	19	99	23	40
PZ	1.75	0.57	22	101	27	39
MC	2.00	0.50	58	100	18	9
HH	4.20	0.24	36	95	13	19
IF	2.50	0.40	34	102	16	42
AF	2.00	0.50	21	105	20	37
SL	6.50	0.15	40	83	0	16
GH	7.85	0.13	42	84	5	4
EP	8.95	0.11	57	79	-7	1
GL	10.50	0.10	50	81	-12	4

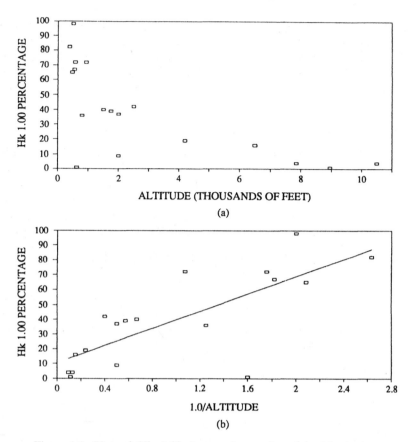

Figure 4.1. Plot of Hk 1.00 frequencies against (a) altitude in thousands of feet, and (b) 1/altitude. The regression line $Y = 10.74 + 29.05X$ is also plotted on (b).

small as possible. As estimate of the variance of ε is given by the mean square for error,

$$\text{MSE} = \text{SSE}/(n - 2) = \sum\left(y_i - a - bx_i\right)^2\Big/(n - 2), \quad (4.3)$$

which is also minimized by the least-squares estimators.

There are several statistical tests that are possible with a simple linear regression. These require the assumption that the model $Y = \alpha + \beta X + \varepsilon$ is correct, with ε being normally distributed with a mean of zero and a constant variance. One approach is based on the idea of what is called the analysis of variance. This involves partitioning the total sum of squares of the Y values about their mean, $SST = \sum(y_i - \bar{y})^2$ into a part that is accounted for by the regression (SSR) and a part that is not accounted for by the regression, which is the sum of squares for error SSE that is shown in equation (4.3). These sums of squares are then related by the equation

$$SST = SSR + SSE.$$

Usually the calculations are summarized in an analysis of variance table, which takes the form shown in Table 4.2. In this table MSR is the mean square for the regression, and MSE is the mean square for error as defined in equation (4.3). The F-ratio MSR/MSE has an expected value close to 1 if there is no relationship between the variables X and Y. A test for a significant linear relationship can therefore be carried out by seeing whether the observed F-ratio is significantly large in comparison with the critical values of the F-distribution with 1 and $n - 2$ degrees of freedom.

Another approach in assessing the significance of a regression relationship is by seeing whether the coefficient of X is significantly different from zero. This can be done by first estimating the standard error of b using the equation

$$\hat{SE}(b) = \sqrt{\left\{ MSE \Big/ \sum(x_i - \bar{x})^2 \right\}}, \qquad (4.4)$$

where the summation is over the n data values. The b value is then significantly different from zero if $b/\hat{SE}(b)$ is significantly different from zero in comparison with the t-distribution with $n-2$ degrees of freedom. This test is exactly equivalent to the F-test from the analysis of variance since it can be shown that $\{b/\hat{SE}(b)\}^2 = F$.

Finally, to assess the accuracy of the estimated regression coefficient, it is useful to remember that a 95% confidence interval for β, the true regression slope, is $b \pm t_{5\%,n-2}\hat{SE}(b)$, where $t_{5\%,n-2}$ is the absolute value from the t-distribution with $n - 2$ degrees of freedom that is exceeded with probability 0.05.

Example 4.2 Inferences concerning gene frequencies related to altitude

As an example, consider again the data on altitudes and Hk 1.00 gene frequencies for 18 colonies of *E. editha* that are provided in

Table 4.2. *The analysis of variance table for a simple linear regression*

Source of variation	Sum of	df	Mean square	F
Regression	SSR = (Difference)	1	MSR	MSR/MSE
Error	SSE = $\sum(y_i - a - bx_i)^2$	$n - 2$	MSE	
Total	SST = $\sum(y_i - \bar{y})^2$	$n - 1$		

Table 4.1. Recall that the regression of gene frequency (Y) on 1/altitude (X) gives the estimated equation $\hat{Y} = 10.74 + 29.05X$, where the 'cap' on Y indicates that it is the value obtained from the equation rather than a data value. The analysis of variance for this regression is shown in Table 4.3. The F-ratio of 23.13, with 1 and 16 degrees of freedom is significantly large at the 0.1% level so that there is clear evidence of a relationship between gene frequencies and altitudes.

The estimated standard error of b is $\hat{SE}(b) = 6.04$. The statistic for testing whether b is significantly different from zero is $b/\hat{SE}(b) = 29.05/6.04 = 4.81$, with 16 degrees of freedom. Since this is the square root of the F-ratio from the analysis of variance, this t-test adds nothing new to the analysis. However, it is of value to indicate the accuracy of the estimated regression coefficient by finding the 95% confidence interval for β. This is $b \pm 2.12 \, \hat{SE}(b)$, where 2.12 is the absolute value from the t-distribution with 16 degrees of freedom that is exceeded with probability 0.05. That is to say, the confidence interval for β is $29.05 \pm (2.12 \times 6.04)$, or 16.20 to 41.85.

4.4 Multiple linear regression

Multiple linear regression is the obvious generalization of simple linear regression for cases where a Y variable is related to p variables $X_1, X_2, \ldots, X_p$. For example, with the data in Table 4.1 there might be interest in relating the percentage of Hk 1.00 genes (Y) to 1/altitude (X_1), the annual precipitation (X_2), the maximum temperature (X_3) and the minimum temperature (X_4).

In the general situation, the data available will consist of n values $y_1, y_2, \ldots, y_n$ of the dependent variable Y, with corresponding values for the X variables. The model that is assumed is

Table 4.3. *The analysis of variance for a regression of Hk 1.00 gene frequencies on 1/altitude for colonies of* Euphydryas editha

Source of variation	Sum of squares	df	Mean square	F
1/altitude	9581.5	1	9581.5	23.13[a]
Error	6576.2	16	411.0	
Total	16157.7	17		

[a]Significantly large at the 0.1% level.

$$Y = \beta_0 + \beta_1 X_1 + \beta_2 X_2 + , \ldots, + \beta_p X_p + \varepsilon, \qquad (4.5)$$

where ε is a random error with a mean of zero and a constant variance σ^2. This model is estimated by finding the coefficients of the X values that make the error sum of squares as small as possible. In other words, if the estimated equation is

$$\hat{Y} = b_0 + b_1 X_1 + b_2 X_2 + , \ldots, + b_p X_p, \qquad (4.6)$$

then the b values are chosen so as to minimize

$$\text{SSE} = \sum (y_i - \hat{y}_i)^2, \qquad (4.7)$$

where the $\hat{y}_i$ is the value given by the fitted equation that corresponds to the data value y_i, the summation being over all n data values. The calculations that are required in order to estimate the regression equation in this way are complicated even when there are only two X variables to be considered. It is therefore best to rely on a standard computer program to produce the required estimates together with their standard errors.

The analysis of variance described in the last section for simple linear regression can be generalized in a straightforward way for multiple regression. The total variation in the Y values is measured by the total sum of squares

$$\text{SST} = \sum (y_i - \bar{y})^2. \qquad (4.8)$$

This can be partitioned into the error sum of squares SSE defined by equation (4.7) and the sum of squares accounted for by the regression, so that SST = SSR + SSE. The proportion of the variation in Y accounted for by the regression equation is then the coefficient of multiple determination,

$$R^2 = \text{SSR}/\text{SST} = 1 - \text{SSE}/\text{SST}. \tag{4.9}$$

As with simple linear regression, there are a variety of inference procedures that can be applied in the multiple regression situation when the regression errors ε are assumed to be independent random variables from a normal distribution with a mean of zero and constant variance σ^2.

A test for whether the fitted equation accounts for a significant proportion of the total variation in Y can be based on the analysis of variance shown in Table 4.4. From this table, the F-ratio can be compared with the F-distribution with p and $n - p - 1$ degrees of freedom to see if it is significantly large. If this is the case then there is evidence that Y is related to at least one of the X variables.

The estimated regression coefficients can be tested individually to see whether they are significantly different from zero. If this is not the case for one of these coefficients then there is no evidence that Y is related to the X variable concerned. More generally, to test the hypothesis that β_j equals the particular value β_{j0} the statistic $(b_j - \beta_{j0})/\hat{\text{SE}}(b_j)$ can be computed, where $\hat{\text{SE}}(b_j)$ is the estimated standard error of b_j. This statistic can then be compared with the percentage points of the t-distribution with $n - p - 1$ degrees of freedom. If $(b_j - \beta_{j0})/\hat{\text{SE}}(b_j)$ is significantly different from zero then there is evidence that β_j is not equal to the hypothetical value β_{j0}. When β_{j0} is taken to be zero the test statistic is simply $b_j/\hat{\text{SE}}(b_j)$.

If the accuracy of the estimate b_j is to be assessed, then this can be done by calculating a 95% confidence interval for β_j as $b_j \pm t_{5\%, n-p-1}\hat{\text{SE}}(b_j)$, where $t_{5\%, n-p-1}$ is the absolute value that is exceeded with probability 0.05 for the t-distribution with $n - p - 1$ degrees of freedom.

4.5 The extra sum of squares principle

One of the difficulties that is often encountered with multiple regression involves the assessment of the relationship between Y and one of the X variables when the X variables themselves are quite highly correlated. In such cases there is often value in considering the variation in Y that is accounted for by a variable X_j when this is included in the regression after some of the other variables are already in. Therefore, if the variables X_1 to X_p are

Table 4.4. *Analysis of variance table for a multiple regression analysis*

Source of variation	Sum of squares	df	Mean square	F
Regression	SSR	p	MSR	MSR/MSE
Error	SSE	$n - p - 1$	MSE	
Total	SST	$n - 1$		

in the order of their importance then it is useful to successively fit regressions relating Y to X_1, Y to X_1 and X_2, and so on up to Y related to all the X variables. The variation in Y accounted for by X_j after allowing for the effects of the variables X_1 to X_{j-1} is then given by the extra sum of squares accounted for by adding X_j to the model.

To be more precise, let $SSR(X_1, X_2, \ldots, X_j)$ denote the regression sum of squares with variables X_1 to X_j in the equation. Then the extra sum of squares accounted for by X_j on top of X_1 to X_{j-1} is

$$SSR(X_j | X_1, X_2, \ldots, X_{j-1}) =$$
$$SSR(X_1, X_2, \ldots, X_j) - SSR(X_1, X_2, \ldots, X_{j-1}).$$

On this basis, the sequential sums of squares shown in Table 4.5 can be calculated. In this table the mean squares are the sums of squares divided by their degrees of freedom, and the F-ratios are the mean squares divided by the error mean square. A test for the variable X_j being significantly related to Y, after allowing for the effects of the variables X_1 to X_{j-1}, involves seeing whether the corresponding F-ratio is significantly large in comparison to the F-distribution with 1 and $n - p - 1$ degrees of freedom.

If the X variables are uncorrelated then the F-ratios indicated in Table 4.5 will be the same irrespective of the order in which the variables are entered into the regression. However, more usually the X variables are correlated and the order may be of crucial importance. This merely reflects the fact that with correlated X variables it is generally only possible to discuss the relationship between Y and X_j in terms of which of the other X variables are controlled for. The problems involved in interpreting regression relationships involving correlated X variables are well known, and are discussed at some lengths in most books on regression analysis under the heading *multicolinearity*. See, for example, Neter *et al.* (1983, Chapters 8 and 11), and Younger (1985, p. 405).

Table 4.5 *Analysis of variance table for the extra sums of squares accounted for by variables as they are added into a multiple regression model one by one*

$X_2|X_1$ indicates the variation accounted for by variable X_2 in addition to variable X_1; and $X_p|X_1, \ldots, X_{p-1}$ indicates the variation accounted for by variable X_p in addition to variables X_1 to X_{p-1}.

Source of variation	Sum of squares	df	Mean square	F
X_1	$\mathrm{SSR}(X_1)$	1	$\mathrm{MSR}(X_1)$	$F(X_1)$
$X_2|X_1$	$\mathrm{SSR}(X_2|X_1)$	1	$\mathrm{MSR}(X_2|X_1)$	$F(X_2|X_1)$
...				
$X_p|X_1, \ldots, X_{p-1}$	$\mathrm{SSR}(X_p|X_1, \ldots, X_{p-1})$	1	$\mathrm{MSR}(X_p|X_1, \ldots, X_{p-1})$	$F(X_p|X_1, \ldots, X_{p-1})$
Error	SSE	$n - p - 1$	MSE	
Total	SST	$n - 1$		

Example 4.3 Gene frequencies related to several environmental variables

Consider again the data for the colonies of the butterfly *Euphydryas editha* that are shown in Table 4.1. In this example a multiple regression relating the Hk 1.00 frequency (Y) to the environmental variables X_1 (1/altitude), X_2 (annual precipitation), X_3 (maximum annual temperature), and X_4 (minimum annual temperature) is examined.

The estimated regression equation is

$$\hat{Y} = -88.5 + 26.10X_1 + 0.47X_2 + 0.87X_3 + 0.25X_4.$$
$$\quad\quad\;\; (8.63) \quad\;\; (0.50) \quad (1.17) \quad (1.02)$$

where the values shown beneath the coefficients are the estimated standard errors associated with the coefficients. The t-statistics for assessing whether the coefficients are significantly different from zero are therefore as follows:

$$b_1: (26.10-0)/8.63 = 3.02$$
$$b_2: (0.47-0)/0.50 = 0.94$$
$$b_3: (0.87-0)/1.17 = 0.74$$
$$b_4: (0.25-0)/1.02 = 0.25$$

Compared with the t-distribution with $n - p - 1 = 18 - 4 - 1 = 13$ degrees of freedom the last three of these statistics are not at all significantly different from zero. However, the first statistic is significantly different from zero at the 5% level, and nearly at the 1% level. It seems, therefore, that X_1 alone is sufficient to account for the variation in Y. This is true even though simple regressions of Y on X_3 and Y on X_4 (that are not presented here) give relationships that are significant at the 5% level.

An analysis of variance partitioning the total variation of Y into regression and error gives the result shown in Table 4.6. Here the F-ratio is significantly large at the 1% level, indicating real evidence of a relationship between Y and at least one of the X variables. The coefficient of multiple determination is $R^2 = 10\,454.0/16\,157.7 = 0.65$.

A more detailed analysis of variance based on adding the variables into the equation one at a time is shown in Table 4.7. Here it can be seen that, when compared with tables of the F-distribution, the F-ratio for X_1 is significantly large at the 0.1% level, but none of the other F-ratios are at all significant. As for

Table 4.6. *Analysis of variance for the multiple regression of gene frequencies of* Euphydryas editha *against environmental variables*

Source of variation	Sum of squares	df	Mean square	F
Regression	10454.0	4	2613.5	5.96[a]
Error	5701.7	13	438.6	
Total	16157.7	17		

[a] Significantly large at the 1% level.

Table 4.7. *Analysis of variance for the multiple regression of gene frequencies of* Euphydryas editha *against environmental variables, with extra sums of squares for variables added one at a time to the equation*

$X_j | X_1, \ldots, X_{j-1}$ indicates the variation accounted for by variable X_j in addition to variables X_1 to X_{j-1}.

Source of variation	Sum of squares	df	Mean square	F
X_1	9581.5	1	9581.5	21.85[a]
$X_2	X_1$	80.8	1	80.8	0.18
$X_3	X_1, X_2$	759.4	1	759.4	1.73
$X_4	X_1, X_2, X_3$	32.3	1	32.3	0.07
Error	5701.7	13	438.6	
Total	16157.7	17		

[a] Significantly large at the 0.1% level.

the *t*-tests, this indicates that X_1 alone accounts for most of the variation that the four variables account for together.

4.6 Assessing the assumptions of a regression model

Whenever a regression model is used to analyse data there should be some assessment of the validity of the assumptions being made. These are:

(a) That the relationship between the dependent variable Y and the independent variables is linear so that it can be represented by equation (4.5)

(b) That the variance of the random error ε is constant for all observations
(c) That the errors ε are normally distributed
(d) That the errors ε_1, ε_2, ..., ε_n for the n observations are independently distributed

Assumption (a) will be invalid if there is a non-linear relationship between Y and the X variables. For example if

$$Y = \surd(\beta_1 X_1 + \beta_2 X_2) + \beta_3 X^2 + \varepsilon$$

then this is not a linear regression situation. Models like this can be estimated from data, but non-linear regression methods have to be used, as described, for example, by Neter *et al.* (1983, Chapter 14) and Ratkowsky (1983). Assumption (a) will also be invalid if an important variable is not measured, so that the 'error' ε includes some systematic effects of that variable, or if squares and products of X variables should be in the equation.

Sometimes a transformation of either the Y variable or some of the X variables will have the effect of turning a non-linear relationship into a linear relationship. This was seen in Example 4.1, where the Hk 1.00 gene frequency of *Euphydryas editha* was seen to be approximately linearly related to 1/altitude, but not to altitude (Figure 4.1). Transformations may also overcome problems with assumptions (b) and (c).

Assumption (b) is required by regression theory for two reasons: first, it is used to justify fitting the regression equation by choosing estimates of the β values so as to minimize the error sum of squares; second, it is needed in the derivation of the t-tests and F-tests that are used for tests of significance concerning regression coefficients. The first of these two reasons is related to the nature of the error sum of squares, which can be written as $\text{SSE} = \sum e_i^2$, where

$$e_i = y_i - (b_0 + b_1 x_{i1} + b_2 x_{i2} + \ldots + b_p x_{ip}), \qquad (4.10)$$

with x_{ij} being the value of X_j associated with the ith Y value. Here e_i is called the ith residual, and is an estimate of the regression error ε_i associated with the ith data point. Clearly in minimizing SSE the implication is that each of the residuals is equally important, and that there is no inherent reason why some residuals should be larger than others.

If assumption (b) is not correct then it can be shown that the usual regression estimates of β values are not biased, so that the fitted equation may still be close to the true equation. However, statistical tests and confidence levels may be seriously upset and better estimates of the β values can be obtained by giving appropriately different weights to different data points using weighted regression, as discussed by Neter *et al.* (1983, p. 263).

Assumption (c) is needed in order to justify the usual tests of significance and confidence levels that are used in regression, but there is some evidence that this is not as crucial as assumptions (a) and (b). Instead, it seems that as long as the distribution of regression residuals is fairly symmetric, with a more or less constant variance, then the tests of significance and confidence limits should behave much as required. That is to say, the tests of significance and confidence limits are fairly robust to the assumption of normality.

Assumption (d) is most likely to be violated when the data are in some sense in a natural order. For example, if one Y value with corresponding X values is collected every day for 30 days then there might well be a tendency for the regression errors ε to be similar for two observations that are taken on successive days.

Lack of independence is also liable to occur when the units that are being measured occur in groups. For example if data are gathered on mice to examine the relationship between the level of a chemical in the blood and other physiological variables then it may well happen that the deviations from a regression equation tend to be similar for sibling mice.

There are a variety of approaches that have been suggested for checking the assumptions of regression analysis, and no attempt will be made here to cover these in detail. Instead, only some of the more straightforward methods will be reviewed briefly. More information is provided by Neter *et al.* (1983) and Younger (1985).

4.7 Residual plots

The simplest approach to assessing the validity of the assumptions (a) to (d) is through residual plots. The idea here is that if the regression model is correct then the residuals $e_1, e_2, \ldots, e_n$ that can be calculated from equation (4.10) will appear to be independent, normally distributed variables with a constant variance. Therefore if these residuals are plotted against the corresponding values of Y predicted from the regression equation, or any of the X values, then there should be no patterns apparent. If patterns do appear in the plots then these may be related to invalid assumptions.

Residual plots of this type may highlight also any outliers that are present in the data. These are data points for which the residuals are unusually large. They may just be valid but unusual values, but if any are present it will be worth checking that they are not due to an incorrect recording or a sampling problem of some type.

Often, standardized residuals are used for plotting instead of the simple residuals. These can be defined by the equation

$$E_i = e_i / \sqrt{(\text{MSE})}. \tag{4.11}$$

Since MSE, the mean square error, is the estimated variance of regression errors, this amounts to scaling the residuals to make them have a mean of zero and a standard deviation of one. Then if they are also approximately normally distributed it is expected that about 68% of the standardized residuals will be within the range from -1 to $+1$, and about 95% of them will lie within the range from -2 to $+2$. In this way it becomes clearer what is meant by a 'large' residual.

Another type of plot that is useful is a normal probability plot. This involves ordering the standardized residuals from the most negative to the most positive, and plotting these ordered statistics against their expected values assuming a standard normal distribution. If E_i is the ith standardized residual when they are placed in order, then the expected value to plot this against is the value for the standard normal distribution that exceeds the proportion $\{i - (3/8)\}/\{n + (1/4)\}$ of the values in the full distribution. What is desired in a plot like this is that the plotted points should fall fairly close to a straight line going through the origin with a slope of unity. If all the ordered standardized residuals equal their expected values then they will all fall exactly on this line.

Example 4.4 Residual plots for gene frequencies related to environmental variables

Table 4.8 shows observed and fitted Hk 1.00 frequencies, ordinary residuals, standardized residuals, and the calculations required for producing a normal probability plot for the multiple regression of

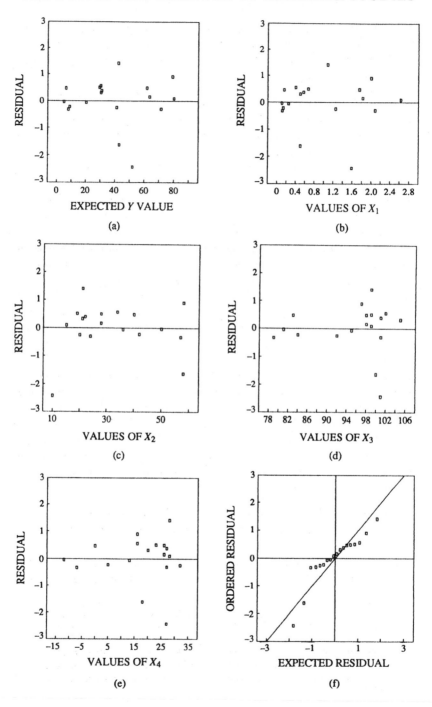

Hk 1.00 gene frequencies against environmental variables for colonies of the butterfly *Euphydryas editha* that was the subject of Example 4.3. In that example, the multiple regression equation was estimated to be

$$\hat{Y} = -88.5 + 26.10X_1 + 0.47X_2 + 0.87X_3 + 0.25X_4.$$

The coefficients of X_2, X_3 and X_4 are not significantly different from zero in this equation, but this is immaterial to the use of residual plots in the present example.

Figure 4.2 has been constructed from the values in Table 4.8. Part (a) of the figure shows standardized residuals plotted against the expected gene frequencies from the fitted equation, parts (b) to (e) are the same residuals plotted against the variables X_1 to X_4 in turn, and part (f) is a normal probability plot.

None of the plots of standardized residuals show any patterns, which suggests that there are no serious problems with the assumptions of the regression model. There is only one large standardized residual, which has the value -2.43. Since this could well have occurred by chance if the regression model is correct, this need not cause any undue concern, although it does indicate that the gene frequency for the colony in question (UO + LO) is something of an outlier.

Overall, the plots in Figure 4.2 suggest that the only concern with the multiple regression should be the effect of the unusual Y value for the colony UO + LO, which results in the negative standardized residual of -2.43. Since this Y value appears to be quite genuine (McKechnie *et al.*, 1975) there are no grounds for omitting it from the regression. The regression equation including this Y value can therefore be accepted as being reasonable.

Example 4.5 The relationship of shop turnover to the catchment population and sales area

For a second example on the use of residual plots, consider the data shown in Table 4.9 which come from a study of retail outlet

---

Figure 4.2. Residual plots from the multiple regression of gene frequencies on environmental variables for *Euphydryas editha*: (a) standardized residuals plotted against Y values from the regression equation, (b) standardized residuals against X_1, (c) standardized residuals against X_2, (d) standardized residuals against X_3, (e) standardized residuals against X_4, and (f) normal probability plot.

Table 4.8. *Residual calculations for the multiple regression of gene frequencies of* Euphydryas editha *on environmental variables.*

Y = observed gene frequency; $\hat{Y}$ = gene frequency from the regression equation; e = residual = $Y - \hat{Y}$; E = standardized residual = $e/\sqrt{(MSE)}$; Ordered E = E values in order of magnitude; $P = (i - 3/8)/(18 + 1/4)$ for the normal probability plot; Z-score = value for the standard normal distribution that exceeds the proportion P of the standard normal distribution.

i	Y	$\hat{Y}$	Residuals		Ordered		Z-score
			e	E	E	P	
1	98	79.1	18.9	0.90	-2.43	0.034	-1.82
2	36	41.3	-5.3	-0.25	-1.63	0.089	-1.35
3	72	61.8	10.2	0.49	-0.33	0.144	-1.06
4	67	63.6	3.4	0.16	-0.31	0.199	-0.84
5	82	80.0	2.0	0.09	-0.25	0.253	-0.66
6	72	42.4	29.6	1.41	-0.23	0.308	-0.50
7	65	71.4	-6.4	-0.31	-0.06	0.363	-0.35
8	1	52.0	-51.0	-2.43	-0.04	0.418	-0.21
9	40	29.5	10.5	0.50	0.09	0.473	-0.07
10	39	31.0	8.0	0.38	0.16	0.527	0.07
11	9	43.1	-34.1	-1.63	0.31	0.582	0.21
12	19	20.3	-1.3	-0.06	0.38	0.637	0.35
13	42	30.3	11.7	0.56	0.47	0.692	0.50
14	37	30.4	6.6	0.31	0.49	0.747	0.66
15	16	6.2	9.8	0.47	0.50	0.801	0.84
16	4	8.7	-4.7	-0.23	0.56	0.856	1.06
17	1	7.9	-6.9	-0.33	0.90	0.911	1.35
18	4	4.9	-0.9	-0.04	1.41	0.966	1.82

Table 4.9. *Data on sales turnover (Y, in thousands of pounds), the catchment population (X_1, in thousands), and the sales area (X_2, in thousands of square feet) for 30 stores. (Hodge and Moore, 1972)*

Shop	Y	X_1	X_2	Shop	Y	X_1	X_2
1	37	23	1.34	16	71	28	1.23
2	43	61	1.60	17	152	43	2.16
3	13	12	0.36	18	470	283	4.40
4	116	70	2.14	19	24	16	0.49
5	281	128	5.65	20	111	33	2.80
6	40	24	1.05	21	20	26	0.66
7	80	35	2.64	22	69	24	0.86
8	52	32	1.39	23	23	4	0.58
9	46	20	1.06	24	31	5	0.43
10	26	8	0.82	25	61	46	0.90
11	138	55	1.39	26	301	332	3.10
12	462	310	3.55	27	26	20	0.84
13	52	25	0.90	28	15	5	0.35
14	24	13	0.40	29	93	56	3.60
15	68	13	1.40	30	49	18	0.89

performance. These data are as provided by Hodge and Moore (1972), with some simplification. The question to be considered in this example is the validity of a multiple regression equation that relates shop turnover (Y) to the catchment population (X_1) and the sales area (X_2).

A regression of Y against X_1 and X_2 produces the equation

$$\hat{Y} = -4.55 + 0.976X_1 + 28.67X_2,$$
$$(0.107) \qquad (7.20)$$

where the values shown in parentheses are the estimated standard errors. The t-statistics for assessing whether the true regression coefficients could be zero are $0.976/0.107 = 9.12$ and $28.67/7.20 = 3.98$, with 12 degrees of freedom. These are both highly significant, so there seems to be a very clear relationship between Y and both X variables. The R^2 value is 0.91, so that most of the variation in Y is accounted for by the regression. However, Figure 4.3 indicates that there may be problems with the assumptions of the regression model. Part (a) of the figure shows standardized residuals plotted against $\hat{Y}$ values (expected turnover in £000s). From this it seems that the residual variance is higher

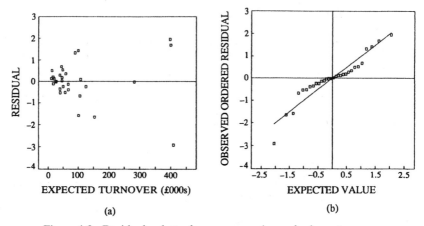

Figure 4.3. Residual plots for a regression of shop turnover against the catchment population and the sales area: (a) standardized residuals plotted against expected turnover from the regression equation, (b) a normal probability plot.

for the large stores than it is for the small stores. A similar impression is also gained if the standardized residuals are plotted against X_1 or against X_2, although these plots are not provided here. Part (b) of Figure 4.3 shows a normal probability plot. This shows some systematic deviations from the expected line, but the distribution of residuals does not seem to be much of a problem.

One way to try to stabilize the residual variance in a situation like this involves transforming the Y values in an appropriate way. If the residual variance seems to increase with magnitude of the Y values, and these Y values are all positive then a logarithmic transformation is usually worth trying, so this was investigated for the data being considered.

A very satisfactory result is obtained if logarithms are taken for both the X and Y variables. The regression equation is then estimated as

$$\log_{10}(Y) = 1.18 + \underset{(0.112)}{0.369\log_{10}(X_1)} + \underset{(0.164)}{0.667\log_{10}(X_2)},$$

where again the estimated standard errors are shown in parentheses below the estimates that they refer to. The residual plots are very much improved for this equation, although the R^2 value of 0.86 is slightly lower than the 0.91 that was found with the untransformed data. Figure 4.4 shows plots of standardized res-

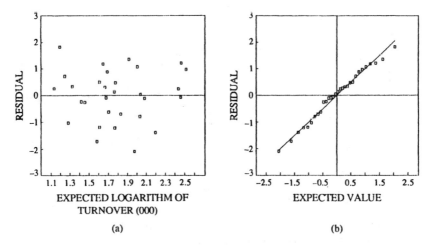

Figure 4.4. Residual plots as in Figure 4.3 but for the regression of log(turnover) against log(catchment population) and log(sales area).

iduals against log(catchment population) and log(sales area). Both plots are completely satisfactory, as are plots of standardized residuals against $\log_{10}(X_1)$ and $\log_{10}(X_2)$ which are not shown here.

4.8 Tests on residuals

Although making residual plots is a useful way of assessing the fit of a regression model, it does suffer from the disadvantage of being rather subjective. For this reason it is sometimes considered worthwhile to carry out some more objective tests also. The main possibilities along these lines are (a) testing for whether the residuals are in a random order, (b) testing for a constant residual variance, (c) testing for outliers, and (d) testing for the normality of the residuals.

There are a large number of tests for randomness that are available, which are designed to find any patterns in a set of observations that are listed in a specific order. For example, some tests are designed to detect a trend in the values while others are designed to detect cycles. These tests can be used appropriately with regression residuals whenever the residuals are in some sense in a natural order. Therefore, if the regression data are collected over a period of time then it is natural to order the residuals according to the times that observations were made and see whether there is any evidence of non-randomness in the resulting series. Similarly, if observations are taken at different points in space then it may be possible to order residuals according to their positions in one dimension. Again, tests of randomness are appropriate. More information about these tests is provided by Gibbons (1986).

One way to test for a constant error variance involves splitting the data into two sets on the basis of the expected values of Y, fitting separate regressions to each half set of data, and comparing the two error mean squares using an F-test (Younger, 1985, p. 271). Another possibility is to test for a significant rank correlation between the absolute residuals and the corresponding expected values of Y (Neter et $al.$, 1983, p. 123).

The detection of outliers is related to the detection of observations that have a particularly influential effect on the values of estimated regression coefficients. Further discussions on these matters and tests of normality are provided by Neter et $al.$ (1983, p. 122 and p. 400) and Younger (1985, p. 265 and p. 574).

4.9 The Durbin–Watson test

One of the tests on regression residuals that is often used is the *Durbin–Watson test*, which is designed to detect serial correlation in a regression model based on data taken at a series of successive points in time. That is to say, it is designed to detect a tendency for observations taken close together in time to have similar residuals (positive serial correlation) or to have different residuals (negative serial correlation). It can be used equally well in any situation where regression observations can be ordered on the basis of the way that they have been collected.

Suppose that the residuals from a regression in a sensible order are $e_1, e_2, \ldots, e_n$. The Durbin–Watson test statistic is then

$$v = \sum_{i=2}^{n} (e_i - e_{i-1})^2 \Big/ \sum_{i=1}^{n} e_i^2,$$

which has an expected value of approximately 2 if the regression errors are independent values from a distribution with constant variance. The Durbin–Watson test also requires the additional assumption that the regression errors are normally distributed variables.

To carry out a two-tailed test at the 5% level of significance, first calculate v and $4-v$. Then take v^* as the minimum of these two values. Next, compare v^* with the limits d_1 and d_2 for critical values that are shown in Table 4.10. If v^* is less than d_1 then there is significant serial correlation; if v^* lies between d_1 and d_2 then it is not possible to decide whether the result is significant or not; if v^* exceeds d_2 then the result is not significant. It is unusual only to be able to quote bounds for critical values for test statistics, but this is the case for the Durbin–Watson test.

Low values of v indicate that the differences $e_i - e_{i-1}$ tend to be small, so that there is positive serial correlation. A one-tailed test for positive serial correlation at the 2.5% level is therefore provided by comparing v with the limits shown in Table 4.10. On the other hand, high values of v indicate that the differences $e_i - e_{i-1}$ tend to be large, so that there is negative serial correlation. A one-tailed test for negative serial correlation is therefore provided by comparing $4 - v$ with the limits shown in Table 4.10.

Table 4.10 is based on the numerical values given by Durbin and Watson (1951) in their original paper. More comprehensive tables are available in some statistics texts, and a very extensive table that has been provided by Savin and White (1977) allows for up to 20 X-variables, with from 6 to 200 observations.

Example 4.6 Testing the residuals from a linear regression of cancer death rates against time

Serial correlation is most likely to occur when the regression being considered has time either as the sole X variable or as one of several X variables. The following example is, therefore, of this type, with the dependent variable being the cancer death rate (deaths per 100 000 population, per year) for Birmingham in the UK, with this rate being regressed against the calendar year.

The first two columns of Table 4.11 show the cancer death rates for the years 1959 to 1977, as provided by Cook-Mozaffari *et al.* (1981). The linear regression equation

$$CDR = -6918.8 + 3.635(\text{YEAR})$$

provides the expected cancer death rates in column three. The last two columns give the residuals e_i and the squared differences

Table 4.10. Bounds for the Durbin–Watson statistic for two-tailed tests at the 5% level of significance: p = the number of X variables in the regression (1 for simple linear regression), and n = the number of data points. (Durbin and Watson, 1951)

n	p = 1		p = 2		p = 3		p = 4		p = 5	
	d_1	d_2	d_1	d_2	d_1	d_2	d_1	d_2	d_1	d_2
15	0.95	1.22	0.83	1.41	0.71	1.61	0.59	1.84	0.48	2.09
20	1.08	1.29	0.99	1.41	0.89	1.55	0.79	1.70	0.70	1.87
25	1.18	1.34	1.10	1.43	1.02	1.54	0.94	1.65	0.86	1.77
30	1.25	1.38	1.18	1.46	1.12	1.54	1.05	1.63	0.98	1.73
35	1.31	1.42	1.25	1.48	1.19	1.55	1.13	1.63	1.07	1.70
40	1.35	1.45	1.30	1.51	1.25	1.57	1.20	1.63	1.15	1.69
45	1.39	1.48	1.34	1.53	1.30	1.58	1.25	1.63	1.21	1.69
50	1.42	1.50	1.38	1.54	1.34	1.59	1.30	1.64	1.26	1.69
60	1.47	1.54	1.44	1.57	1.40	1.61	1.37	1.65	1.33	1.69
70	1.51	1.57	1.48	1.60	1.45	1.63	1.42	1.66	1.39	1.70
80	1.54	1.59	1.52	1.62	1.49	1.65	1.47	1.67	1.44	1.70
90	1.57	1.61	1.55	1.64	1.53	1.66	1.50	1.69	1.48	1.71
100	1.59	1.63	1.57	1.65	1.55	1.67	1.53	1.70	1.51	1.72

Table 4.11. *Cancer death rates (CDR, deaths per 100 000 per year) in Birmingham, UK, with calculations for determining the Durbin–Watson test statistic*

Year	Observed CDR	Expected CDR	Residual e_i	$(e_i - e_{i-1})^2$
1959	219	202.3	16.7	
1960	209	206.0	3.0	185.9
1961	207	209.6	−2.6	31.8
1962	211	213.2	−2.2	0.1
1963	215	216.9	−1.9	0.1
1964	208	220.5	−12.5	113.1
1965	221	224.1	−3.1	87.7
1966	221	227.8	−6.8	13.2
1967	228	231.4	−3.4	11.3
1968	243	235.1	7.9	129.2
1969	237	238.7	−1.7	92.8
1970	234	242.3	−8.3	44.0
1971	248	246.0	2.0	107.4
1972	246	249.6	−3.6	31.8
1973	267	253.2	13.8	301.5
1974	263	256.9	6.1	58.3
1975	254	260.5	−6.5	159.6
1976	269	264.1	4.9	129.2
1977	266	267.8	−1.8	44.0
			$\sum e_i^2 = 975.0$	$\sum(e_i - e_{i-1})^2 = 1541.2$

between residuals $(e_i - e_{i-1})^2$, that are needed to calculate the Durbin–Watson statistic, which is found to be $1541.2/975.0 = 1.58$.

For a two-tailed test, the statistic to be compared with tabulated critical values is the minimum of 1.58 and $4 - 1.58 = 2.42$, i.e. $v^* = 1.58$. To use Table 4.10, note that the number of X variables is $p = 1$, and the number of data points is $n = 19$. The limits for the critical value of v^* are not given in Table 4.10 for this value of n. However the d_1 and d_2 values for $n = 15$ and $n = 20$ show that the observed v^* is certainly not significantly far from the expected value of 2 for independent residuals. There is, therefore, no evidence of serial correlation on a two-tailed test at the 5% level of significance.

Figure 4.5 shows the regression residuals plotted against the years that they correspond to. This plot confirms the absence of any obvious time trends in the residuals.

4.10 Summary and further reading

This chapter has provided a review of the most important aspects of the use of simple and multiple regression methods for data

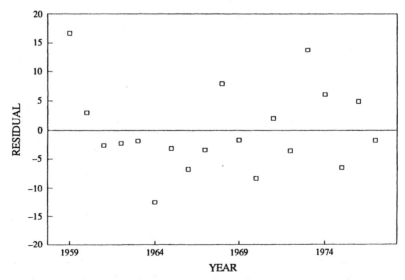

Figure 4.5. Residuals from the regression of cancer death rates in Birmingham against years.

analysis, including hypothesis tests and confidence limits for regression coefficients, the use of analysis of variance, and the assessment of the validity of the assumptions made when these methods are used. For further information on these and related topics, one of the many specialist texts such as that of Neter *et al.* (1983) or Younger (1985) should be consulted. Regression methods are also developed further in the chapters that follow, and some generalizations for the analysis of count data and proportions are discussed in Chapter 8.

The case study that follows gives some indication of the power of regression methods for addressing questions that are difficult to approach in a systematic way by any other means.

Exercises

(1) Table 4.12 shows some data that come from an experiment on sampling for modelling in terms of the classification of Figure 1.1. There are three experimental variables that were varied (the reactor temperature, the ratio of H_2 to n-heptane, and the contact time), and one response variable (the percentage of n-heptane converted to acetylene). These data were used by Marquardt and Snee (1975) as an example for a modification of multiple regression called *ridge regression*, and by Snee (1977) in a discussion of methods for validating regression models.

(i) Use the extra sum of squares principle with a computer program for multiple regression to compare the fit of the three models

$$Y = \beta_0 + \beta_1 X_1 + \beta_2 X_2 + \beta_3 X_3 + \varepsilon,$$

$$Y = \beta_0 + \beta_1 X_1 + \beta_2 X_2 + \beta_3 X_3 + \beta_4 X_1^2 + \beta_5 X_2^2 + \beta_6 X_3^2 + \dot{\varepsilon},$$

and

$$Y = \beta_0 + \beta_1 X_1 + \beta_2 X_2 + \beta_3 X_3 + \beta_4 X_1^2 + \beta_5 X_2^2 + \beta_6 X_3^2 + \beta_7 X_1 X_2 + \beta_8 X_1 X_3 + \beta_9 X_2 X_3 + \varepsilon.$$

(Note that the squares and products of the three X variables can be used in their own right as predictor variables in regression equations.)

Table 4.12. *Percentage conversion of n-heptane to acetylene for different combinations of the reactor temperature, ratio of H_2 to n-heptane, and the contact time. (Marquardt and Snee, 1975; Snee, 1977)*

Reactor temperature (°C) (X_1)	Ratio of H_2 to n-heptane (mole ratio) (X_2)	Contact time (seconds) X_3	Conversion of n-heptane to acetylene (%) (Y)
1300	7.5	0.0120	49.0
1300	9.0	0.0120	50.2
1300	11.0	0.0115	50.5
1300	13.5	0.0130	48.5
1300	17.0	0.0135	47.5
1300	23.0	0.0120	44.5
1200	5.3	0.0400	28.0
1200	7.5	0.0380	31.5
1200	11.0	0.0320	34.5
1200	13.5	0.0260	35.0
1200	17.0	0.0340	38.0
1200	23.0	0.0410	38.5
1100	5.3	0.0840	15.0
1100	7.5	0.0980	17.0
1100	11.0	0.0920	20.5
1100	17.0	0.0860	29.5

(ii) Determine whether any of the terms can be removed without making a significant reduction in the goodness of fit of the model chosen in part (i).

(iii) Plot the residuals from the model that you choose against the expected values of Y and against each of the X variables.

(2) Table 4.13 shows some data used for an example by McCullagh and Nelder (1989, p. 204), and originally collected by J. Crilley and L. N. Heminway of Lloyd's Register of Shipping. The data concern a type of damage caused by waves to the forward section of some types of cargo ships, and this exercise addresses the question of how the frequency of damage incidents relates to the months of service, the type of ship, the period of construction, and the period of operation. McCullagh and Nelder analysed these data using a generalized linear model, which is a type of model

114

that will be described in Section 8.10. For the present exercise the data are analysed using multiple linear regression.

(i) Plot the number of damage incidents against the months in service, the type of ship, the year of construction and the period of operation. Repeat the plots but using the transformed variables log(number of incidents + 1) and log(months in service). (Note that a transformation of the type $\log(Y + 1)$ is often used as a near alternative to a logarithmic distribution in cases where some of the Y values are zero. Also, other things being equal, it is reasonable to expect that the number of incidents will be proportional to the months in service.)

(ii) Explain why the plots in (i) indicate that a regression of log(number of incidents + 1) against log(months in service) will give better results than a regression of number of incidents against months in service.

(iii) The five types of ship can be accounted for in a multiple regression by constructing four 'dummy' 0–1 variables in the same manner that 'dummy' seasonal variables are set up in Case Study 4. Thus the fifth ship type can be considered to be the standard type, from which the other four types differ. Similarly, the four periods of construction of ships can be allowed for by using three 'dummy' variables, and the two periods of operation can be allowed for by using one 'dummy' variable. This leads to the construction of the regression data shown in Table 4.14. Using these data and a suitable computer program, fit the regression models

$$Y = \beta_0 + \beta_1 X_1 + \varepsilon,$$

$$Y = \beta_0 + \beta_1 X_1 + \beta_2 X_2 + \beta_3 X_3 + \beta_4 X_4 + \beta_5 X_5 + \beta_6 X_6 + \varepsilon,$$

$$Y = \beta_0 + \beta_1 X_1 + \beta_2 X_2 + \beta_3 X_3 + \beta_4 X_4 + \beta_5 X_5 + \beta_6 X_6 + \beta_7 X_7 + \beta_8 X_8 + \varepsilon,$$

and

$$Y = \beta_0 + \beta_1 X_1 + \beta_2 X_2 + \beta_3 X_3 + \beta_4 X_4 + \beta_5 X_5 + \beta_6 X_6 + \beta_7 X_7 + \beta_8 X_8 + \beta_9 X_9 + \varepsilon.$$

Table 4.13. *Data from Lloyd's Register of Shipping on damage incidents of a certain type. (McCullagh and Nelder, 1989)*

The cases refer to all ships defined by the third to fifth columns of the table, for which the total months of service are given by column two and the total number of damage incidents by the last column. There are five types of ship, four periods of construction (1960–64, 1965–69, 1970–74 and 1975–79), and two periods of operation (1960–74 and 1975–79).

Case	Months of use	Ship type	Period of construction	Period of operation	Number of incidents
1	127	1	1	1	0
2	63	1	1	4	0
3	1095	1	2	1	3
4	1095	1	2	4	4
5	1512	1	3	1	6
6	3353	1	3	4	18
7	2244	1	4	4	11
8	44882	2	1	1	39
9	17176	2	1	4	29
10	28609	2	2	1	58
11	20370	2	2	4	53
12	7064	2	3	1	12
13	13099	2	3	4	44
14	7117	2	4	4	18
15	1179	3	1	1	1
16	552	3	1	4	1
17	781	3	2	1	0
18	676	3	2	4	1
19	783	3	3	1	6

20	1948	3	3	4	2
21	274	3	4	4	1
22	251	4	1	1	0
23	105	4	1	4	0
24	288	4	2	1	0
25	192	4	2	4	0
26	349	4	3	1	2
27	1208	4	3	4	11
28	2051	4	4	4	4
29	45	5	1	1	0
30	789	5	2	1	7
31	437	5	2	4	7
32	1157	5	3	1	5
33	2161	5	3	4	12
34	542	5	4	4	1

Table 4.14. Regression data derived from Table 4.13

'Dummy' variables are used: four to allow for the ship type; three to allow for the period of construction; and one to allow for the period of operation. The 'dummy' variables are constructed so that the last levels of the factor being allowed for (the fifth type of ship, the fourth period of construction and the second period of operation) are the standard levels that are represented by all dummy variables being zero.

Case	Log months in use X_1	Ship type				Period of construction			Period of operation	Log (number incidents + 1)
		X_2	X_3	X_4	X_5	X_6	X_7	X_8	X_9	Y
1	4.84	1	0	0	0	1	0	0	1	0.00
2	4.14	1	0	0	0	1	0	0	0	0.00
3	7.00	1	0	0	0	0	1	0	1	1.39
4	7.00	1	0	0	0	0	1	0	0	1.61
5	7.32	1	0	0	0	0	0	1	1	1.95
6	8.12	1	0	0	0	0	0	1	0	2.94
7	7.72	1	0	0	0	0	0	0	0	2.48
8	10.71	0	1	0	0	1	0	0	1	3.69
9	9.75	0	1	0	0	1	0	0	0	3.40
10	10.26	0	1	0	0	0	1	0	1	4.08
11	9.92	0	1	0	0	0	1	0	0	3.99
12	8.86	0	1	0	0	0	0	1	1	2.56
13	9.48	0	1	0	0	0	0	1	0	3.81
14	8.87	0	1	0	0	0	0	0	0	2.94
15	7.07	0	0	1	0	1	0	0	1	0.69
16	6.31	0	0	1	0	1	0	0	0	0.69

17	6.66	0	0	1	0	0	1	0	1	0.00
18	6.52	0	0	1	0	1	1	1	0	0.69
19	6.66	0	0	1	0	0	0	1	1	1.95
20	7.57	0	0	1	0	0	1	1	0	1.10
21	5.61	0	0	1	0	1	0	0	0	0.69
22	5.53	0	0	0	1	1	0	0	1	0.00
23	4.65	0	0	0	1	1	0	0	0	0.00
24	5.66	0	0	0	1	0	1	1	1	0.00
25	5.26	0	0	0	1	1	1	1	0	0.00
26	5.86	0	0	0	1	1	0	1	1	1.10
27	7.10	0	0	0	1	0	0	1	0	2.48
28	7.63	0	0	0	1	0	0	0	0	1.61
29	3.81	0	0	0	0	1	1	0	1	0.00
30	6.67	0	0	0	0	0	1	0	1	2.08
31	6.08	0	0	0	0	0	1	1	0	2.08
32	7.05	0	0	0	0	0	0	0	1	1.79
33	7.68	0	0	0	0	0	0	1	0	2.56
34	6.30	0	0	0	0	0	0	0	0	0.69

Use the extra sum of squares principle to assess the goodness of fit of this hierarchy of models, and decide which model seems to be most appropriate.

(iv) Use residual plots to assess whether the assumptions involved in the model chosen in (iii) seem to be realistic.

(v) Comment on which types of ship, periods of construction and periods of operation appear to be associated with the highest rates of damage incidents.

CASE STUDY 4

The loss of sales in a store due to a fire

This case study is based on a real situation but some of the details have been changed in order to protect the confidentiality of the data. The background is that a certain retail and wholesale hardware company had two stores in Dunedin, New Zealand over the period from 1974 to 1980. Store A was considerably larger than store B, with the total value of sales being in the ratio of about 4:1 in favour of store A in 1974. In November 1977 there was a fire in Store A, which damaged much of the stock. A fire sale was held to clear this stock with the result that the store A sales were, if anything, higher than usual in the month of the fire. However sales were depressed for a considerable period from that time on because damage to the store considerably reduced the sales area.

The hardware company was insured against the loss of sales as a result of a fire. However, when an insurance claim was made on these grounds early in 1980 there was a wide discrepancy between the loss of sales estimated by the hardware company on the one hand and the loss of sales estimated by the insurance company on the other hand. As a result, an independent third party was called in to produce an unbiased assessment of the loss. Several ways to assess the likely loss were suggested by this third party, one of which was similar to the multiple regression method that will now be described.

Table 4.15 shows the data that were considered to be relevant to the study, together with values of some seasonal effect and fire effect variables that are discussed below. It was thought that sales in store B would account for the local trading conditions to some extent, while the national sales figures R1 and R2 would reflect the general economic environment as it related to the goods sold by the hardware company. Figure 4.6 shows plots of the total sales for stores A and B over the study period. It can be seen that in store A there seems to have been a drop in sales to some extent after the fire, but in store B there was a slow but consistent growth in sales over the whole period.

If the effects of the fire are ignored then a plausible regression model that can be used to relate the store A sales to the other variables is

$$Y = \beta_0 + \beta_1 X_1 + \beta_2 X_2 + \beta_3 X_3 + \beta_4 X_4 + \beta_5 X_5 + \beta_6 X_6$$
$$+ \beta_7 X_7 + \beta_8 X_8 + \beta_9 X_9 + \beta_{10} X_{10} + \beta_{11} X_{11} + \beta_{12} X_{12}$$
$$+ \beta_{13} X_{13} + \beta_{14} X_{14} + \varepsilon,$$

where X_1 is the store B sales, X_2 is the national sales R1, X_3 is the national sales R2, and X_4 to X_{14} account for seasonal effects. Here the use of the store B sales and the national sales is straightforward, but the seasonal effects variables need more explanation.

It is well known that shop sales are highly seasonal, with the main peak in most cases occurring just before Christmas. For this

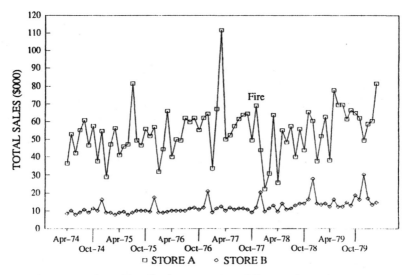

Figure 4.6. Monthly sales in stores A and B over the period April 1974 to March 1980.

Table 4.15. *Data available to assess the loss of sales resulting from a fire in a hardware store.*

Store A had the fire in November 1977. The national sales series are: R1 = national sales of retail household appliances, electrical goods, radios, televisions, etc., and R2 = national sales of retail hardware, builders hardware, paint, etc., both in millions of dollars. The seasonal effects and fire effects are explained in the text.

Period (Month-Year)	Store A sales ($000)	Store B sales ($000)	National statistics R1	National statistics R2	Monthly seasonal effects M	J	J	A	S	O	N	D	J	F	M	Fire effects 1	2
Apr-74	36.4	8.5	12.2	16.2	0	0	0	0	0	0	0	0	0	0	0	0	0
May-74	53.0	10.2	14.8	19.4	1	0	0	0	0	0	0	0	0	0	0	0	0
Jun-74	42.1	7.9	14.2	16.3	0	1	0	0	0	0	0	0	0	0	0	0	0
Jul-74	55.2	9.1	15.6	20.2	0	0	1	0	0	0	0	0	0	0	0	0	0
Aug-74	60.9	10.8	16.1	18.7	0	0	0	1	0	0	0	0	0	0	0	0	0
Sep-74	46.7	9.1	14.9	19.9	0	0	0	0	1	0	0	0	0	0	0	0	0
Oct-74	57.5	11.4	16.7	19.8	0	0	0	0	0	1	0	0	0	0	0	0	0
Nov-74	37.6	10.2	16.0	22.4	0	0	0	0	0	0	1	0	0	0	0	0	0
Dec-74	54.7	16.5	20.4	25.2	0	0	0	0	0	0	0	1	0	0	0	0	0
Jan-75	29.0	9.1	13.0	17.0	0	0	0	0	0	0	0	0	1	0	0	0	0
Feb-75	47.3	9.1	14.9	18.1	0	0	0	0	0	0	0	0	0	1	0	0	0
Mar-75	56.4	7.9	16.5	18.6	0	0	0	0	0	0	0	0	0	0	1	0	0
Apr-75	41.0	9.1	18.2	18.3	0	0	0	0	0	0	0	0	0	0	0	0	0
May-75	46.1	9.6	20.1	19.6	1	0	0	0	0	0	0	0	0	0	0	0	0
Jun-75	47.3	7.9	19.3	17.7	0	1	0	0	0	0	0	0	0	0	0	0	0

Month					d1	d2	d3	d4	d5	d6	d7	d8	d9	d10	d11
Jul-75	81.5	9.1	21.0	18.7	0	0	0	0	0	0	0	0	1	0	0
Aug-75	49.5	10.2	20.3	18.8	0	0	0	0	0	0	1	0	0	0	0
Sep-75	46.7	10.2	22.1	21.6	0	0	0	0	0	1	0	0	0	0	0
Oct-75	55.8	10.2	23.5	22.7	0	0	0	0	1	0	0	0	0	0	0
Nov-75	51.8	9.6	20.3	20.7	0	0	0	0	0	0	0	1	0	0	0
Dec-75	57.0	17.6	27.3	26.5	0	0	0	0	0	0	1	0	0	0	0
Jan-76	31.9	9.1	17.5	17.6	0	0	0	0	0	1	0	0	0	0	0
Feb-76	44.4	9.1	18.6	20.8	0	0	0	0	1	0	0	0	0	0	0
Mar-76	66.1	9.6	25.0	27.5	0	0	0	1	0	0	0	0	0	0	0
Apr-76	39.9	10.2	23.6	24.6	1	0	0	0	0	0	0	0	0	0	0
May-76	50.1	10.2	26.0	25.2	0	0	0	0	0	0	1	0	0	0	0
Jun-76	49.5	10.2	28.0	24.5	0	0	0	0	1	0	0	0	0	0	0
Jul-76	62.1	10.2	33.0	25.3	0	0	0	1	0	0	0	0	0	0	0
Aug-76	59.8	11.4	27.7	25.3	0	0	1	0	0	0	0	0	0	0	0
Sep-76	62.1	11.9	24.8	26.1	0	0	0	0	0	0	0	1	0	0	0
Oct-76	55.2	10.8	22.6	26.7	0	0	0	0	0	0	1	0	0	0	0
Nov-76	62.1	11.9	26.6	29.3	0	0	0	0	1	0	0	0	0	0	0
Dec-76	64.4	21.0	40.8	35.7	0	0	0	1	0	0	0	0	0	0	0
Jan-77	33.6	9.1	21.5	22.4	0	0	1	0	0	0	0	0	0	0	0
Feb-77	67.2	11.4	21.8	26.9	0	0	0	0	0	0	0	0	1	0	0
Mar-77	111.7	12.5	28.2	32.2	0	0	0	0	0	0	0	0	0	0	0
Apr-77	50.1	10.2	24.0	27.8	0	0	0	0	0	0	1	0	0	0	0
May-77	52.4	11.9	29.2	29.2	0	0	0	0	1	0	0	0	0	0	0
Jun-77	57.5	10.8	27.7	27.0	0	0	0	1	0	0	0	0	0	0	0
Jul-77	61.5	11.4	27.6	26.1	0	0	1	0	0	0	0	0	0	0	0
Aug-77	63.8	11.4	27.7	29.7	0	0	0	0	0	0	0	0	1	0	0
Sep-77	64.4	10.8	27.1	29.0	0	0	0	0	0	0	1	0	0	0	0
Oct-77	49.5	9.1	25.5	28.1	0	0	0	0	1	0	0	0	0	0	0
Nov-77 (fire)	68.9	11.9	26.4	31.8	0	1	0	0	0	0	0	0	0	0	0

Table 4.15. (continued)

Period (Month-Year)	Store A sales ($000)	Store B sales ($000)	National statistics R1	R2	Monthly seasonal effects M	J	J	A	S	O	N	D	J	F	M	Fire effects 1	2
Dec-77	43.8	20.5	31.7	35.6	0	0	0	0	0	0	0	1	0	0	0	0	1
Jan-78	22.2	9.6	20.8	24.7	0	0	0	0	0	0	0	0	1	0	0	0	1
Feb-78	30.7	11.4	21.7	27.5	0	0	0	0	0	0	0	0	0	1	0	0	1
Mar-78	63.8	13.1	26.2	33.4	0	0	0	0	0	0	0	0	0	0	1	0	1
Apr-78	25.6	9.6	25.2	27.5	0	0	0	0	0	0	0	0	0	0	0	0	1
May-78	55.2	14.2	32.1	32.4	1	0	0	0	0	0	0	0	0	0	0	0	1
Jun-78	48.4	10.8	30.5	28.9	0	1	0	0	0	0	0	0	0	0	0	0	1
Jul-78	57.5	11.4	31.1	27.7	0	0	1	0	0	0	0	0	0	0	0	0	1
Aug-78	39.9	13.1	33.1	31.5	0	0	0	1	0	0	0	0	0	0	0	0	1
Sep-78	55.8	14.2	29.5	31.7	0	0	0	0	1	0	0	0	0	0	0	0	1
Oct-78	43.8	14.2	30.8	33.3	0	0	0	0	0	1	0	0	0	0	0	0	1
Nov-78	65.5	16.5	33.7	37.9	0	0	0	0	0	0	1	0	0	0	0	0	1
Dec-78	60.4	27.9	39.1	40.2	0	0	0	0	0	0	0	1	0	0	0	0	1
Jan-79	37.6	14.2	26.8	32.0	0	0	0	0	0	0	0	0	1	0	0	0	1
Feb-79	51.8	13.6	26.8	33.1	0	0	0	0	0	0	0	0	0	1	0	0	1
Mar-79	62.7	14.2	34.0	38.6	0	0	0	0	0	0	0	0	0	0	1	0	1
Apr-79	38.1	12.5	28.3	32.8	0	0	0	0	0	0	0	0	0	0	0	0	0
May-79	78.0	16.5	41.5	40.1	1	0	0	0	0	0	0	0	0	0	0	0	0
Jun-79	69.5	12.5	35.4	35.4	0	1	0	0	0	0	0	0	0	0	0	0	0
Jul-79	69.5	12.5	33.1	34.6	0	0	1	0	0	0	0	0	0	0	0	0	0

Aug-79	61.5	14.8	36.3	38.5	0	0	0	0	0	1	0	0	0	0	0	0
Sep-79	66.6	13.1	30.4	35.6	0	0	0	0	0	0	1	0	0	0	0	0
Oct-79	64.9	18.8	33.5	40.5	0	0	0	0	1	0	0	0	0	0	0	0
Nov-79	62.1	16.5	34.7	44.1	0	0	0	0	0	0	1	0	0	0	0	0
Dec-79	49.5	30.2	39.8	44.7	0	0	0	0	0	0	0	0	0	0	0	0
Jan-80	58.7	17.1	30.8	36.1	0	0	0	0	0	0	1	0	0	0	0	0
Feb-80	60.4	13.6	32.6	40.4	0	0	0	0	0	0	0	1	0	0	0	0
Mar-80	81.5	14.8	35.6	44.2	0	0	0	0	0	0	0	0	1	0	0	0

reason, any equation that attempts to relate sales to other variables needs to take seasonal effects into account. In the present case, this is done to some extent by including store B sales and national sales in the regression equation, since these other sales series will themselves display seasonal patterns. However, it is quite conceivable that part of the seasonal pattern of sales in store A sales is not reflected in the other series. This suggests that it is worth making a direct allowance for seasonal effects in the regression equation, in addition to using the other sales series. This can be done by using what are sometimes called 'dummy' variables. One month, say April, is regarded as the standard month. Each of the other months is then given its own X variable which is 0 except for observations taken in the month in question, in which case it is 1. Thus X_4, which is the dummy variable for May in the above equation, is 0 for all observations not taken in May, and is 1 for observations in May. Similarly, X_5 is 1 for June, but otherwise 0. Since there are 12 months, it needs 11 dummy variables (X_4 to X_{14}) to account for the differences between May, June, ..., March and the standard month of April. Table 4.15 shows all the values that are obtained in this way, under the general heading 'Monthly seasonal effects', where the column headings for the individual 0–1 variables are the first letters of the months that these variables refer to. With these definitions, the coefficients of the X variables in the regression equation (β_4 to β_{14}) are the monthly seasonal effects for the months May to March relative to zero for April.

Dummy variables are used quite often in regression analysis to allow for the effects of different levels of a qualitative variable. A further discussion of their use is provided in Section 7.14.

When the regression equation containing variables X_1 to X_{14} was fitted to the data it accounted for a substantial part of the variation in store A sales, with $R^2 = 0.564$. However a plot of standardized residuals (Figure 4.7) gives a clear indication that the model should include some allowance for the effects of the fire. The residuals are very low, with all but one being negative from the time of the fire until April 1979.

This suggests that two variables (X_{15} and X_{16}) should be included in the regression equation to allow for the effects of the fire. The first of these can take account of the immediate effects of the fire sale. This is achieved by making X_{15} equal to 0 for every observation except for the one for November 1977. In this way, the coefficient β_{15} in the regression equation is a direct estimate of

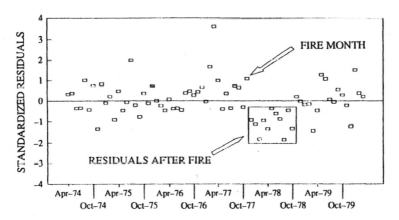

Figure 4.7. Standardized residuals plotted against time for the regression of store A sales on store B sales, two national sales variables, and seasonal effects.

the effect of the fire in the month when the fire occurred. The second variable for the fire effect, X_{16}, can be set at 0 for every month up to and including November 1977, 1 for the following months through to March 1979, and then 0 again from April 1979 on. This implies that the sales from December 1977 to March 1979 were all changed by the same fixed amount as a result of the fire, with no effects after March 1979. Values for the two fire effect variables are shown in the last two columns of Table 4.15.

The fitted regression equation with all the variables included has the coefficients shown in Table 4.16. From this table it can be seen that the estimate of the fire effect in the month of the fire is 11.49, with standard error 9.77. From a t-test, the t-ratio, $11.49/9.77 = 1.18$ with 55 degrees of freedom, is not significantly different from zero at the 5% level. However, the estimate of the fire effect from December 1977 to March 1979 is -12.80, with standard error 2.70. This gives the t-ratio $-12.80/2.70 = -4.74$, with 55 degrees of freedom, which is significantly different from zero at the 0.1% level. Hence, there is strong evidence of sales losses over the period in question.

Of course, the way that the second fire effect variable was determined (to remove the negative residuals shown in Figure 4.7 for the months subsequent to the fire) means that the significance of the coefficient for this variable was more or less inevitable. It can therefore by argued that the 'true' significance level of the fire effect may be exaggerated here to some extent.

127

Table 4.16. *Coefficients for the fitted regression equation for sales in store A as a function of sales in store B, national sales, seasonal effects, and fire effects, with standard errors and t-statistics with 55 degrees of freedom*

Variable	Estimated coefficient	Estimated standard error	t
Constant	18.11	—	—
Store B sales	1.02	0.82	1.25
National sales			
R1	0.58	0.45	1.29
R2	−0.01	0.52	−0.02
Seasonal effect			
May	12.08	5.36	2.25[a]
June	11.60	5.40	2.57[a]
July	22.52	5.47	4.12[c]
August	12.56	5.37	2.34[a]
September	15.33	5.16	2.97[b]
October	11.50	5.23	2.20[a]
November	12.33	5.52	2.24[a]
December	−0.30	9.21	−0.03
January	−2.12	5.22	−0.41
February	12.14	5.23	2.32[a]
March	32.13	5.31	6.05[c]
Fire effect November 1977	11.49	9.77	1.18
Fire effect December 1977–March 1979	−12.80	2.70	−4.74[c]

[a]Significant at the 5% level.
[b]Significant at the 1% level.
[c]Significant at the 0.1% level.

It is interesting to see from Table 4.16 that the coefficients of the store B sales and the national sales R1 and R2 are not significantly different from zero. This implies that one or more of these variables can be removed from the equation without making much difference to the goodness of fit of the regression equation. However, this possibility has not been pursued here, since finding the equation with the smallest number of predictor variables is not of any particular concern. However, it is of some interest to see the analysis of variance that is obtained when the variables are added to the equation in the order: store B sales, then the national sales R1 and R2, then seasonal effects, and lastly fire effects. This

Table 4.17. *Extra sums of squares explained by different terms in the regression of store A sales on store B sales, national sales, seasonal effects, and fire effects*

Source of variation	Sum of squares	df	Mean square	F
Store B	845.5	1	845.5	10.80[a]
+R1+R2	2205.0	2	1102.5	14.08[b]
+Seasons	5066.8	11	460.6	5.88[b]
+F1+F2	1943.7	2	971.8	12.41[a]
Error	4306.0	55	78.3	
Total	14367.0	71		

[a]Significant at the 1% level.
[b]Significant at the 0.1% level.

analysis of variance is shown in Table 4.17. It appears that with this ordering all the terms add extra predictive power to the equation since all the F-values are significantly large.

The assumptions involved in using the regression model seem to be reasonable. The standardized residuals show no patterns when plotted against time (Figure 4.8), or against predicted sales from the fitted regression equation (not shown). A normal probability plot indicates the existence of two relatively large residuals, one positive and one negative (Figure 4.9). The corresponding sales figures (for March 1977 and December 1980) are certainly unusual, but they are correct. There is, therefore, no sound reason for not including them in the data. The Durbin–Watson statistic for testing serial correlation is 1.89. This falls within the uncertainty region according to the tables of Savin and White (1977), but is so close to 2 that it suggests little evidence of high serial correlation.

According to the regression model, the total effect of the fire was to raise sales by \$11 490 in the fire month of November 1977, and then lower sales by \$12 800 per month for the 16 months from December 1977 to March 1979. The total loss is therefore estimated as $-\$11\,490 + (16 \times \$12\,800) = \$193\,310$. This is a substantial sum, and an insurance company wanting to minimize the claim would no doubt look carefully at the assumptions involved in calculating it.

There are two weaknesses that the insurance company could choose to exploit here. First, and most important is the fact that, since the study is purely observational, a causal link between the

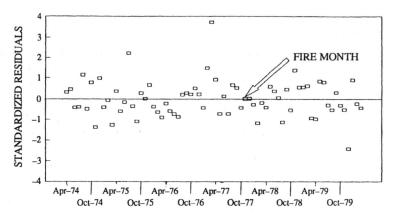

Figure 4.8. Standardized residuals plotted against time for the regression of store A sales on store B sales, two national sales variables, seasonal effects, and fire effects.

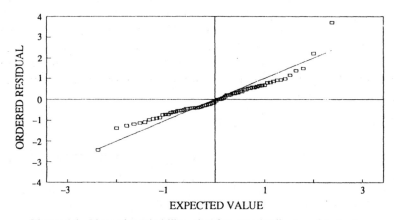

Figure 4.9. Normal probability plot for standardized residuals for the regression of store A sales on store B sales, two national sales variables, seasonal effects, and fire effects.

loss of sales and the fire is not firmly established. Therefore, any alternative explanation for low sales from December 1977 to March 1979 can also be entertained. This means that if the insurance company can find anything else unusual in the trading conditions over this period then they can claim that part or all the loss is associated with this alternative factor. For example, if there was a relatively low level of expenditure on advertising over the period then the insurance company could argue that this was part of the reason for low sales and reduce the allowable claim accordingly.

The second weakness in the method for estimating the effect of the fire is the way that the second fire effect variable was defined so as to change the mainly negative residuals shown in Figure 4.7 for the period December 1977 to March 1979. It has already been mentioned that letting the data decide the variable in this way is likely to lead to a bias, and that it is hardly surprising to find that the coefficient of the second fire effect variable is highly significant. However, there seems little alternative in the present case since there was no way of knowing in advance what the nature of the fire effect would be, apart from the fact that sales were likely to be high in the month of the fire because of the fire sale, but then low for some later period.

This case study is an example of what is called an intervention analysis in Eberhardt and Thomas' (1991) classification of types of research study that has been discussed in Section 1.2, and is shown schematically in Figure 1.1. The 'intervention' is, of course, the fire. The sales series for the store with the fire would also often be called an interrupted time series. Situations of this type, where there is an interest in the effects of a specific controlled or uncontrolled event occur quite often and are discussed at greater length in Chapter 6.

Experimental designs to assess the effect of a treatment

5.1 Introduction

As was pointed out in Section 1.6, the subject of experimental design is usually thought of beginning with the work of Sir Ronald Fisher at Rothamstead Experimental Station in Britain, in the early part of this century. Two of his classical books on the subject were *Statistical Methods for Research Workers*, first published in 1925, and *The Design of Experiments*, first published in 1935. The subject has come a long way in the years since then, and yet there are still aspects of it that are not covered well in most textbooks. One reason for this is that the theory of experimental design began with applications in agriculture, an area where the researcher has a great deal of freedom to manipulate the experimental materials and to apply different treatments. However, in many other areas there are very real constraints as to what can be done, either for ethical reasons, or because the experimental units are human subjects with minds of their own.

The example of assessing the effect on heart disease of a high or low salt diet that was discussed in Section 1.6 suggests that it is important, at least in some disciplines, to consider potential experimental designs that are less than perfect but at least can be used. It is important, then, to understand the weaknesses of these *quasi-experimental designs*. Much of the theoretical work in this area has been done by those working in the areas of education research and in the evaluation of social programmes. However, this work is relevant to experimenters in many other subject areas as well.

This chapter is concerned mainly with the simplest type of experiment where the *experimental units* (for example, human or animal subjects) are in two groups. One of the groups is a *control group*, which receives the usual conditions, while the other group is the *treatment or experimental group*, which receives some special treatment. The question of interest is whether some measurement taken on the experimental units is changed by the special treatment. Situations where a treatment can take several different forms, so that several experimental groups are needed, are also considered to some extent in this chapter. For these, the question is whether some or all the treatments change a measurement on the experimental units.

More complicated types of experiment are discussed in the next two chapters. Chapter 6 is concerned with cases where the question of interest is whether a treatment has an impact on the values in a time series, while Chapter 7 is concerned with experiments in which two or more factors are manipulated at the same time. It is the material in Chapter 7 that is usually emphasized in books on the statistics of experimental designs.

In Chapter 1 a distinction has been made between an experimental study, where events are controlled by the investigator, and an observational study, where events are uncontrolled. However, in practice this distinction may be somewhat blurred because an observational study would have been an experimental study if it were not for the fact that the assignment of the treatment to experimental units was either an accident, or made by some agency for reasons unconnected with the assessment of the effects of the treatment.

For example, consider Case Study 4, which was concerned with the effects of a fire on the sales in a hardware store. Here the 'treatment' was the fire, which was not started deliberately, so that this is an observational study. However, the data would presumably have been exactly the same if the fire had been started deliberately to see what would happen. Therefore, this can be considered to be a type of unplanned experiment.

Apart from situations of this type, there are also, of course, factors that cannot be manipulated because of their essential nature, such as sex, ethnic origins, age, and so on. The point here is that to all intents and purposes many observational studies can be thought of as unplanned 'experiments' to which the discussions in this and later chapters are relevant.

5.2 External and internal validity

In the social science literature the terms *internal validity* and *external validity* are used in the assessment of the problems that may occur with particular types of experimental design. Internal validity concerns whether the apparent effects or lack of effects shown by the experimental results are due to the factor being studied, rather than some alternative factor. External validity concerns the extent to which the results of an experiment can be generalized to some wider population of interest.

An experiment without internal validity is useless because what is being measured is wrong. In other words, the treatment effect is confounded with the effects of other factors. To take a specific example, suppose that an experimenter is interested in the effect of four different diets on the growth of rats. The available rats are divided at random into four groups, each of which is given one of the diets. The weight gain in one month is then measured for each rat, and significantly different mean weight gains for different diets are required as evidence of diet effects. This seems straightforward, but the internal validity of the experiment would be completely lost if all the rats on one diet were kept in the same cage, since the differences in diets would be completely confounded with the differences in cages. This means that one plausible explanation for the different weight gains with different diets is that the weight gains were dependent on the cages rather than the diets. In other words, all the rats in some cages would have had relatively high growth and all the rats in other cages would have had relatively low growth, irrespective of which diet they were given.

With care, the internal validity of an experiment like this can be ensured so that it is possible to say with confidence that there is either evidence for a diet effect or not, under the conditions used. However, it would still be questionable to use the experiment to draw conclusions about the effect of different diets on wild rats. Hence the external validity of the experiment may be low in this respect, although generalization to what will happen in other laboratories might be realistic.

The potential threats to the internal validity of an experiment are the *alternative explanations* for a treatment effect. To a large extent these threats depend on the specific situation, but the following list gives an idea of the possibilities (Campbell and Stanley, 1963):

(a) History: specific events occur during the course of the experiment in addition to what is required by the design
(b) Maturation: the experimental units change during the experiment simply as a result of the passing of time
(c) Testing: taking one measurement on a unit changes the

values of later measurements

(d) Instrumentation: there are changes either in the method for measuring the responses of experimental units or in the agents making the measurements

(e) Regression to the mean: if the allocation of experimental units to the experimental and control groups is made on the basis of pretest scores, with those with low scores going to one group and those with high scores going to the other, then on retesting there is a tendency for the two groups to have closer means than on the original test

(f) Differential selection: because of the method for selecting groups, certain types of experimental unit are mainly in either the experimental or the control group

(g) Experimental mortality: there are losses of experimental units during the experiment, which are at different rates for the experimental and control groups

Factors which effect the extent to which the results of an experiment can be generalized (the external validity) are:

(a) Testing interaction: where a pretest changes the sensitivity of experimental units to the experimental treatments in such a way that the measured treatment effect is not what it would be in the population of interest

(b) Selection interaction: where the nature of the process for selecting experimental units means that treatment effects are likely to be higher or lower than for units in the population of interest

(c) Reactions to experimental arrangements: where the changed circumstances necessary for an experiment cause changes in the measurements on experimental units

(d) Multiple treatment effects: where each unit gets several treatments and some effects of earlier treatments are present when later treatments are applied

These threats to the internal and external validity of experiments are considered further throughout the remainder of this chapter.

5.3 Pseudoreplication

One of the pitfalls in designing an experiment is the inadvertent use of *pseudoreplication*, which has been defined by Hurlbert

(1984 p. 190) as: 'the use of inferential statistics to test for treatment effects with data from experiments where either treatments are not replicated (though samples may be) or replicates are not statistically independent'.

The problem here is that if pseudoreplication is treated as if it were true replication then treatment effects may appear significant when in fact they are not.

In the discussion in the previous section concerning an experiment to compare weight gains of rats on different diets, it was pointed out that if all the rats on one diet are put in one cage then the diet effect becomes confounded with the cage effect, and the internal validity of the experiment is thereby compromised. Another way of looking at this is to say that the rats within cages provide only pseudoreplication since their weight gains may not be independent. In fact in terms of the treatment allocation the true experimental unit is a cage of rats on the same diet rather than a single rat. From this point of view there is no replication at all.

Generally, pseudoreplication is likely to occur when the experimental units being used tend to have similar measurements when they are close in time or in space, and the method of assigning individuals to treatment groups means that individuals with the same treatment tend to be close together. Therefore, n observations of the same child at hourly intervals are not equivalent to n observations of different children, and n observations that are taken at one location in a river are not equivalent to n observations that are taken at different locations. More generally, it is not valid to treat observations obtained by *cluster sampling* as if they were obtained by random sampling.

Although this may seem obvious, it appears that in the past pseudoreplication has often been treated as true replication. This is indicated by a survey carried out by Hurlbert (1984) of 156 papers published in biology journals. He found that 27% of these papers involved pseudoreplication, which represented 48% of the papers using formal methods of statistical inference.

Pseudoreplication can be avoided by ensuring that the observations taken are really independent, for example by randomly allocating experimental units to treatments. If this is not possible then the analysis of the observations should take into account any correlations. For example, if several observations have to be taken on each experimental unit then a repeated measures analysis may be appropriate, as discussed in Chapter 7.

5.4 The one-group pretest–posttest design

The description 'pre-experimental designs' has been used to describe those designs that are so weak that it is difficult to draw any sound conclusions from the results. Perhaps the simplest of these that could be contemplated for a serious study is the one-group pretest–posttest design, which can be represented as:

$$O_1 \ X \ O_2,$$

where O_1 represents pretest observations taken on a group of experimental units, X represents an experimental intervention, and O_2 represents posttest observations taken on the same units. Here a major weakness is the absence of a separate control group, although under certain circumstances the change in observations between the pretest and the posttest might be considered to be a valid measure of the effect of the treatment.

Example 5.1: Assessing the environmental impact of a power station

An example of the one-group pretest–posttest design would be the assessment of the effect of a new power station on the level of a chemical in a stream that the station discharges into. Suppose that before the station is built 10 samples of sediment taken at different locations in the discharge area give chemical levels 4, 7, 5, 8, 9, 3, 3, 8, 6 and 2. Then, after the power station has been running for a year, further readings from the same locations are found to be 10, 16, 9, 12, 15, 10, 11, 12, 13 and 19.

A paired comparison t-test suggests itself here for the determination of whether or not a significant change has taken place. The mean change in level for the 10 locations is $\bar{d} = 7.2$, with standard deviation $s_d = 3.85$. The t-value is therefore $\bar{d}/(s_d/\sqrt{n}) = 7.2/(3.85/\sqrt{10}) = 5.91$, with 9 degrees of freedom, which is significantly different from zero at the 0.1% level.

There is little doubt that a change has occurred. However, the important question is whether this change is due to the operation of the power station. The experimental design makes it difficult to say this with confidence since there are many alternative explanations for the experimental results. Some possibilities are:

(a) A flood which had a large effect on the sediment (history)

(b) Discharges from factories upstream which are causing a gradual increase in the level of the chemical in the area where the power station is located (maturity)

(c) The calibration of the measuring instrument changed in the year between the samples, or a different instrument was used (instrumentation)

The only way that the experimental results can be accepted at their face value is by arguing that these and all other explanations that do not include the effect of the power station are not correct.

5.5 The static group comparison

Another simple pre-experimental design is the static group comparison, which can be represented as follows:

$$X \quad O_1$$
$$O_2.$$

This is a simple comparison between an experimental group which receives a treatment (X) and a control group with no treatment, with O_1 and O_2 indicating measurements on the experimental units taken after the treatment has been applied. Here, the basic problem is that there is no way of knowing whether the two groups were comparable before the treatment. Therefore, treatment effects that are measured by the mean value for treated units minus the mean value for control units may really be differences that would have been there anyway.

Example 5.2: Is the study of philosophy valuable training for business?

The following letter in a newspaper concerning the relative values of different types of undergraduate training for potential managers is a good illustration of the difficulty of assessing the results of a static group comparison. The letter has been changed in minor ways to shorten it, and to protect the identity of the writer, but is otherwise as printed in the *Otago Daily Times*, a New Zealand newspaper.

Sir, — Sir Robert Jones' article was a welcome defence of the humanities. In case readers suppose his claims to be mere opinion, I shall give some striking evidence for his assertion that a traditional education in the humanities is the best training for management.

In a comparison of the performance of United States undergraduates taking the graduate management aptitude test in 1981–2, students in philosophy scored on average 11% above the mean, while students of management scored 7.7% below the mean. Philosophy students did better than students in any other subject except maths (13.3% above the mean). The same pattern appears in results for the law school admission test. Philosophy scored 8.7% above the mean, beaten only by maths (12.8% above) and economics (9.6% above). Management students scored 5.4% below the mean.

The lesson is clear: philosophy, a supposedly useless subject, is good training for business and the professions.

In fact, the lesson here is not at all clear. There is no way of knowing from the quoted results how the different groups of students compared before receiving their different 'treatments' (studying different subjects for a first degree). However, it is possible that students who choose to study philosophy are above the average in ability, and this is the reason why they do better than management students in graduate tests. It is quite possible that if these students had chosen to study management instead of philosophy for their first degrees then they would have had higher average scores on the graduate tests. In truth, there is no way of knowing from the data presented whether studying philosophy helps or hinders high scoring on these tests.

5.6 The importance of a comparable control group

Examples 5.1 and 5.2 suggest that in most situations a satisfactory experiment to assess the effect of a treatment requires that there is a control group that is similar to the experimental group except as far as the treatment is concerned. Without a comparable control group there is no way to be sure about what might have happened in the absence of the treatment, and it becomes necessary to compare the experimental group results with a rather hypothetical 'what might have been'.

Of course, a control group is of little use unless it was clearly comparable with the experimental group before the treatment was imposed, which raises the question how comparability can be assured. In this respect, modern notions of experimental design only recognize one completely satisfactory way to achieve comparability: the random allocation of subjects to groups. By this means, any differences between groups can be expected to average out, and there is no need to make any assumptions about the nature of these differences. One definition of a 'true' experimental design is therefore a design that incorporates appropriate randomization.

5.7 Regression to the mean

Regression to the mean is a phenomenon that it is important to understand as a possible explanation for apparent treatment 'effects'. It may occur whenever an experimental group is chosen because of low or high values on a variable of interest, and a correlated variable is used to measure the experimental outcome at a later time. The following artificial example demonstrates the problem.

Example 5.3: Testing the effectiveness of a new drug for asthma

Suppose that a study is carried out to test the effectiveness of a new drug for the treatment of asthma. At the start of the trial a group of patients is asked to assess the effectiveness of current treatment on a scale from 1 to 15. The new treatment is then introduced to the patients who give the lowest scores for satisfaction. After one month they are tested again and the mean satisfaction score has increased significantly. It is concluded, therefore, that the new treatment is effective. However, in fact the new treatment is no better than the old one.

To see how this can occur, suppose that the pretest and posttest scores are as shown in Table 5.1. The distribution is the same for pretest and posttest scores, as can be seen by looking at the frequency distribution in the last two rows and the last two

Table 5.1. *Satisfaction scores for patients from a trial for a new treatment of asthma*

The main body of the table shows the numbers of patients with different pretest and posttest scores. For example, there were two patients with a pretest score of 12 and a posttest score of 11

Pretest Scores	Posttest scores							Total frequency	Posttest mean
	7	8	9	10	11	12	13		
13				1	1	1	1	4	11.5
12			1	1	2	1	1	6	11.0
11		1	2	3	3	2	1	12	10.55
10	1	1	3	4	3	1		14	10.0
9	1	2	3	3	2	1		12	9.5
8	1	1	2	1	1			6	9.0
7	1	1	1	1				4	8.5
Total frequency	4	6	12	14	12	6	4	58	
Pretest mean	8.5	9.0	9.5	10.0	10.5	11.5	11.0		

columns of the table. In particular, both distributions have the same overall mean of 10. The fact that the pretest and posttest scores are not the same for each patient comes about only because these scores depend to a certain extent on chance factors such as the number of asthma attacks just before patients are asked to assess their treatment, their general state of mind, etc.

Consider the patients with a score of 7 on the pretest. On the posttest their mean is 8.5, so they seem to have improved. However, this merely reflects the fact that these individuals have pretest scores that are so low that they can only produce either another 7 or a higher score on the retest. On the other hand, consider the patients with a pretest score of 13. On retesting, their mean becomes 11.5 so they seem to have got worse. However, this just reflects the fact that for these patients the only possibility is to remain the same or decline.

Table 5.1 shows that patients with pretest scores that are above the mean (11, 12 and 13) have posttest means which are lower (10.5, 11.0 and 11.5, respectively), patients with a pretest score of 10 have the same posttest mean, and patients with pretest scores that are below the mean (9, 8 and 7) have increased posttest means (9.5, 9.0 and 8.5, respectively).

This effect is called *regression to the mean* because any group that is chosen because it is extreme will tend to look less extreme on the retest: the posttest mean will regress towards the population mean. The effect occurs irrespective of whether or not there is a treatment effect. Therefore, it may have the appearance of being a treatment effect when none is really there, or it may exaggerate or hide the true treatment effect. To take proper account of regression to the mean requires an appropriate analysis such as that described in Section 5.11 on the *regression discontinuity design*.

5.8 The comparative posttest design

The problems with the static group comparison are largely overcome by randomly allocating experimental units to the treatment and control groups before the treatment is applied. This design, which is sometimes called the *comparative posttest design*, can be represented as shown below, where R indicates the random allocation of subjects to groups:

$$R \quad X \quad O_1$$
$$R \qquad \quad O_2$$

Randomization ensures that the two groups are initially comparable, so that the posttest mean difference between the groups is a valid measure of the treatment effect, providing that the sole difference between the two groups after randomization is that only one gets the treatment. Therefore, the only two threats to validity are (a) that the treatment is not the sole difference between the groups, and (b) that the experimental subjects might not be representative of subjects in general as far as the treatment effects are concerned.

The statistical analysis of the comparative posttest design is quite straightforward in most cases. A t-test (or possibly a non-parametric alternative) to compare the means for the treatment and control groups will usually be quite sufficient. The treatment effect is estimated by the difference $\bar{X}_1 - \bar{X}_2$ between the experimental group mean $\bar{X}_1$ and the control group mean $\bar{X}_2$. A 95% confidence interval for this is then just

$$\bar{X}_1 - \bar{X}_2 \pm t_{5\%,n-2} \cdot \text{SÊ}(\bar{X}_1 - \bar{X}_2),$$

where n is the total number of experimental units in both groups, $t_{5\%,n-2}$ is the absolute value from the t-distribution table with $n-2$ degrees of freedom that is exceeded with probability 0.05, and $\text{SÊ}(\bar{X}_1 - \bar{X}_2)$ is the estimated standard error of $\bar{X}_1 - \bar{X}_2$.

Although randomization will go some way towards eliminating differences between the control and experimental groups, there will usually be some residual differences left in potentially confounding variables that are sometimes referred to as *covariates*. These are variables that can be expected to account for some of the differences between groups in the absence of a treatment effect. For example, in assessing a new treatment for cancer, a measure of the seriousness of the illness before treatment begins is a natural covariate. Other covariates in this case might be the age and sex of patients.

When the values of covariates are known for all experimental units it is natural to be interested in an estimate of the effect of the treatment after allowing for the effects of these covariates. This can be obtained in the case of the cancer treatment by considering the control and experimental patients separately for groups with similar values for the covariates or, alternatively, by using multiple regression to assess the difference between the experimental and control groups that is accounted for by the treatment after allowing for the effects of the covariates. This type of analysis, which is sometimes called the *analysis of covariance*, is discussed further in Section 5.12.

5.9 The comparative change design

Under some conditions, the comparative posttest design can be improved by taking observations on the experimental units after randomization but before the treatment is applied. This gives the *comparative change experiment*, as indicated below, where R indicates the initial randomization of the experimental units to the two groups:

$$R \quad O_1 \quad X \quad O_2$$
$$R \quad O_3 \qquad O_4$$

The advantage of having pretests is that if the randomization has not quite produced equal groups then this can be allowed for by comparing the change between the pretest and the posttest in the experimental group with the same change in the control group.

A pretest is not desirable when there is the possibility that the pretest has the effect of somehow making the subjects more sensitive to the treatment than they would have been without the pretest. For example, suppose that it is desirable to assess the effect of seeing a certain film on racial prejudice. To do this, a group of subjects is randomly divided into two groups, which are given the pretest. One group sees the film, and the posttest is given to both groups. The group seeing the film shows a significantly larger change (towards less prejudice) than the other group, which is certainly evidence of an effect of the film. However, as noted by Campbell and Stanley (1963), there may be some doubt about whether this effect would have occurred in the absence of the pretest.

The problem is that to measure racial prejudice it is necessary to ask questions that will lead subjects to think about their attitudes, and may make them more sympathetic to the message in the film. Indeed, it is quite possible that without the pretest many subjects would treat the film as pure entertainment. On these grounds it seems that the experimental design is improved by not having a pretest and relying on randomization to produce comparable groups.

With the comparative change design, two types of analysis are possible. The first is based on a simple comparison of changes in score for the treated and the control subjects. The second is based on a regression of posttest scores on pretest scores, including variables that allow for treatment effects. These two types of analysis are illustrated in the following example.

As discussed in Section 5.12, if the second approach is used then it may be possible to include covariates (confounding variables) in regression models, with the idea that these may take into account some differences between the control and treated groups that still exist after the experimental units have been allocated to groups. However, since most of these differences should be captured in the pretest scores, the use of covariates may not be as useful here as it is with the comparative posttest design.

Example 5.4: The effects of a drug on the level of a blood chemical

The data in Table 5.2 are from a hypothetical experiment on assessing the effect of a drug on the level of a chemical in the blood of human subjects. It is assumed that 32 patients were randomly assigned to two groups of 16. The first group was given the drug and the second group was given a placebo. Table 5.2 shows chemical levels before (X_1) and after (X_2) the treatment for each of the patients.

An analysis based on the change scores, $D = X_2 - X_1$, can simply involve seeing whether the mean changes are significantly different for the control and experimental group. Here a t-test will be used, on the assumption of normally distributed data with the same standard deviation for each group.

From the data, the following statistics are obtained: treated subjects, sample size, $n_1 = 16$; mean change, $\bar{D}_1 = 0.12$; standard deviation of changes, $s_{D1} = 0.16$; control subjects, sample size, $n_2 = 16$; mean change, $\bar{D}_2 = 0.06$; standard deviation of changes, $s_{D2} = 0.19$. The pooled estimate of the common population standard deviation is therefore

$$s = \sqrt{[\{(n_1 - 1)s_{D1}^2 + (n_2 - 1)s_{D2}^2\}/(n_1 + n_2 - 2)]} = 0.175,$$

with 30 degrees of freedom. Hence, the usual t-statistic for testing for a significant difference between $\bar{D}_1$ and $\bar{D}_2$ is

$$t = (\bar{D}_1 - \bar{D}_2)/\{s\sqrt{(1/n_1 + 1/n_2)}\} = 0.91.$$

This t-value can be tested by seeing whether it is significantly different from zero by comparison with the critical values from the t-distribution with 30 degrees of freedom. On this basis there is no evidence of a treatment effect from a two-tailed test at the 5% level.

145

Table 5.2. *The results of a comparative change experiment to assess the effect of a drug on the level of a chemical in the blood of patients*

	Experimental Group			Control Group		
	Pretest X_1	Posttest X_2	Change D	Pretest X_1	Posttest X_2	Change D
1	11.7	11.8	0.1	12.5	12.5	0.0
2	3.9	3.9	0.0	13.2	13.6	0.4
3	21.5	21.7	0.2	10.6	10.7	0.1
4	12.5	12.6	0.1	9.6	9.5	-0.1
5	10.6	10.7	0.1	9.2	9.0	-0.2
6	15.4	15.4	0.0	11.6	11.8	0.2
7	16.0	15.9	-0.1	14.0	13.8	-0.2
8	11.7	11.6	-0.1	13.8	13.8	0.0
9	9.7	9.7	0.0	9.3	9.1	-0.2
10	19.5	19.9	0.4	10.0	10.2	0.2
11	13.7	13.9	0.2	17.7	18.0	0.3
12	12.0	12.3	0.3	12.2	12.3	0.1
13	13.0	13.0	0.0	7.3	7.6	0.3
14	6.8	6.8	0.0	14.2	14.3	0.1
15	14.6	15.0	0.4	11.6	11.6	0.0
16	10.3	10.6	0.3	14.3	14.3	0.0
Mean			0.12			0.06
SD			0.16			0.19

An alternative analysis using linear regression allows for the possibility of treatment effects on both the level and slope of the regression. To begin with, a mean difference between the control and experimental groups is allowed by fitting the model

$$X_2 = b_0 + b_1G + b_2X_1,$$

where $G = 0$ for subjects in the control group and $G = 1$ for subjects in the experimental group. This model says that there is a linear regression relationship between the posttest score X_2 and the pretest score X_1, and that the treatment causes the level of the chemical being studied to shift by an amount $+b_1$. The estimated equation is

$$\hat{X}_2 = -0.106 + \underset{(0.061)}{0.046}\ G + \underset{(0.0087)}{1.014}\ X_1,$$

with the standard errors of the regression coefficients indicated in parentheses. The coefficient of G is not at all significant ($t = 0.046/0.061 = 0.75$; with 29 degrees of freedom (df)), but the coefficient of X_1 is very highly significant ($t = 1.014/0.0087 = 116.5$; with 29 df). Hence, there is no evidence that the treatment causes a simple shift in the mean level of the chemical in the blood, but there is very strong evidence that the posttest scores are related to the pretest scores.

Next, a model allowing different intercepts and different slopes can be considered with the equation

$$X_2 = b_0 + b_1G + b_2X_1 + b_3(G \cdot X_1).$$

Here the product $G \cdot X_1$ will be zero for all the controls, and equal to X_1 for all the treated patients. In effect, this allows the coefficient of X_1 to be different for the two groups. The estimated equation is

$$\hat{X}_2 = -0.103 + \underset{(0.0253)}{0.042}\ G + \underset{(0.017)}{1.014}\ X_1 + \underset{(0.0201)}{0.0003}\ (G \cdot X_1).$$

There is no evidence from t-tests that either of the coefficients of the terms involving G are significantly different from zero. Therefore, it can be concluded that there is no evidence of any treatment effects.

Although the analysis based on change scores has the merit of being very straightforward, it can be argued that the regression

147

analysis is better since it allows for a more general type of response to the experimental treatment. In fact, the change score analysis is really assuming that the regression of X_2 on X_1 has a coefficient of exactly 1 for X_1, and the effect of the treatment is just to shift the mean of X_2 by a fixed amount.

The analysis of a comparative change experiment should always be supplemented by plots of the posttest scores against the pretest scores, and plots of the differences D against the pretest scores, to ensure that the regression models being used are sensible for the data being considered. However, these are not provided for this example.

5.10 The comparative change design without randomization

The description *quasi-experimental designs* is used for a range of designs that are better than the one-group pretest–posttest and static group designs, but fall short of 'true' experiments, which involve the random allocation of treatments to experimental units. They are designs that an experimenter might consider worthy of use when nothing better is feasible.

One of the simplest quasi-experimental designs is the comparative change experiment, but without randomization to groups. It can, therefore, be represented as follows:

$$O_1 \quad X \quad O_2$$
$$O_3 \qquad O_4.$$

An analysis of the results of such an experiment can be carried out using regression, in a similar way to the analysis given above for the comparative change with randomization. It is helpful always to try to account for differences between the control and experimental group before the treatment by measuring relevant covariates at that point in time and using regression analysis to adjust for their effects, as discussed in Section 5.12. However, it is a mistake to think that this will produce a design that is as good as one that uses randomization.

5.11 The regression discontinuity design

The *regression discontinuity design* is appropriate when, for some reason, it is necessary to define the treatment group and the control group in terms of a cut-off value on a pretest. For example, this design is applicable for assessing the effect of giving scholarships to all high school students that exceed a certain score on a qualifying examination, or for assessing the effect of giving nutrition advice to all families with a total income below a certain level.

Figure 5.1 indicates the idea behind analysing the results from this type of experiment. Here all the experimental units with pretest scores (X) above 100 receive the treatment, which is designed to reduce their posttest scores (Y). It is assumed that in the absence of the treatment the scores for the treated units would have been what is obtained by extrapolating beyond 100 using a regression fitted to the control data only. The fact that the scores for treated units are lower than the regression line is evidence of a treatment effect.

There are two threats to this type of experimental design. First, it is crucial that all experimental units are correctly allocated to the control and experimental groups, without a 'fuzzy' cut-off point. Problems in this area may well occur in experiments where the allocation is not strictly controlled, and there may be an advantage

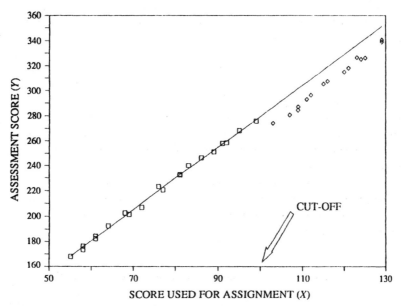

Figure 5.1. The regression discontinuity design with a treatment cut-off point at a pretest score of 100.

in receiving the treatment. This might be the case in a school setting, for example, if children below a certain level on a test are given remedial education. Parents with children just above the cut-off point on the test may then attempt to get their children into the remedial group by putting pressure on teachers. This may not matter very much if it is not done systematically. However, if the tendency is to move children who have done better than expected on the pretest from the control group into the remedial group then there is a possibility that a regression discontinuity will be falsely introduced.

The other threat is non-linearity in the regression relationship between X and Y since a curved regression line might account for the experimental results just as well as a straight regression line with a shift where the treatment is introduced. To some extent this threat to validity must always be a possibility that needs to be ruled out as unrealistic. If possible, data should be collected to verify that there is a linear relationship between the posttest and pretest scores when there is no treatment. If a relationship is not linear then it may be possible to use another regression model (for example including an X^2 term in the equation).

Example 5.5: Reducing delinquency of female teenagers

As an artificial example of the regression discontinuity design, suppose that it is decided to attempt to reduce delinquency among problem female teenagers living at home. The problem mainly concerns girls with poor home conditions, so that extra counselling is introduced to girls with a home condition index (X) above the median (high scores indicating poor conditions). An index of delinquency (Y) is determined for all girls six months later, with the results shown in Table 5.3.

Figure 5.2 shows the observed delinquency scores plotted against the home condition scores, together with the expected values obtained from fitting a regression model of the form

$$Y = \beta_0 + \beta_1 X + \beta_2 C + \varepsilon,$$

where $C = 1$ for the girls that received counselling and $C = 0$ for the other girls. This is a simple linear regression, except that the constant term is β_0 when there is no counselling and $\beta_0 + \beta_2$ when there is counselling. Therefore, it allows for counselling to produce a constant shift in the delinquency score. The significance of this

Table 5.3. *Results from a regression discontinuity experiment to assess the effect of counselling on problem teenage girls (X = index of home conditions, Y = delinquency score after six months)*

	No counselling group		Counselling group	
	X	Y	X	Y
1	2.5	26.8	5.1	26.9
2	3.0	25.4	5.3	31.6
3	3.3	21.6	5.4	23.2
4	3.3	24.0	5.4	25.0
5	3.6	20.9	5.6	23.1
6	3.7	24.9	5.7	28.0
7	3.7	21.9	5.9	30.3
8	3.8	24.4	5.9	27.5
9	4.1	23.0	6.0	25.4
10	4.2	23.2	6.0	20.3
11	4.3	28.2	6.0	27.3
12	4.4	31.1	6.1	24.7
13	4.5	26.6	6.2	25.8
14	4.5	29.9	6.2	27.7
15	4.7	28.3	6.3	30.6
16	4.7	27.1	6.4	31.3
17	4.9	25.9	6.5	26.7
18	5.0	30.3	6.7	30.9
19	5.0	24.1	6.9	30.0
20	5.1	28.8	7.3	25.7

shift can be tested by seeing whether the estimate of β_2 is significantly different from zero.

The fitted regression equation is

$$\hat{Y} = 18.79 + 1.70X - 2.02C.$$

The estimated standard errors associated with the coefficients of X and C are 0.72 and 1.65, respectively. These give t-statistics for the coefficients of X and C to be 2.39 and -1.22, respectively, each with 37 degrees of freedom. Before carrying out the experiment, it was expected that the coefficient of X would be positive and the coefficient of C would be negative. One-tailed tests are therefore appropriate when assessing the significance of the t-values. On this basis, the coefficient of X is significantly greater than zero at the 5% level, but the coefficient of C is not

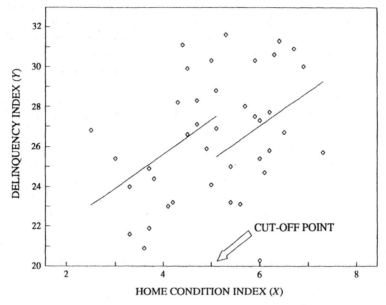

Figure 5.2. Delinquency scores plotted against home conditions for problem teenage girls. The lines shown are the expected frequencies from the fitted regression equation $\hat{Y} = 18.79 + 1.70X - 2.02C$, which allows counselling to shift the regression line relating the delinquency score to the index of home conditions.

significantly less than zero at the 5% level. It seems that the level of delinquency is related to the home conditions, but there is no real evidence that counselling is effective in reducing delinquency.

5.12 Regression adjustments for confounding variables

In Section 5.9 the possibility of making a regression adjustment to an estimated treatment effect to allow for differences between a control and an experimental group on some confounding variables was mentioned. This is done by assuming a linear regression relationship between the variable Y that is being used to measure the treatment effect and the confounding variables of the form

$$Y = \beta_0 + \beta_1 X_1 + \ldots + \beta_p X_p + \tau T + \varepsilon,$$

where X_1 to X_p are values for the confounding variables measured on the experimental units, and T is a treatment indicator that is 1 for units in the treatment group and 0 for units in the control group. With this model the coefficient τ of T can be interpreted as the change in Y caused by the treatment, after allowing for the effects of the X variables. Therefore, the regression estimate of τ is the estimated treatment effect after adjusting for the confounding variables.

The regression can include a pretest of some type as an omnibus covariate to capture all the differences between experimental units that exist before the treatment and are related to the posttest. However, as noted in Section 5.9, when a pretest is used it is likely that this will substantially reduce the value of the other covariates.

An advantage of this approach, which is sometimes called the *analysis of covariance*, is that with the right choice of confounding variables it is possible to have a very sensitive experiment. However, there are a number of problems. The linear model may be too simple, in which case regression adjustments may introduce a bias into the estimated treatment effect. Also, important confounding variables may not be measured. For this reason, it is best to randomly allocate experimental units to groups even when a regression adjustment is planned.

It is important to realize the limitations of using regression adjustment as proposed here in cases where the assignment of experimental units to treatment and control groups depends on the response variable Y as well as the confounding variables. That there are limitations can be seen by considering the controversial question of whether busing of school children (transporting them from the area where they live to schools some distance away) to achieve racial balances in public schools in the United States would raise the educational achievements of black children. The problems of regression adjustments in this context are discussed at length by Achen (1986, Chapter 2). Here, only a brief review will be given.

The Coleman (1966) report was based on measuring the educational achievements of black children in schools with different social class and racial mixtures. It was claimed in the report that, while the racial composition of schools seemed to make little difference to performance, poor black children in schools with a high percentage of middle class children do better than poor black children in schools with a low percentage of middle class children. This seems to suggest that moving black children into middle class schools is worthwhile since it will raise their performance.

To simplify the discussion, suppose that two groups of black children are being compared. One group (the controls) are in schools with predominantly lower class children. The 'treated' group are in schools with predominantly middle class children. The educational performance (Y) is measured for each black child, along with the family income (X). The regression equation

$$Y = \beta_0 + \beta_1 X + \tau T + \varepsilon$$

is then estimated, where T is 0 for a black child in the control group and 1 for a black child in the 'treated' group.

It seems that τ is a measure of the effect on the educational achievement of a black child of being in a middle class school, after adjusting for the effect of the income of the black child's family. However, this may not be the case since the black children were not assigned at random to the control and treated groups. In fact, many of the black children in middle class schools were probably there because their parents were more ambitious and more concerned about education than the majority of parents with the same family income. In other words, the way that children were assigned to schools is itself a possible explanation of why black children in middle class schools do better than black children in lower class schools.

Although the Coleman report involved a more complicated situation than this, the problem is still the same: any apparent effects of black children being in middle class schools are easily explained by black parents having an element of choice about the schools that their children attend. The only way to be sure of the affect of school characteristics on educational performance in a situation like this is to conduct a true randomized experiment, since without randomization it will always be possible to argue for alternative explanations for apparent treatment effects. If this is not possible then ordinary regression methods for adjusting for confounding variables are of doubtful value, although more complicated methods from the econometric literature may be applicable (Achen, 1986, Chapter 3).

Some of the most interesting contributions to the debate on the value of the analysis of covariance for adjusting for group differences were made by Lord (1967, 1968, 1973), who put forward a number of examples to illustrate potential difficulties. The most famous of these examples provides what is called *Lord's paradox*, which was introduced by Lord (1967, p. 304) as follows: 'A large university is interested in investigating the effects on the students of the diet provided in the university dining hall and any sex differences in these effects. Various types of data are gathered. In particular, the weight of each student at the time of arrival in September and his weight the following June are recorded'. No other information is provided, and Lord suggests how two statisticians might analyse the data. It can be assumed that the samples of males and females are so large that sampling errors in any estimated diet effects are negligible.

Statistician 1 decides to calculate the weight change for each student between the start and end of the study as the measure of the diet effect. This statistician finds that the average weight change is zero for males and females and therefore concludes that there is no effect of diet for either males or females. Statistician 2 decides to regress the weights at the end of the study (Y) against the weights at the start (X), and fits the regression equation

$$Y = \alpha + \beta X + \tau S + \varepsilon,$$

where S is a dummy variable that is 1 for males and 0 for females. This statistician finds that τ is positive, and concludes that males gain more weight than females on the diet provided. The paradox, then, is that two statisticians can both make a reasonable analysis of the data and come to opposite conclusions.

This, and other examples provided by Lord, led to an extensive discussion on the merits of the analysis of covariance. However, as pointed out by Holland and Rubin (1986), there really is no paradox since the two statisticians have both made different unverifiable assumptions in order to estimate the diet effects for males and females. It should really come as no surprise that it is possible to reach different conclusions when starting from different assumptions.

Statistician 1 is assuming that the change in weight of a student over the academic year measures the diet effect (although it is not clear what this means without a control diet). In other words, in the absence of any diet effects, the expected weight of a student at the end of the year is equal to his or her initial weight. However, statistician 2 is assuming that in the absence of a sex effect the expected weight of a student at the end of the academic year is given by $\alpha + \beta X$, where X is the initial weight. Therefore, the two statisticians are implicitly defining the effect of sex differently. It is, in fact, quite possible for both the following statements to be true: (a) the average weight changes of males and females are equal; (b) when males and females of the same initial weight are compared, then the males always have a higher expected weight gain.

As Holland and Rubin (1986) point out, the key problem in this area is deciding on the appropriate assumptions to make when measuring treatment effects. Their paper should be consulted for a further discussion on these matters.

An interesting recent development in the theory of the use of the analysis of covariance has been the idea of observing what effect a covariance adjustment has on some variables for which the effect of a treatment is known. The type of argument that can be used is shown by the following two examples:

(a) Several groups of former soldiers were compared with respect to medical histories, using a grouping that was related to the extent to which the soldiers had earlier been exposed to chemical agents. The different groups were not random samples from the population of all soldiers in the different groups, and it was suspected that in some cases individuals with the most exposure and the worst medical problems were under-represented. In this case, if the groups are similar with respect to the frequency of diseases that are unlikely to be related to exposure to chemical agents (such as back and knee injuries from accidents many years after exposure to chemicals), but differ significantly with respect to diseases that are likely to arise from exposure to chemical agents, then this seems to strengthen the evidence for a treatment effect

(b) A study of the effects of exposure to benzene found an excess of leukaemia deaths among benzene workers but a deficit of deaths overall. The deficit of deaths overall suggested some hidden bias in the study, probably in the direction of underestimating the effect of benzene

These ideas are formalized by Rosenbaum (1989) who uses these two examples as the basis for a theory for using information on supplementary variables that are measured in a study in order to provide information about pretreatment differences between different groups of subjects. See his paper for more details.

5.13 Matching

There are three ways for making an allowance for confounding variables when assessing the effect of a treatment by means of an experiment: by randomization, by making a regression adjustment, or by the matching of experimental units. The first two have already been discussed. Matching will now be considered.

The idea with matching is the same as for the *method of paired comparisons*, and it is a special case of what is called *blocking* in experimental design. Experimental units are paired up so that each pair consists of two comparable units on relevant confounding variables, with one in the pair receiving the treatment and the other not. Preferably, in each pair the unit getting the treatment should be randomly chosen, since this removes the possibility of any bias in the allocation. However, even if randomization is not possible it can be hoped that the difference in responses between treated and untreated members of a pair is a valid estimate of the treatment effect.

Matching is often used for medical studies, with two or three variables such as age, sex and the severity of the illness being used for this purpose. Trying to match on more variables is likely not to work because of the difficulty of finding so much agreement between subjects.

When matching variables are classifications, a 'match' usually means two subjects who are in exactly the same classes. For example, suppose that matching is to be done on sex (male, female), age (under 21, 21–45, over 45) and socio-economic status (I, II, III). There are then $2 \times 3 \times 3 = 18$ possibilities and subjects match only if they are in the same cell for the classification.

When the matching variables are discrete or continuous, two procedures are common. The variable values can be considered in ranges (as was done with age in the previous example) so that a match consists of two individuals in the same class. This is *within-class matching*. Alternatively, two individuals can be considered to match on a variable if the difference between them on this variable is less than or equal to some amount D. This is called *calliper matching*.

The idea of matching is easy to understand, and the statistical analysis is straightforward. If two experimental units have the same values for confounding variables X_1 to X_p then the difference between those units on some other variable Y will be independent of the confounding variables, irrespective of the nature of the relationship between Y and the X variables. Therefore, if one unit is treated and the other is not then the difference in their Y values is an estimate of the treatment effect that is unaffected by the X variables. However, it may be difficult to form matches from the subjects available, so that for some pairs the residual differences on confounding variables between treated and untreated individuals may be too large to be ignored.

In a study originally described by Douglas (1960) and later reviewed by Billewicz (1965) and Cochran (1983), children from premature births were found to have inferior school performance at ages 8 to 11 when compared to normal birth children. The original sample size was 675 and samples were matched on sex, the age of the mother, social class, birth rank in the family and the degree of crowding in the home. The matching was done by starting with the low birth weight cases and selecting from a reservoir of 12 000 normal births to match them. However, it became apparent that even after matching there were systematic differences between the two groups on social class, maternal care, and the degree of parental interest in school progress. An analysis confirmed that these variables could explain differences in school performance to some extent and, in fact, the investigators considered that the differences in these variables were likely to be the cause of differences in school performance rather than differences in birth weights. Furthermore, it was also considered unlikely that the differences in social class, maternal care and the degree of parental interest in school progress were themselves caused by birth weight differences. This example shows that even matching on five variables may not guarantee that differences between pairs are valid measures of a treatment effect.

The process of matching on several variables may be quite difficult if there are more than a few subjects to deal with. In medical situations there may be a relatively small sample of treated cases, all of which should be used, and a much larger reservoir of 'normal' individuals. Then, if the cases tend to be unusual in some respect it may require large numbers of normal individuals to be searched to find each match.

There are a number of different algorithms that can be used to choose matches. With *available pair matching*, treated cases are matched from a reservoir of controls. Starting with an arbitrary order for the cases, the first is considered and the best matching control is found. The pair is then set aside and the second case is matched with the closest control. This process continues until all cases are matched. The difference between cases and controls on matching variables will vary from pair to pair, and sometimes these differences may be quite large.

With *mean matching* an attempt is made to ensure that the mean values of confounding variables are similar for the two groups. The mean of the cases is first found for all variables. From the reservoir of controls the case that matches these means is chosen as the first control. The second control is then chosen to make the mean of controls 1 and 2 match the mean for the cases as closely as possible for all variables. This process continues, trying always to introduce controls so as to have the cases and controls with the same means. The idea is that if the means agree for cases and controls on all the confounding variables then the effects of these variables will average out in the estimation of a treatment effect.

With good matching the effect of a treatment can be measured by the differences $D = Y - X$, where Y is the score for the treated member of a pair and X is the score for the other member. The question of interest is then whether the mean difference $\bar{D}$ is significantly different from zero. A paired comparison t-test might be used to assess this, although other tests are also possible. It may also be valuable to regress the D values on the values of the matching variables to see whether there is any evidence that the effect of the treatment varies with these variables, and, if so, to adjust for the residual effects of these variables.

Example 5.6: Matching rats on a biochemical variable

As an example, consider an experiment where rats were paired up on the basis of their values for a biochemical variable X, and one of each pair was randomly chosen to receive a certain treatment. The rats were then sacrificed to measure a second biochemical Y. In Table 5.4, X_1 and Y_1 are measures on untreated rats and X_2 and Y_2 are measures on treated rats. Important questions are: is there any evidence of a treatment effect, and, if so, is this effect related to the level of X?

The differences $D = Y_2 - Y_1$ are direct measures of treatment effects. An analysis can begin, therefore, by seeing whether $\bar{D}$, the mean of D, is significantly different from zero. A test statistic is $\bar{D}/(s_d/\sqrt{n}) = 0.435/(1.134/\sqrt{20}) = 1.714$, where s_d is the sample standard deviation of D and n is the sample size. This is not significantly different from zero at the 5% level when compared with critical values from the t-distribution with 19 degrees of freedom.

Although this indicates that there is no overall effect of the treatment, it is still conceivable that the D values are significantly

Table 5.4. *Results from an experiment on the effect of a treatment on a biochemical variable for rats*

X_1 and X_2 are values for an easily measured biochemical variable for the treated and untreated rat in each pair, respectively; Y_1 and Y_2 are values for the variable used to assess the treatment effect, again for the treated and untreated rat in each pair, respectively; $D = Y_2 - Y_1$; $\bar{X} = (X_1 + X_2)/2$.

Pair	X variables		Y variables		D	$\bar{X}$
	X_1	X_2	Y_1	Y_2		
1	11.0	11.0	23.3	24.1	0.8	11.0
2	11.3	11.3	24.7	24.3	−0.4	11.3
3	11.5	11.8	24.2	27.0	2.8	11.7
4	11.9	11.8	26.1	26.0	−0.1	11.9
5	12.6	12.3	27.1	27.3	0.2	12.5
6	13.2	12.6	29.3	27.8	−1.5	12.9
7	13.0	13.2	28.9	28.1	−0.8	13.1
8	13.6	13.9	29.3	31.1	1.8	13.8
9	14.2	14.1	30.5	30.1	−0.4	14.2
10	14.5	14.8	30.4	32.9	2.5	14.7
11	14.8	14.8	32.4	32.3	−0.1	14.8
12	15.1	14.9	33.2	32.4	−0.8	15.0
13	15.5	15.7	33.9	34.2	0.3	15.6
14	16.1	16.2	34.0	34.3	0.3	16.2
15	16.4	16.2	35.3	34.9	−0.4	16.3
16	17.0	16.8	35.8	35.7	−0.1	16.9
17	17.4	17.2	36.6	37.2	0.6	17.3
18	17.6	17.5	36.7	38.4	1.7	17.6
19	18.0	18.0	37.3	38.7	1.4	18.0
20	18.8	18.3	39.4	40.3	0.9	18.6

Mean = 0.435
SD = 1.134

related to the X values. Since the matching on X values is quite close, this possibility can be examined by regressing the D values against the mean of the X values for pairs. The estimated regression equation is:

$$\hat{D} = -0.47 + 0.062\bar{X},$$

with an estimated standard error for the coefficient of $\bar{X}$ of 0.112.

The coefficient of $\bar{X}$ is not significantly different from zero at the 5% level, so again there is no evidence of a treatment effect. This is confirmed by plotting the D values against $\bar{X}$, although that plot is not provided here.

5.14 Summary and further reading

This chapter should have demonstrated that there are many potential pitfalls in the design of even simple experiments involving the comparison of two groups, particularly if the experimenter does not have the ability to randomly allocate experimental units to groups. It is important to achieve internal and external validity, to understand the advantages of different types of experimental design, to appreciate the problems involved with using the analysis of covariance to adjust for differences between groups prior to treatment. Pseudoreplication and regression to the mean should not be allowed to produce fallacious 'treatment effects'.

Those interested in reading more about the experimental and quasi-experimental designs that have been discussed in this chapter should consult the books by Achen (1986), Cook and Campbell (1979), Campbell and Stanley (1963) and Mohr (1988).

Exercises

(1) A psychologist was interested in the effect of a drug on the learning ability of rats. In particular, she wanted to know whether there is any difference between the effect of the drug on 'slow learners' and 'fast learners'. To study this, she took 40 rats and gave them a learning test. On the basis of the results, she divided them into the slow group and the fast group, where these were the bottom and top halves of the scoring distribution. Then each group was given the drug for one month, and retested. The data obtained are shown in Table 5.5. (Ignore the values of the variable I for the moment.)

(i) Use a t-test to compare the two group mean values for D and report your conclusions.

(ii) Suppose that, in fact, some of the rats were incorrectly classified from the pretest because this test has an

Table 5.5. *Results from an experiment involving giving a drug to rats classified as 'slow learners' and 'fast learners' (X_1 = pretest score, X_2 = posttest score, D = difference, I = error free indicator of slow and fast learners)*

	Slow learners				Fast learners		
I	X_1	X_2	D	I	X_1	X_2	D
1	2.5	4.1	1.6	1	5.1	7.5	2.4
1	3.0	6.0	3.0	2	5.3	5.0	−0.3
1	3.3	6.1	2.8	2	5.4	6.3	0.9
2	3.3	7.6	4.3	1	5.4	5.9	0.5
1	3.6	5.7	2.1	2	5.6	6.5	0.9
1	3.7	6.9	3.2	2	5.7	8.0	2.3
1	3.7	5.4	1.7	1	5.9	5.2	−0.7
2	3.8	5.4	1.6	2	5.9	5.6	−0.3
1	4.1	6.0	1.9	2	6.0	6.5	0.5
1	4.2	5.2	1.0	2	6.0	6.5	0.5
1	4.3	6.3	2.0	2	6.0	7.2	1.2
1	4.4	7.1	2.7	2	6.1	7.8	1.7
2	4.5	7.0	2.5	2	6.2	7.2	1.0
1	4.5	5.3	0.8	2	6.2	7.0	0.8
1	4.7	6.4	1.7	1	6.3	5.7	−0.6
2	4.7	7.3	2.6	1	6.4	6.8	0.4
2	4.9	7.6	2.7	1	6.5	4.9	−1.6
1	5.0	4.7	−0.3	2	6.7	7.0	0.3
1	5.0	5.4	0.4	2	6.9	5.1	−1.8
2	5.1	6.6	1.5	2	7.3	6.1	−1.2
		Mean	1.99			Mean	0.34
		SD	1.05			SD	1.15

associated sampling error, and that the slow and fast learners are really given by the variable I, with 1 for slow learners and 2 for fast learners, respectively. Repeat the analysis of part (i) but with the correct allocation to groups. Explain why your results are not quite different. (There is no 'trick' in this question. The results are precisely what might be expected to be obtained.)

(iii) Assuming that the correct allocation of rats as slow and fast learners is not known, analyse the data as coming from a regression discontinuity design since this is the true situation.

(2) You are on the local school committee, and the Principal is discussing some of his problems. He says that one worry is that the school is not doing well for the high achievers, although he is pleased with results for low achievers. When asked to explain he says that at the start of the year he gave all classes a general test of ability to determine the position of every student. Later in the year he gave everyone another version of the same type of test, and was surprised to find that in most classes the score of the best students had deteriorated on average. This alarmed him. However he was pleased to see that, in most cases, the students at the bottom of the classes had improved. He proposes to introduce special (expensive) extra classes for the brightest students. What do you say to the committee?

(3) A comparative change experiment was carried out to examine the effect of a hormone on the growth of mice. The 35 young mice available were divided at random into a group of 17 and a group of 18. Then the group of 17 were given the hormone for one month while the other group were fed normally. The length of a body part (mm) was measured on each mouse before (X_1) and after (X_2) the treatment, with the results that are shown in Table 5.6.

  (i) Analyse the results by comparing the mean values of the differences (length gains) for the two groups. State your conclusions.
  (ii) Analyse the results by regression X_2 scores on X_1 scores. State your conclusions.

(4) How much external validity does the experiment in question (3) have as a means of determining the effect that the hormone would have on wild mice?

CASE STUDY 5

The Lanarkshire milk experiment

The Lanarkshire milk trial took place many years ago, but it is still a good example of a large scale experiment which went wrong because of a well-intentioned attempt to improve on the random selection of subjects. The trial took place over four months in 1930, in Lanarkshire in Scotland. During this time 5000 school

Table 5.6. *Results of a comparative change experiment to assess the effects of a hormone on the growth of mice (X_1 = initial length of a body part, X_2 = final length of the same body part)*

	Experimental group				Control group		
	X_1	X_2	Diff		X_1	X_2	Diff
1	18.6	22.2	3.6	1	29.4	33.4	4.0
2	29.7	33.7	4.0	2	17.1	19.7	2.6
3	20.7	24.3	3.6	3	34.5	38.8	4.3
4	22.0	25.5	3.5	4	17.6	20.4	2.8
5	33.9	38.0	4.1	5	14.8	17.2	2.4
6	37.5	42.1	4.6	6	20.6	23.6	3.0
7	23.0	26.7	3.7	7	38.1	42.9	4.8
8	8.7	11.6	2.9	8	22.0	24.9	2.9
9	16.7	20.0	3.3	9	22.8	26.1	3.3
10	21.2	24.7	3.5	10	22.6	25.9	3.3
11	23.6	27.3	3.7	11	25.6	29.2	3.6
12	21.6	25.4	3.8	12	32.5	36.6	4.1
13	24.6	28.3	3.7	13	12.2	14.4	2.2
14	11.0	14.0	3.0	14	25.9	29.5	3.6
15	28.5	32.6	4.1	15	19.0	22.1	3.1
16	26.7	30.4	3.7	16	23.4	26.7	3.3
17	22.0	25.8	3.8	17	24.4	27.8	3.4
				18	25.6	28.9	3.3

children were given three-quarters of a pint of raw milk per day, another 5000 school children were given the same quantity of pasteurized milk per day, and 10000 school children acted as controls. The height and weight of the children were measured at the start and end of the study period, and it was concluded in the official report (Taylor, 1931) that:

(a) The addition of milk in the diet of school children is reflected in a definite increase in the rate of growth, both in height and weight

(b) There is no obvious or constant difference in this respect between the sexes. There is little evidence of a definite relationship between the age of the child and the amount of improvement.

(c) The effects of raw and pasteurized milk are equal.

Subsequently, there was some criticism of the way the trial was carried out and of these conclusions. A paper by W. S. Gossett, writing under the pseudonym 'Student' (1931), summarizes the problems.

First, the sampling method was not satisfactory. The 20000 children used for the trial were chosen from 67 schools, not more than 400 or less than 200 being chosen from each school, with half the chosen children in each school being assigned as 'feeders' and half as 'controls'. Some schools were assigned raw milk and some were assigned pasteurized milk, with no school getting both. Within each school the selection of children as 'feeders' or 'controls' was left to the Principal. Initially this was done essentially randomly by using either a ballot or an alphabetic system, but unfortunately was marred by the fact that ('Student', 1931, p. 399): 'In any particular school where there was any group to which these methods had given an undue proportion of well fed or ill nourished children, others were substituted in order to obtain a more level selection'

The result of this seems to have been that teachers felt that the poorer nourished children in their schools needed milk more than others so that the 'control' children were definitely superior to the 'feeders' both in height and weight at the start of the study.

The unfortunate effect of allowing teachers to change the selected children was that a fully valid comparative change experimental design as discussed in Section 5.10 became a quasi-experimental design of the type discussed in Section 5.11, with all the difficulties that this introduces because of the possible effects of confounding variables.

A second problem was that the study began in winter and ended in summer, but the children were weighed in their clothes. As a result, at least part of any weight gains during the experiment would have been offset by summer clothing being lighter than winter clothing. This would not have mattered if children were randomly assigned to groups. However, since the milk groups appear to have had more poor children than the control group, and poor children would have had fewer clothes, it is likely that the clothing effect would have been more pronounced in the control group. This would have tended to reduce the apparent effect of milk. It is also possible that effects of changes of clothing were related to age, and therefore upset the comparisons of treatment effects for children of different ages.

A third problem was that in the analysis of the results the control children were combined together irrespective of whether they were from a school given raw milk or a school given pasteurized milk. Since it is quite possible that schools were quite different in their racial and social composition, the combined controls may not have been comparable with either the raw milk or the pasteurized milk groups.

After discussing all these problems 'Student' reviewed the conclusions from the official report and suggested that:

(a) It was probably true that the addition of milk to the diet of the school children increased their rate of growth in height and weight, but this is shifted from the sure ground of scientific inference to guesswork by the fact that allocation to the control and experimental groups was not random

(b) The report may well be wrong in saying that there is no evidence of age effects. The effect of the shedding of clothes may well have introduced a different bias in weight gains for different ages and, in any case, the data in the report do give some evidence of systematic differences between ages

(c) The report is wrong in saying that there is no evidence of a difference between the effects of raw and pasteurized milk, since in most comparisons growth rates were higher with raw milk than with pasteurized milk. However, the effect of non-random sampling means that this result may or may not reflect what would occur in the population of interest

'Student' ended his paper with some suggestions about how an experiment like this could be improved. Most of the difficulties would have been avoided by using a purely random allocation of subjects to groups, either with some attempt at measuring the weight of clothes or ensuring that the experiment took place in one season. However, matching could have been used within schools by pairing up children of the same age, height and weight and then assigning milk by the toss of a coin. In this case the observations would be the differences between the growth rates for the two children in a pair. Measuring confounding variables related to social class would also be valuable.

6

Interrupted time series

6.1 Introduction

In many studies, the data that are available consist of values measured on some process at successive points in time, and the question that needs to be addressed is whether there is any evidence that a change to the process that takes place part way through the observation period results in a change in the nature of the observations. This is the interrupted time series situation for which the Eberhardt and Thomas (1991) classification of research studies (Figure 1.1) calls for an intervention analysis.

Examples of interrupted time series occur with environmental impact studies where measurements are made before and after the impact occurs; behaviour modification experiments where measures of behaviour are taken before and after some treatment designed to alter the behaviour of an individual or a group of individuals; studies on the effect of government legislation on economic indicators, etc.

In terms of an experimental design, the interrupted time series can be thought of as an improvement on the one group pretest–posttest experimental design:

$$O_1 \; X \; O_2,$$

which has been discussed in Section 5.4. The improvement involves having replication in time, so that, for example, if there are four pretreatment (baseline) observations and four posttreatment (intervention) observations the design takes the form:

$$O_1 \; O_2 \; O_3 \; O_4 \; X \; O_5 \; O_6 \; O_7 \; O_8.$$

The same structure can occur with an observational study where the intervention is unplanned. For example, in Case Study 4 the monthly sales in a hardware store before and after a fire were considered. This is an interrupted time series, with some complications due to seasonal effects and the possibility of trends that were unrelated to the fire.

The comparative time series design is an extension of the interrupted time series design where there is a control series as well as a treated series. Hence the design can be represented as

$$O_{11} \; O_{12} \; O_{13} \; O_{14} \; X \; O_{15} \; O_{16} \; O_{17} \; O_{18}$$
$$O_{21} \; O_{22} \; O_{23} \; O_{24} \quad\;\; O_{25} \; O_{26} \; O_{27} \; O_{28}.$$

The idea is that the effect of the treatment X is confirmed if it is displayed in the first series but not in the second one. There may be several control and several treated series.

A major complication with analysing data from these time series designs comes from the fact that successive observations from a time series often display serial correlation. What this means is that the Pearson correlation coefficient between observations a distance k apart in time is non-zero, at least for some values of k. Usually, the correlation between close observations is positive, which means that high values tend to be followed by high values and low values tend to be followed by low values. However, negative correlation is also possible so that high values tend to be followed by low values, and vice versa.

There are three methods that are used to analyse time series designs: a graphical analysis, which attempts to make a subjective allowance for any serial correlation; a regression analysis, which assumes that the serial correlation in the regression residuals is small enough to be ignored; and an analysis based on a time series model that takes serial correlation into account. In the remainder of this chapter these methods are considered first for a single time series and then for multiple time series.

6.2 Analysis with the interrupted time series design

There is not just one situation with the interrupted time series design, since there are a multitude of possibilities for the pattern of observations before and after a treatment. In some cases the evidence that something has happened will be clear and unambiguous. In other cases there will always be doubts about conclusions, whether or not there is a statistically significant change in a series. The context in which observations are made is crucial.

An example of an experiment where the outcome is unambiguous would be the assessment of the effect of dipping a bar of iron into nitric acid. Suppose that measuring the weight before and after this treatment gives the following results in grams, where X indicates when the treatment occurred:

98.03 98.04 98.03 98.04 X 97.01 97.00 97.02 97.00.

There is no doubt that the weight loss is due to the treatment, here. No control is needed because it is known that iron bars retain their weight under normal circumstances, and the treatment is the only plausible explanation for the weight loss.

The situation for deciding whether raising the minimum drinking age to 21 has had an effect on the number of fatal car accidents involving people under 21 is much less clear. For example, suppose that over a period of eight months the counts:

16 21 12 8 X 9 10 3 12

are obtained, where X indicates the point where the minimum drinking age was raised. Drawing a conclusion here about an effect of the treatment is much harder than it was with the case of the iron bar for several reasons: there is a good deal of purely random variation in the results from month to month; seasonal effects may be present; other relevant events were occurring at the same time, etc. Even though a change seems apparent there is still room for doubt about whether the explanation was the change in the minimum drinking age.

In most situations it will be important to take the *pattern* of observations into account in deciding whether a change in a time series has occurred. Therefore, in cases A to C in Figure 6.1 it is difficult to argue for a treatment effect, even if a significant change in the mean can be demonstrated for the observations before and after the treatment. In these cases, the change is obviously typical of what happens without the treatment. However, with cases D to F a treatment effect might be thought likely since the change at the time of the intervention does not seem to fit within the pattern seen at other times.

This does not mean to say that the inspection of the graph of a time series is sufficient to determine whether an intervention has had an effect, since studies have shown that the scales used in graphs can influence whether or not observers judge an effect to be present and that even experienced observers show low levels of agreement in assessing presence and absence (Sharpley, 1986). The point being made is that significant effects should be interpreted in the light of the general pattern in a series.

The formal analysis of an interrupted time series is most

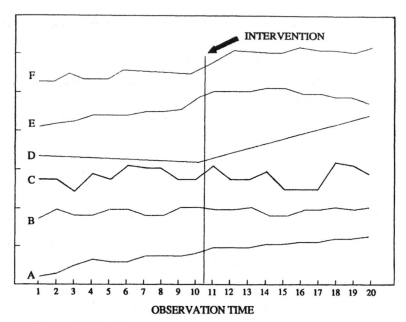

Figure 6.1. Possible patterns of changes with interrupted time series with the treatment occurring between the observations at times 10 and 11: A–C, cases where an effect is not suggested; D–F, cases where a change is suggested.

straightforward when the assumptions of a regression model seem realistic. For example, if a series appears to exhibit a linear trend before the intervention takes place then it may be realistic to assume that in the absence of the intervention the structure of the observations for the whole series is given by

$$Y_t = \alpha + \beta t + \varepsilon_t. \tag{6.1}$$

Here Y_t is the observed value at time t, α and β are constants, and ε_t represents a random 'disturbance', which has a mean of zero, a variance which is the same for all values of t, and is uncorrelated with the 'disturbances' for other observations. On this basis, the effect of the intervention can be assessed by comparing the model (6.1) with two other models. First, an intervention effect that shifts the mean level of the series by the amount δ can be allowed for by fitting the model

$$Y_t = \alpha + \beta t + \delta I + \varepsilon_t, \tag{6.2}$$

where $I = 0$ before the intervention and $I = 1$ after the intervention. Second, an intervention effect that changes the trend can be allowed for by fitting the model

$$Y_t = \alpha + \beta t + \delta I + \tau(It) + \varepsilon_t, \tag{6.3}$$

where (It) is the product of I and t. According to equation (6.3) the equation for the time series is

$$Y_t = \alpha + \beta t + \varepsilon_t$$

before the intervention, and

$$Y_t = (\alpha + \delta) + (\beta + \tau)t + \varepsilon_t$$

after the intervention.

With these regression models the assessment of the effect of the intervention can be based either on the significance of the estimates of δ and τ, or on the significance of the extra sums of squares accounted for by adding first I and then (It) to the regresssion equation (Section 4.5).

It is important to verify that the assumptions of regression are realistic. An analysis of residuals should always be made, and the *Durbin–Watson test* for serial correlation that has been discussed in Section 4.9 should be carried out to make sure that serial correlation in the regression residuals is not a serious problem.

If serial correlation in the regression residuals seems to be present then it should be allowed for in the analysis. In fact, some commentators such as Sharpley and Alavosius (1988) suggest that serial correlation should be taken into account even when it is not statistically significant, since even low levels can introduce a substantial bias with test procedures that ignore it. In other words, it is safer to assume that some serial correlation exists in all time series.

An important contribution to the theory in this area was provided by Box and Tiao (1975), who developed the use of modern time series modelling methods to accommodate sudden changes in series. They used these methods to assess the effect of two interventions on the oxidant pollution level in downtown Los Angeles, and the effect of government controls on the monthly inflation rate in the United States. Other examples of data analysis along the same lines are provided by Bhattacharyya and Layton (1979) (studying the effectiveness of seat belt legislation in Queensland, Australia), and by Madenjian et al. (1986) (studying the impact of a power station on fish populations).

In the past, a major objection that has been raised to the use of these methods has been the fact that a large number of observations are needed in order to identify time series models. A minimum of 50 to 100 observations is often quoted, and this is simply far more than can conceivably be obtained with many studies. However, recent research that is reviewed by Sharpley and Alavosius (1988) suggests that this objection is based on the incorrect assumption that a valid test for the effect of an intervention on a time series requires the correct model to be identified. In practice, simulations indicate that tests for the effect of an intervention give essentially the same result whenever any reasonable model is used to account for serial correlation, even when that model is incorrect. Furthermore, this result holds even with time series consisting of just five observations before and five observations after the intervention.

On the basis of these results, Crosbie and Sharpley (1989) have produced the computer program DMITSA for analysing interrupted time series. This program assumes that the time series being analysed has a model of the form of equation (6.1) before the intervention takes place, with serial correlation between the residuals occurring because they are related by the autoregressive equation

$$\varepsilon_t = \tau_1 \varepsilon_{t-1} + \tau_2 \varepsilon_{t-2} +, \ldots, + \tau_k \varepsilon_{t-k} + \delta_t, \qquad (6.4)$$

where δ_t is a random error and k can be chosen by the user. The program then tests to see whether the constants α and β in equation (6.1) change significantly at the time of the intervention.

Crosbie and Sharpley recommend that k in equation (6.4) should be set equal to 1 on the grounds that the first order model obtained thereby is all that is required to allow for the serial correlation in data. If this point of view is accepted than there are a range of methods that have been suggested for fitting the resulting model (Judge *et al.*, 1988, pp. 388–93 and pp. 532–8).

Example 6.1: Deaths of motorcycle riders and the compulsory use of helmets

This example is concerned with the question of whether there is any evidence that making the use of helmets compulsory for riders of motorcycles in New Zealand led to a significant reduction in the number of deaths from motorcycle accidents. Helmets were made compulsory at speeds in excess of 30 miles per hour (48.2 kilometres per hour) in 1956, and at all speeds shortly afterwards. As shown in Figure 6.2, the 1956 law change appears to have had quite a strong effect.

When the model of equation (6.3) is fitted to the data by standard regression methods, the fitted equation is

$$\hat{Y} = 38.30 + 7.10\ t + 2.55\ I - 7.39(It),$$
$$\quad\quad\quad (1.71)\quad\quad (7.21)\quad\quad (1.74)$$

where t is the number of years after 1950 and I is a dummy variable which is 0 up to 1955 and 1 thereafter. The estimated standard errors for coefficients are shown in parentheses below the coefficients. The t-statistics for testing whether the coefficients are significantly different from zero, with 16 degrees of freedom, are $7.10/1.71 = 4.14$, $2.55/7.21 = 0.35$, and $-7.39/1.74 = -4.23$, respectively. Hence the coefficients of time t and (It) are significantly different from zero at the 0.1% level but the coefficient of I is not significant at all.

According to the fitted model, the expected number of accidents for the years 1951 to 1955 was

$$\hat{Y}_t = 38.30 + 7.10t,$$

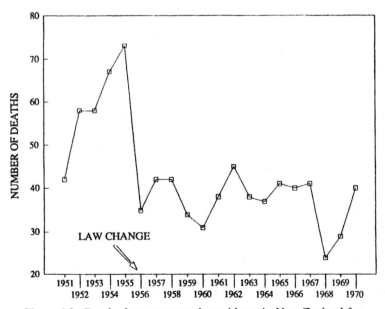

Figure 6.2. Deaths from motorcycle accidents in New Zealand for the years 1951 to 1970. A law making the use of motorcycle helmets compulsory was introduced in 1956.

and from then on was

$$\hat{Y}_t = 38.30 + 2.55 + (7.10 - 7.39)t = 40.55 - 0.29t.$$

This indicates a substantial drop in the number of accidents, and a halt to the upward trend.

A plot of the standardized residuals from the regression equation indicates that there are no particularly large residuals (Figure 6.3), although there is a run of positive residuals from 1961 to 1967. The Durbin–Watson test statistic is $v = 1.856$, which is not significant at the 5% level in comparison with the critical values in Table 4.10. Therefore, the regression model seems to be reasonable in this application.

An analysis of the data was also carried out using Crosbie and Sharpley's (1989) program DMITSA, which makes an allowance for serial correlation by assuming that the regression residuals are given by Equation 6.4. Following the suggestion of Crosbie and Sharpley, the value for k in this equation was assumed to be 1. It was then estimated that for the years 1951 to 1955 prior to the introduction of the helmet law the expected number of accidents

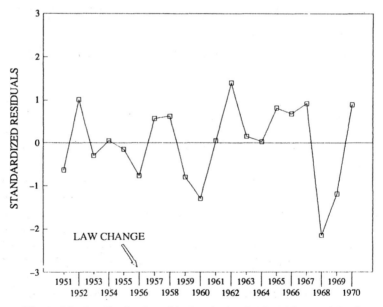

Figure 6.3. Standardized residuals obtained when the model of equation (6.3) is fitted to the data on the number of deaths from motorcycle accidents.

was

$$\hat{Y}_t = 51.84 + 5.59t,$$

and was thereafter

$$\hat{Y}_t = 40.15 - 0.37t.$$

The change in the constant term and the change in the slope were both found to be significant. Essentially this analysis leads to the same conclusions as the regression analysis ignoring serial correlation, whch is not surprising, since the regression residuals give little indication that serial correlation exists.

There is certainly evidence of a change in the time series in 1956. However, this does not necessarily mean that the change was 'caused' by the helmet law, although this does seem to be the most plausible explanation. As always in this type of study, the evidence is circumstantial only, and its meaning is open to debate. Before accepting that the helmet law was responsible for a drop in the number of deaths, the alternative explanations of instrumentation (a change in the method of recording deaths) and history (the other events that occurred in 1956) must be ruled out. This requires some further information and will not be pursued here.

6.3 Analysis with the comparative time series design

With the comparative time series design there is at least one interrupted series and at least one control series. As noted earlier, if the series really are comparable then the observation of changes in the interrupted series but not in the control series is stronger evidence of an effect of interruption than is provided from the results of interrupted series only.

As for the single interrupted time series, there are basically three approaches that can be used for analysing comparative time series data. Graphs can be examined to see whether effects are displayed in the interrupted series but not in the control series; regression models can be fitted on the assumption that serial correlation in the residuals is negligible; or time series models that allow for serial correlation can be fitted.

Graphical analyses here suffer from the usual limitation of being subjective. As noted by Stewart-Oaten *et al.* (1986, p. 930):

'graphs and tables that are used to justify conclusions
... require at least as many assumptions as inferen-

tial statistical procedures do. Since these assumptions are frequently implicit, these graphs and tables usually provide a less reliable basis for conclusions, rather than a more reliable one.'

In other words, a graphical analysis does not really overcome the difficulties that apply with an analysis that involves model fitting.

There are two types of regression analysis that are possible. One approach involves fitting a regression model that attempts to account for the values in both the control and intervention series, allowing for any trends that are present in both series and for an intervention effect. The precise model fitted obviously depends on the circumstances. The other approach involves using the control series as predictor variables in the regression equation with the idea that this will allow for the effect of history.

The second approach is exemplified in Case Study 4 on the estimation of the loss of sales that resulted from a fire in a hardware store. In that example, a second hardware store in the same town and owned by the same company was used as a control series which reflected the local retailing conditions. Two national sales series were also used to allow for national sales. A multiple regression including the second store sales, the national sales, seasonal effects, and fire effects gave a reasonable fit to the data, with residuals that appeared to be random. The coefficients of the fire effect variables could then be used to estimate the total sales loss from the fire.

In situations where there is one control time series and one time series with intervention, it may be possible to allow for factors that affect both series by considering the difference between the two series to be a random time series in the absence of an intervention effect, with a possible shift in the mean as a result of the intervention. This approach was advocated by Stewart-Oaten *et al.* (1986) in the context of the assessment of environmental impacts, as a response to Hurlbert's (1984) paper on pseudoreplication in biological studies. Stewart-Oaten *et al.* used nine years of data on an arthropod population near the San Onofre Nuclear Generating Station in California as an example. Later, Carpenter *et al.* (1989) developed the idea further by suggesting that randomization methods (as discussed in Chapter 9 of the present book) should be used for significance tests. Results were provided using data on various measures such as the chlorophyll concentration and the *Daphnia* density from three manipulated lakes and nine control lakes over a three-year period.

The more complicated methods of time series modelling for impact assessment that were proposed by Box and Tiao (1975) can be extended to permit the values in a control series to be used to account for the effects of history on a series subjected to an intervention. An example of how this can be done is provided by Bhattacharyya and Layton (1979) in the context of estimating the effect of seat belt legislation on deaths from road accidents in Queensland, Australia, taking into account the quarterly sales of motor spirits. These methods are usually considered to require fairly large numbers of observations, but the results discussed by Sharpley and Alavosius (1988) concerning the analysis of a single interrupted time series suggest that a simple model allowing for serial correlation may give quite acceptable results for the analysis of comparative time series data even when this model is not correct and the time series are quite short.

A general problem with the comparative time series design is that the time series may not in fact be very comparable, and may be affected in different ways by events, although superficially they seem similar. Also, the relationship between two series may change for reasons that are unconnected with the treatment applied to one for the series during the course of the experiment. For example, with the fire example in Case Study 4 it may well be that even if the fire had not occurred the relationship between the sales in the store concerned and the other sales series would have changed between the early and the late part of the observational period.

6.4 Summary and further reading

This chapter has provided a review of methods for assessing whether a specific event has changed the course of a time series. Graphical and regression methods of data analysis are discussed, including simple methods which allow for serial correlation and yet should give good results even with quite short series.

For more information on methods for modelling interventions in a time series, with a number of relevant references, the paper by Abraham (1983) is a useful starting point. The point of view that large numbers of observations are not needed for a valid statistical analysis of time series data exhibiting serial correlation was apparently first argued by Sharpley (1987), and his paper should be consulted for the evidence supporting this point of view.

Exercises

(1) 'Roadshow' was a travelling safety campaign that involved presentations in secondary schools throughout New Zealand in 1983 (Harte, 1986). The show started in Whangarei in the north of the country in February of that year, and ended in Christchurch in the south in June. At the conclusion of the campaign, a question of some interest to the Ministry of Transport was whether or not there was any evidence that Roadshow had reduced accidents in the targeted group of children aged 15–19 years. The data available to assess Roadshow are the number of reported accidents involving drivers aged 15–19 years, in two-weekly periods, for both 1982 and 1983, in each of the towns visited. However, for the present example the simplified data that are shown in Table 6.1 will be considered, with accident counts on a monthly rather than a two-weekly basis, and with the counts combined for all towns for which the Roadshow presentation started in the same month.

(i) Plot the number of accidents against time separately for each of the five groups of towns. Comment on the existence of trends and seasonal effects. Is there a clear indication of a reduction in accidents following Roadshow?

(ii) Assume that the accident count depends only on which group of towns is considered, so that the observed counts Y can be represented by the multiple regression equation

$$Y = \beta_0 + \beta_1 T_1 + \beta_2 T_2 + \beta_3 T_3 + \beta_4 T_4 + \varepsilon,$$

where T_i is a dummy variable for the ith group of towns, and is 1 for counts from that group, or is otherwise zero. Take Group E towns as the 'standard' group for which $T_1 = T_2 = T_3 = T_4 = 0$. Fit this model to the data using a computer program for multiple regression.

(iii) Add seasonal effects to the model in (ii) by assuming that

$$Y = \beta_0 + \sum_{i=1}^{4} \beta_i T_i + \sum_{i=1}^{11} \tau_i M_i + \varepsilon,$$

178

Table 6.1. *The Roadshow data in a simplified form*

The counts shown are the numbers of accidents in each month involving drivers aged 15–19 years. Group A towns (Whangarei and Auckland) were visited in February 1983, group B towns (Hamilton, New Plymouth, Rotorua and Taupo) were visited in March 1983, group C towns (Gisborne, Napier, Wanganui and Palmerston North) were visited in April 1983, group D towns (Masterton and Wellington) were visited in May 1983, and group E towns (Nelson, Invercargill, Dunedin, Timaru and Christchurch) were visited in June 1983. The more comprehensive data from which these counts are derived were kindly supplied to the author by D. S. Harte (Harte, 1986), formerly of the Ministry of Transport, Wellington, New Zealand.

Towns	Year	Jan	Feb	Mar	Apr	May	Jun	Jul	Aug	Sep	Oct	Nov	Dec	Total
Group A	1982	45	39	62	70	81	59	68	56	65	56	45	53	699
	1983	48	49[a]	73	41	59	45	63	68	55	63	78	64	706
Group B	1982	38	43	34	50	28	25	40	31	37	38	42	44	450
	1983	29	30	33[a]	32	25	26	23	40	39	37	30	31	375
Group C	1982	24	34	45	41	36	37	33	38	27	40	26	25	406
	1983	24	38	34	29[a]	27	35	36	29	40	35	30	34	391
Group D	1982	40	49	53	48	37	54	39	45	39	38	48	49	539
	1983	48	41	37	40	46[a]	43	38	39	39	34	34	50	489
Group E	1982	46	48	71	57	73	63	61	51	54	67	63	56	710
	1983	48	53	67	71	67	53[a]	66	47	48	65	61	47	693
Total		390	424	509	479	479	440	467	444	443	473	457	453	5458

[a] Visit by Roadshow

where the dummy variables for towns are defined in the same way as for the first model, and M_i is a dummy variable for month i such that $M_i = 1$ for this month, or is otherwise zero. Take month 12 (December) as the 'standard' month for which M_1 to M_{11} are zero. Fit this model to the data and compare it with the model in (ii).

(iv) Make an allowance for a difference between 1982 and 1983 by adding a dummy variable A to the model, which is 0 for observations in 1982 and 1 for observations in 1983 so that

$$Y = \beta_0 + \sum_{i=1}^{4} \beta_i T_i + \sum_{i=1}^{11} \tau_i M_i + \Theta A + \varepsilon,$$

where the coefficient Θ measures the effect of 1983 relative to 1982. Fit this model to the data and compare it with the model in (iii).

(v) Add an effect for Roadshow into the model from (iv) by introducing the variable R, so that

$$Y = \beta_0 + \sum_{i=1}^{4} \beta_i t_i + \sum_{i=1}^{11} \tau_i M_i + \Theta A + \delta R + \varepsilon,$$

where the coefficient δ indicates the magnitude of the effect. For simplicity assume that half of the effect was felt in the month when Roadshow occurred, and accident rates returned to their normal levels in the fourth month after the presentation. Then $R = 0$ for the months prior to Roadshow, $R = \frac{1}{2}$ in the Roadshow month, $R = 1$ for the three following months, and $R = 0$ thereafter. (The argument for assuming half the effect of Roadshow in the Roadshow month is that on average the presentation occurred about half-way through the month for each group of towns.)

(iv) Summarize the results of fitting the different models in an analysis of variance table, showing extra sums of squares for the terms added to the model in (ii). Plot residuals from the model that seems most appropriate. Report your conclusions stating in particular what you estimate to have been the effect of Roadshow. What reservations, if any, do you have about the validity of your estimate of the effect of Roadshow?

(2) Bhattacharyya and Layton (1979) used the data shown in Table 6.2 to discuss the effect of seat belt legislation on the

Table 6.2. *Numbers of deaths from road accidents in Queensland, 1950–76, excluding deaths of pedal cyclists, motor cyclists and pedestrians. (Bhattacharyya and Layton, 1979)*

Year	Quarter				Year	Quarter			
	1	2	3	4		1	2	3	4
1950	18	16	5	14	1964	70	53	76	74
1951	14	30	23	15	1965	73	33	63	94
1952	17	20	31	48	1966	62	39	85	67
1953	22	26	26	22	1967	74	36	91	82
1954	16	21	23	38	1968	93	70	89	93
1955	26	23	32	29	1969	103	104	98	94
1956	33	36	47	40	1970	75	93	110	98
1957	27	41	34	45	1971	86	108	103	121
1958	35	51	39	54	1972	84	97	109	85
1959	28	46	61	52	1973	90	120	96	101
1960	44	35	50	67	1974	79	99	102	80
1961	40	50	45	46	1975	99	89	132	96
1962	31	56	75	62	1976	73	71	85	123
1963	53	45	60	67					

number of deaths from road accidents in Queensland, Australia. In this case there were three interventions:

(a) on 1 January 1969 it became compulsory for new cars to be fitted with from seat belts
(b) on 1 January 1971 it became compulsory for new cars to be fitted with front and back seat belts
(c) on 1 January 1972 the wearing of seat belts became mandatory on cars in which belts were fitted.

Analyse these data to assess the effect of the legislation on the numbers of deaths.

CASE STUDY 6
Fluoridation in Birmingham

The subject of Example 1.2 was a comparative time series analysis of cancer death rates in United States cities with and without fluoridation of drinking water. The present case study is on the same topic, but concerns the suggestion by Burk (1980) that the fluoridation of drinking water in Birmingham, UK, in 1964 resulted in a sharp increase in cancer death rates in that city.

Burk's claim is based on the crude cancer death rates per 100 000 of population for Birmingham and Manchester for the years 1959 to 1977 that are shown in Table 6.3. When these are plotted against time, as shown in Figure 6.4, it can be seen that the cancer death rates in Birmingham showed little trend up to 1964, but then began a steady upward trend, whereas in Manchester, which was not fluoridated, there was a steady upward trend through the whole period.

For the moment the question of whether the apparent change in the time series of Birmingham cancer death rates in 1964 was caused by fluoridation will be left aside. Instead, consider the question of whether the change is statistically significant. One approach in deciding this involves using linear regression methods to estimate the 'effect' of fluoridation by fitting the model

$$Y = \beta_0 + \beta_1 t + \beta_2 F + \beta_3(Ft) + \varepsilon,$$

to the Birmingham data, where t is the calendar year, and F is a dummy variable which is 0 up to and including 1964 and 1 for 1965

Table 6.3. *Cancer death rates (CDR) per 100 000 of population in Birmingham and Manchester, UK, from 1959 to 1977. Fluoridation of the drinking water in Birmingham was carried out in 1964*

1959	Birmingham CDR	Manchester CDR
1959	219	228
1960	209	244
1961	207	243
1962	211	242
1963	215	247
1964	208	242
1965	221	254
1966	221	249
1967	228	260
1968	243	263
1969	237	260
1970	234	264
1971	248	284
1972	246	286
1973	267	290
1974	263	291
1975	254	297
1976	269	305
1977	266	301

and subsequent years. According to this model, cancer death rates up to and including 1964 are given by

$$Y = \beta_0 + \beta_1 t + \varepsilon,$$

and are given thereafter by

$$Y = \beta_0 + \beta_1 t + \beta_2 + \beta_3 t + \varepsilon.$$

Thus, the parameters β_0 and β_1 reflect the average level and trend in cancer death rates up to 1964, β_2 reflects any immediate change to the level in the series that took place in 1965, and β_3 reflects any change in the trend starting in 1965.

The fitted equation, with the standard errors of estimated coefficients shown in parentheses below them, is

$$\hat{Y} = 2060.9 - 0.94t - 9893.9F + 5.04(Ft).$$
$$\quad\quad\quad\quad (1.47) \quad\quad (3025.1) \quad\quad (1.54)$$

The coefficient of F is significantly different from zero at the 1%

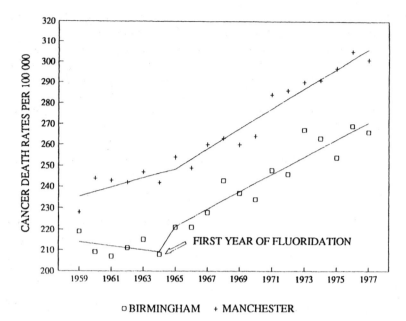

Figure 6.4. Crude cancer death rates in Birmingham and Manchester, UK from 1959 to 1977, with trend lines determined by linear regression.

level according to a t-test with 15 degrees of freedom $(-9893.9/3025.1 = -3.27)$. There is, therefore, strong evidence of a change in the level of the time series in 1965. The coefficient of (Ft) is also significantly different from zero at the 1% level on a t-test $(5.04/1.54 = 3.27)$, indicating a change of trend in 1965 as well.

Although Manchester was never fluoridated, it is interesting to see what happens if the regression model fitted to the Birmingham data is also fitted to the data for this city. The result is the equation

$$\hat{Y} = \underset{}{-4130.3} + \underset{(1.28)}{2.23\,t} - \underset{(2620.5)}{5079.2F} + \underset{(1.34)}{2.58\,(Ft).}$$

Here, the coefficients of F and (Ft) are not significantly different from zero at the 5% level, although they are not far from being so with t-values of $-5079.2/2620.5 = -1.94$ and $2.58/1.34 = 1.93$.

The trend lines shown in Figure 6.4 are the values produced from the fitted regression equations. Indeed, it does seem that

184

there was a sharp change in the trend for Birmingham from 1965 onwards, with no corresponding change in Manchester.

The standardized residuals from the regression equations are shown plotted against the year in Figure 6.5. These appear to be random, with no suggestion of serial correlation. The Durbin–Watson test statistic is $v = 2.27$ for Birmingham and 2.15 for Manchester. Since both values are greater than 2 they suggest negative serial correlation between the regression residuals in successive years. However, neither value is significantly different from 2 when tested using the critical values shown in Table 4.10 (with $p = 3$ and $n = 18$), so there is no real evidence of serial correlation.

To examine the effect of allowing for serial correlation, the time series for each of the cities was analysed using Crosbie and Sharpley's (1989) computer program DMITSA. Following their recommendation, k was assumed to be equal to 1 in the autoregressive model for the correlation between regression residuals that is given by equation (6.4). For Birmingham this indicates a significant change in both the level and trend of the cancer death rate series at the time of fluoridation. For Manchester the same

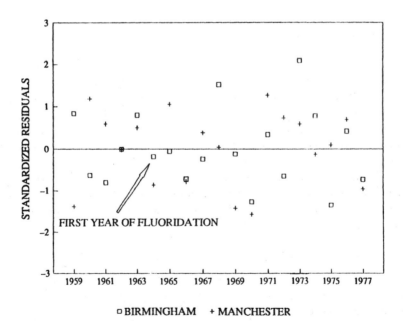

□ BIRMINGHAM   + MANCHESTER

Figure 6.5. Standardized residuals for the regression of Birmingham and Manchester cancer death rates against time and the fluoride effect variables F and (Ft).

analysis indicates no significant change in the level of the series, but a change in the trend which is significant at the 5% level. The significant change in the trend in the Manchester series is obviously hard to explain since fluoridation was not carried out in this city.

Usually, making an allowance for serial correlation will reduce the significance of any effects displayed in data below the level of significance that is obtained from tests which ignore this correlation. This is because serial correlation tends to be positive for real time series, which means that the information contained in the data is less than would be provided by the same number of independent observations. The reverse has happened for the Manchester data because the program DMITSA estimates that the correlation between successive cancer death rates is negative for this city, which implies that the data provide more information than would be obtained from a series with uncorrelated regression residuals.

It has been found from the regression analysis that there is clear evidence of a change at the time of fluoridation in the intercept and the slope for the regression of Birmingham cancer death rates against time, which was not matched by corresponding changes in the regression for the control city of Manchester. The analysis using the computer program DMITSA indicates a change in the intercept and slope for Birmingham at the time of fluoridation, and a change in the slope for Manchester. From these results and Figure 6.4 it can be argued that there is evidence of some change to the series of cancer death rates in Birmingham in 1965 that either did not occur, or occurred to a lesser extent in Manchester.

However, Cook-Mozaffari *et al*. (1981) and Cook-Mozaffari and Doll (1981), among others, have objected strongly to the inference that the changes in Birmingham was *caused* by fluoridation. They argue that the use of crude cancer death rates is quite misleading, just as it is with United States data (Example 1.2), since it takes no account of changes in the demographic structure of the population in the city. In other words, they suggest that the true explanation of the change in the regression is that other events occurred at about the same time as fluoridation.

To allow for the effect of a changing age and sex distribution, Cook-Mozaffari *et al*. (1981) estimated the cancer death rates that would have applied in Birmingham and Manchester over the periods 1959–63, 1969–73 and 1974–78 if the age and sex structures of the populations in the cities were the same as for a 'world standard population'. They also estimated similar age-standardized

Table 6.4. *Changes in crude and standardized mortality rates in the seven largest cities in the United Kingdom. (Cook-Mozaffari et al., 1981)*

	Crude rates		Standardized rates	
	1959–63 to 1969–73	1969–73 to 1974–78	1959–63 to 1969–73	1969–73 to 1974–78
England and Wales	+10.9%	+5.0%	+5.2%	+1.7%
Non-fluoridated				
London	+14.6%	+2.4%	+6.5%	−6.4%
Bristol	+17.2%	+3.3%	+8.7%	0.0%
Liverpool	+28.9%	+9.9%	+9.5%	+0.9%
Leeds	+17.2%	+2.3%	+7.0%	−2.1%
Sheffield	+11.1%	+9.1%	+2.7%	+3.4%
Manchester	+17.5%	+5.9%	+4.3%	−1.0%
Fluoridated 1964				
Birmingham	+19.1%	+6.9%	+6.4%	+1.0%

rates for the large United Kingdom cities of London, Bristol, Liverpool, Leeds and Sheffield, which were not fluoridated, and for England and Wales as a whole. This produced the estimated percentage changes in standardized mortality rates that are shown in Table 6.4, from which it can be seen that the change in the standardized mortality rate in Birmingham (+6.4% from 1959–63 to 1969–73, and +1.0% from 1969–73 to 1974–78) were quite typical of the change in other areas, and much lower than the changes seen in the crude cancer mortality rates (+19.1% and +6.9%, respectively).

It seems that this is a clear example of a situation where a simple comparison between a treated and a control time series analysis points to conclusions that are invalid because of the effects of confounding variables (changing population structures) that exaggerate real changes in cancer death rates, and make the two time series far from being comparable.

7

More advanced experimental designs

7.1 Introduction

The previous two chapters have been concerned with relatively simple experiments involving for the most part the comparison between a control group and a treated group of experimental units. In the present chapter the discussion turns to designs that can be used to compare either the effects of several levels of a single type of treatment or several levels of different types of treatment.

The designs to be discussed have quite complex structures in some cases, with correspondingly complex analyses of data. As such, a detailed review of all methods of analysis is beyond the scope of this book. Instead, the treatment here will be largely restricted to the description of the designs and to the assumptions involved in their use. It is assumed that most researchers will have at their disposal one of the standard computer packages for analysing the results of designed experiments, so that what is important is a knowledge of which designs can be used and a general knowledge of the principles that are used for their analysis rather than the ability to carry out the calculations.

7.2 Factorial experiments and the analysis of variance

In the terminology of experimental design a *factor* is simply a classification of experimental units, and a factorial experiment is one in which all combinations of the factors being considered are tested. Three examples are as follows:

(a) Thirty subjects are allocated at random to three groups of ten subjects, each group is given a different dose of a drug, and the mean scores for the three groups are compared. This is a one factor experiment

(b) Thirty males are allocated at random to three groups of size ten. Thirty females are also randomly allocated to three groups of ten. One male group and one female group are given a placebo, another male group and another female group are given a low level of a drug, and the remaining male and female groups are given a high level of the drug. This is a 2×3 factorial experiment replicated 10 times, with the two factors being sex and drug

(c) There are 48 subjects available in six groups of eight subjects. The six groups consist of males aged 20 to 29 years, males aged 30 to 39 years, males aged 40 years or over, females aged 20 to 29 years, females aged 30 to 39 years, and females aged 40 years or over. Two subjects in each group are randomly chosen to receive a placebo, two are randomly chosen to receive a low level of a drug, two are randomly chosen to receive a medium level of the drug, and the remaining two receive a high level of the drug. This is a $2 \times 3 \times 4$ factorial experiment replicated twice, with the three factors being sex, age and drug

Examples (b) and (c) illustrate the fact that an experiment can involve both classification and treatment factors. Classification factors such as the sex or the age of subjects represent inherent differences that cannot be manipulated by the experimenter. They are included in the experimental design in order to control for any effects that they might have. On the other hand, treatment factors, such as the dose given for a drug, can be manipulated, and often the main point of the experiment is to see the effect of this manipulation. The difference between classification and treatment factors is important since they have to be treated differently by experimental procedures.

Whenever possible, the experimental units that are used for the different levels of a classification factor should be chosen at random from the populations of experimental units at the different levels. Therefore, in an experiment using human subjects in several different age groups, the subjects in each age group should be a random sample from the relevant population of subjects in that age group. This makes it possible to use the experimental results to draw conclusions about the populations of subjects: the experiment has external validity.

The concept of random sampling from a population is not relevant with a treatment factor. However for these types of factor it is highly desirable that the groups of experimental units that are given different levels should be randomly chosen from the original pool of units. This ensures that any initial differences between the units are equalized within the bounds of random sampling so that estimates of treatment effects are unbiased. Thus, the random allocation of levels of the factor ensures that the experiment has internal validity.

The standard tool for analysing designed experiments in general, and factorial experiments in particular, is the analysis of variance. The basic idea with this method, which has already been discussed in Chapter 4 in the context of linear regression, is that the total sum of squares about the mean of all the available observations,

$$\text{SST} = \sum (X - \bar{X})^2,$$

can be partitioned into sums of squares that are accounted for by the effects of factors, and a residual or error sum of squares, SSE. That is,

$$\text{SST} = \text{Sums of squares for factors} + \text{SSE}.$$

With one factor, there are only two sums of squares on the right-hand side of this equation, one for the factor and one for error. With two or more factors there is the possibility of having sums of squares that are accounted for by the interactions between these factors, in addition to sums of squares for the factors themselves.

The sum of squares for a factor or interaction in a factorial experiment can be thought of as the extra sum of squares accounted for when variables that allow for that factor or interaction are included in the regression model (Section 4.5). An important property of many designed experiments from this point of view is that the extra sums of squares for the different factors and interactions are the same, irrespective of the order in which they are added to the model. Indeed, ensuring that the sums of squares of factors and interactions have this property is a key aspect of experimental design in general. In this respect, it is worth mentioning that the property is not generally maintained when there is more than one factor in an experiment and the number of replicate observations is not the same for all factor combinations. This is a good reason to ensure, if it is possible, that the number of replicates is constant.

Example 7.1: Percentages of yellow snails in different types of habitat

As an example of a situation where a one factor analysis of variance can be used, consider the data shown in Table 7.1. These

190

Table 7.1. *Percentages of yellow* Cepaea nemoralis *in samples taken from 17 locations, with six different types of habitat, in southern England. (Cain and Sheppard, 1950)*

Habitat	Percentage yellow snails	Mean	SD
Downland beech	25.0 26.9	26.0	1.3
Oakwood	8.1 13.5 3.8	8.5	4.9
Mixed deciduous wood	9.1 30.9 17.1 37.4 26.9	24.3	11.2
Hedgerows	76.2 40.9 58.1 18.4	48.4	24.7
Downside long coarse grass	64.2 42.6	53.4	15.3
Downside short turf	45.1	45.1	—

data, which come from a study by Cain and Sheppard (1950), are percentages of yellow *Cepaea nemoralis* snails found in 17 colonies from six different types of habitat in southern England. On the assumption that the samples from different habitats are random samples from their respective populations, an interesting question that can be addressed by an analysis of variance is whether there is any real evidence that the mean percentage of yellow snails varies with the habitat.

In a one factor case like this, the analysis of variance table takes the form shown in Table 7.2 when there are I levels of the factor, n_i observations taken at level i, and a total of $n = \sum n_i$ observations altogether. The derivation of the equations for sums of squares that are shown in this table will not be considered here. For those interested in more details it can be noted that these equations can be obtained by setting up a regression model for the effects of the factor using dummy 0–1 variables as explained later in Section 7.14, although most books on experimental design adopt a different approach. The justification for having $I - 1$ degrees of freedom for the effects of the factor is that $I - 1$ dummy variables are needed to account for these effects. Hence, the extra sum of squares accounted for by allowing for the factor, has $I - 1$ degrees of freedom.

The F-ratio shown in Table 7.2 is the mean square for differences between factor level (MSB) divided by the mean square for

Table 7.2. *The form of the analysis of variance table when there is one factor at I levels*

$x_{ij} =$ the jth observation in the ith group; T_i is the sum of the n_i observations in the ith group; $T = \sum T_i$ is the sum of all the observations; and $n =$ the total number of observations.

Source of variation	Sum of squares	df	Mean square	F
Between groups	$SSB = \sum_i T_i^2/n_i - T^2/n$	$I - 1$	$MSB = SSB/(I - 1)$	MSB/MSE
Error	$SSE = \sum_i \sum_j x_{ij}^2 - \sum_i T_i^2/n_i$	$n - I$	$MSE = SSE/(n - I)$	
Total	$SST = \sum_i \sum_j x_{ij}^2 - T^2/n$	$n - 1$		

error (MSE). If this is significantly large in comparison with critical values from the F-distribution with $I - 1$ and $n - I$ degrees of freedom then there is evidence that the mean of the observations is not the same for all the factor levels. The usual assumptions for a regression model are required for this test to be valid. In particular, the residual term in the regression model should be normally distributed with a constant variance. Therefore, there should be a normal distribution for the observations at any one of the factor levels, with the variance being the same for all factor levels.

Table 7.3 shows the analysis of variance for the snail data of Table 7.1. The F-value is 3.54, with 5 and 11 degrees of freedom, and a comparison of this value with the F-distribution table gives a significance level between 5% and 1%. It seems, therefore, that there is some evidence that the percentage of yellow *Cepaea nemoralis* varies with the type of habitat.

Example 7.2: Counts of aquatic insects in creeks

For a second example, consider the data in Table 7.4, which can be analysed by a two factor analysis of variance. Here the observations, which were used as an example by Simpson *et al.* (1960, p. 284), are counts of total numbers of aquatic insects collected in samples from two creeks in North Carolina in each of four months. The factors are creeks and months, and there are six replicate values for each creek–month combination.

In this case there are three types of effect that there might be interest in detecting: differences between the results for the four months, differences between the two creeks, and an interaction between these two effects. If it exists, the interaction effect can be interpreted as a difference between creeks that changes in magnitude from month to month. Alternatively, the interaction can be interpreted as a difference between months that is not the same for each creek.

The analysis of variance table for these data is provided in Table 7.5. Comparing the F-ratios with tables of the F-distribution it is found that the effect of months is significant at the 0.1% level, the effect of creeks is not at all significant (being less than one), and the interaction effect is significant at the 5% level. There is, therefore, very strong evidence of changes in density from month to month, and some evidence of an interaction. The small F-value

Table 7.3. *One factor analysis of variance on the snail data given in Table 7.1*

Source of variation	Sum of squares	df	Mean square	F
Habitats	4196.0	5	839.2	3.54[a]
Residual	2610.3	11	237.3	
Total	6806.3	16		

[a] Significantly large at the 5% level.

for creeks shows that the difference between creeks averages out to about zero over the four months. However, if the existence of an interaction term is accepted then this itself implies that there are different results for the two creeks for some months since, as noted above, the interaction can be interpreted as meaning that there are changes in the difference between the two creeks from month to month.

One of the assumptions behind the analysis of variance is that the error variance is the same for all factor levels. However, a consideration of the data in Table 7.4 suggests that this might not be true for the example being considered. In fact, the range of values is much greater for the factor combinations with a high mean count than the range for the factor combinations with a low mean count. For this reason the data are considered further in Section 7.4. However, before that matter is considered there are a number of general aspects of the nature of factors and experimental designs that will be discussed in the context of this example and the earlier one on samples of *Cepaea nemoralis* from different habitats.

7.3 Some general considerations

The example on counts of aquatic insects does not involve a treatment factor. Both the classifications creek and month occur naturally and it makes no sense to speak about randomly allocating experimental units to levels of these factors. Therefore, inferences have to be based on the assumption that the six observations taken

Table 7.4. *Number of aquatic insects taken by a square-foot bottom sampler in Shope Creek and Ball Creek, North Carolina, in the months of December, 1952 and March, June and September, 1953. (Simpson et al., 1960)*

Month	Shope Creek						Ball Creek					
December	7	9	19	1	18	15	25	9	16	28	10	14
March	29	37	114	49	24	64	35	45	22	29	18	27
June	124	51	63	81	83	106	20	44	26	127	38	52
September	72	87	100	68	67	9	40	45	263	100	129	115

Table 7.5. *The analysis of variance table for the data shown in table 7.4 (SS = sum of squares, df = degrees of freedom and MS = mean square)*

Source of variation	SS	df	MS	F
Months	39 932	3	13 311	9.60[b]
Creeks	9	1	9	0.01
Interaction	12 065	3	4 022	2.90[a]
Error	55 482	40	1 387	
Total	107 488	47		

[a] Significantly large at the 5% level.
[b] Significantly large at the 0.1% level.

for each creek–month combination are a random sample from the population of possible observations for this combination. On this basis it can be argued that this is an example of an observational study rather than an experiment that involves the manipulation of conditions. In a similar way, the earlier example on the comparison of the percentage of yellow snails for samples of *Cepaea nemoralis* from different habitats might also be considered to be more correctly described as an observational study than as an experiment.

The point of view adopted here is that this distinction between studies that involve a treatment factor and those that do not is not of much importance since the observations from both types of studies can be analysed in essentially the same way by analysis of variance. In fact, as noted by Hurlbert (1984), an observational study is often called an 'experiment' simply because the measurement procedure is somewhat complicated.

A more important distinction is between an *experimental design* and a *quasi-experimental* design. The first of these descriptions covers situations in which experimental units are randomly sampled from the populations that exist for different levels or combinations of levels of control factors, and levels of the treatment factor or factors are randomly allocated to experimental units. The second description covers situations where either random sampling or random allocation is not possible. As has been discussed in the previous two chapters, quasi-experimental designs suffer from the difficulty that inferences are only valid to the extent that the apparent effects of factors do not have alternative explanations.

In fact, quasi-experimental designs are used more often than is generally appreciated. For example in the study of the percentage of yellow *Cepaea nemoralis* from different habitats in southern England it seems unlikely that any attempt was made to list all the colonies of these snails within the area of interest and then sample some at random from each habitat type. Instead, samples were probably taken from known colonies that were convenient to visit. In that case, useful inferences from the data are possible only on the assumption that somehow or other this convenience sampling was equivalent to random sampling. In truth, there is no way of knowing whether this is true or not.

Another aspect of experimental design that must not be forgotten is the avoidance of *pseudoreplication*. This has been discussed already in Section 5.3, but still the importance of the topic makes it worth mentioning again. Essentially, pseudoreplication occurs when the replicates in an experiment are not really true replicates at all (Hurlbert, 1984). This would be the case with Example 7.2 on counts of aquatic insects in two creeks in four months if the six samples taken for each creek–month combination came from a small part of the creek being sampled, since this would mean that the variation in counts from different parts of the creek at the same time is not included in the experimental error. This could easily result in 'significant' differences occurring between months and creeks simply because the error mean square is smaller than it should be.

The same example can be used as the starting point for the consideration of the difference between what are called *fixed* and *random* effects factors for analysis of variance. This is an important distinction since it affects the way that F-ratios should be calculated for testing the effects of factors and interactions.

The F-ratios shown in the analysis of variance in Table 7.5 were calculated by dividing the factor and interaction mean squares by the error mean square. This is appropriate if the month and creek factors are regarded as having fixed effects, which means that no other months or creeks are considered to be relevant to the question of whether any effects exist. In other words, inferences about effects are only relevant to Shope Creek and Ball Creek in the months of December, March, June and September.

With factors that have random effects, a different point of view is adopted. In this case the factor levels that are used in an experiment are regarded as being a random sample from a population of levels that could have been used, and inferences are aimed at this populations of levels rather than just the levels that are used in the experiment. The obvious case where the assumption of random effects is called for is when random sampling really is used to determine which levels of a factor to use in an experiment. For example, there might be a large number of lakes that could be used in a study, with ten of these being randomly chosen. Inferences about differences between lakes can then be concerned with differences for the population of lakes rather than just those that are sampled.

Often it is assumed that the choice of factor levels is effectively random even though no random process is used in their selection. Thus, in a psychology experiment the subjects used might be regarded as being equivalent to a random sample from the population of relevant subjects although in fact a random sample is not used.

With a two factor experiment with replication there are the following possibilities for testing for factor effects:

(a) With two fixed effects factors the error mean square should be used as the denominator in the F-ratio for testing all the effects

(b) With two random effects factors the error mean square should be used as the denominator of the F-ratio for testing for an interaction, but the interaction mean square should be used as the denominator for testing for the main effects of the two factors

(c) With one fixed effects factor and one random effects factor (the so-called 'mixed model'), the error mean square should be used as the denominator of the F-ratio for testing for interaction and the main effect of the factor with randomly chosen levels, but the interaction mean square should be used as the denominator for the F-ratio for testing for the main effect of the factor with fixed levels

With three or more factors, of which some are fixed and some are random, there are rules for deciding on what F-ratios to use for testing different effects. These rules are quite complicated and will not be discussed further here. For most researchers the important point to appreciate is that the distinction between fixed and random effects is important when it comes to the analysis of data. Many computer programs for analysis of variance will automatically decide what F-ratios to use for testing once a decision is made about which factors are fixed and which are random.

7.4 Transformation of data

It was mentioned in Example 7.2 that there is some cause for concern with the analysis of the data in Table 7.4 on counts of aquatic insects since it appears that the amount of variation between the results of replicated samples was not constant for the eight month–creek combinations. Means and standard deviations for these combinations are shown in Table 7.6, and the standard deviations are plotted against the means in Figure 7.1(a). It is presumably no accident that the combination with the smallest mean (11.5) has the smallest standard deviation (7.0) while the combination with the largest mean (115.0) has the largest standard deviation (81.0). The assumption of a constant residual variance that is required for the validity of an analysis of variance is, therefore, clearly questionable.

The usual approach for correcting this type of problem involves transforming the data. A few standard rules are:

(a) If the standard deviations for different factor combinations are proportional to the mean values for those factor combinations then replacing each observation X by $\log(X)$ will produce a constant standard deviation. The base used for logarithms is not important

(b) If the variances for different factor combinations are proportional to the mean values for those factor combinations, then replacing each observation X by $\sqrt{X}$ will produce a constant standard deviation. This transformation is particularly useful for data consisting of counts

(c) If data values are proportions of the form $P = X/N$, where X is the number of 'successes' in N trials, then the arc-sine transformation may be effective in producing a constant variance. This involves replacing each P value with $\sin^{-1}(\sqrt{P})$

Since the data being considered are counts of aquatic insects, rule (b) suggests that a square root transformation should be carried out before an analysis of variance. However, the plot of standard deviations against means after this transformation shown

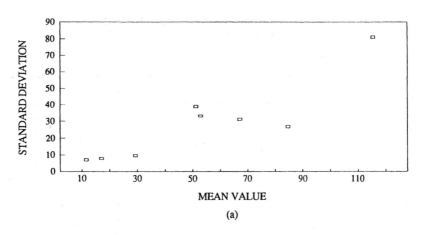

(a)

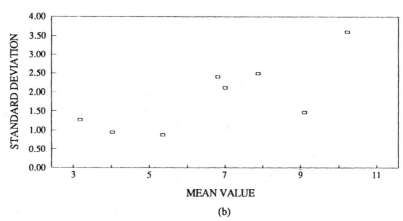

(b)

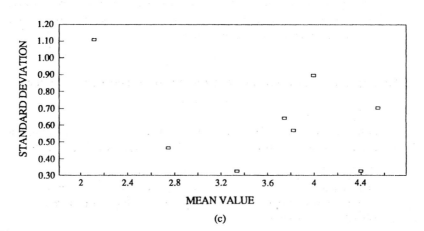

(c)

Table 7.6. *Means and standard deviations for the month and creek combinations for the data in Table 7.4*

Month	Shope Creek		Ball Creek	
	Mean	SD	Mean	SD
December	11.5	7.0	17.0	7.8
March	52.8	33.2	29.3	9.6
June	84.6	26.9	51.1	38.9
September	67.1	31.2	115.0	81.0

in part (b) of Figure 7.1 indicates that there is still a tendency for the standard deviation to increase with the mean. This suggests that a 'stronger' transformation is required, and in fact a logarithmic transformation (using base e) seems to work quite well, as shown in part (c) of Figure 7.1.

An analysis of variance on the log-transformed data provides the analysis of variance shown in Table 7.7. The F-ratios for creeks and interaction are very close to the values for the untransformed data, but the F-ratio for months is much larger. The conclusions from the analysis are essentially unaltered by using the transformation.

7.5 Experiments with three or more factors

Many factorial experiments involve three or more factors. In these cases, analysis of variance can still be used to analyse the results. All that happens is that the total sum of squares is split into more components, as in the following example.

Example 7.3: An experiment on the time required to carry out a task

The data shown in Table 7.8 come from a $3 \times 3 \times 2$ factorial experiment without replication that involved recording the times

---

Figure 7.1. Plots of standard deviations against means for the eight combinations of creek and month from the data in Table 7.4: (a) untransformed data; (b) square root transformed data; (c) log transformed data.

Table 7.7. *The analysis of variance table for the data shown in Table 7.4, after a logarithmic transformation*

Source of variation	SS	df	MS	F
Months	24.50	3	8.17	17.71[b]
Creeks	0.00	1	0.00	0.00
Interaction	4.09	3	1.36	2.95[a]
Error	18.44	40	0.46	
Total	47.03	47		

[a] Significantly large at the 5% level.
[b] Significantly large at the 0.1% level.

Table 7.8. *Times (seconds) required to carry out a task from a three factor experiment*

Time of day	Machine 1 Operator			Machine 2 Operator			Machine 3 Operator		
	a	b	c	a	b	c	a	b	c
AM	63	62	61	59	64	62	61	61	61
PM	63	60	61	61	64	61	60	60	58

required by the operators of machines to carry out a certain task. The factors considered are:

(A) the machine used for the task (1, 2, 3)
(B) the operator carrying out the task (a, b, c)
(C) the time of day (AM, PM)

If the three factors are regarded as having fixed effects then the analysis of variance table is as shown in Table 7.9. Since there is no replication, the three factor interaction has to be assumed to be negligible in order to test the other factors and interactions. With this assumption the three factor interaction mean square becomes an estimate of the error variance which can be used as the denominator in all the F-ratios.

Table 7.9. *Analysis of variance on the data in Table 7.8 on the times required to carry out a task, assuming fixed effects*

Source of variation	Sum of squares	df	Mean square	F
Machine (A)	10.11	2	5.06	7.59[a]
Operator (B)	4.11	2	2.06	3.07
Time of day (C)	2.00	1	2.00	3.00
Interactions				
A × B	18.89	4	4.72	7.08[a]
A × C	3.00	2	1.50	2.25
B × C	2.33	2	1.17	1.75
A × B × C (Error)	2.67	4	0.67	
Total	43.11	17		

[a]Significantly large at the 5% level.

The only significant effects are for machines, and the interaction of machines and operators. Therefore, it appears that the time required to carry out the task is not the same for each machine, and the difference between machines varies from operator to operator. The non-significant F-ratio for the operators just indicate that their average times are not very different.

The interpretation of the experimental results changes considerably if one or more of the factors are considered to have random effects. This is hardly appropriate with the third factor, since AM and PM cannot be regarded as a random choice of times of day. However, it could be that the three machines used were randomly chosen from a larger population of available machines, or that the three operators were randomly chosen from a population of potential operators.

For example, suppose that the three operators were randomly chosen from a large pool of operators that could be used, but the three machines were the only ones available. Then the variation between operators must be taken into account in assessing the effects of the machines and the time of day. It is no longer straightforward (or particularly sensible) to test for a difference between operators, and appropriate F-ratios for testing for the effects of the machines and the times of day are as follows:

Main effect of machines

$F = $ (Machine mean square)/(Machine × Operator

interaction mean square) $= 5.06/4.72 = 1.07$, with 2 and 4 degrees of freedom.

Main effect of time of day

$F =$ (Time of day mean square)/(Operator × Time of day interaction mean square) $= 2.00/1.17 = 1.71$, with 1 and 2 degrees of freedom.

Interaction between machines and time of day

$F =$ (Machine × Time of day interaction mean square)/(Three factor interaction mean square) $= 1.50/0.67 = 2.25$, with 2 and 4 degrees of freedom.

None of these three F-ratios are significantly large at the 5% level, so there is no real evidence of any effects.

7.6 Higher order interactions

It is not possible to test for the existence of the three factor interaction in a factorial experiment with three factors unless there is some replication (i.e. repeated independent observations collected with the same factor levels). If there is replication then it becomes possible to calculate an error mean square that is separate from the three factor interaction mean square, so that there is one more line in the analysis of variance table. The appropriate F-ratios for testing effects still depend on the assumptions made about whether factors have fixed or random effects.

Although the three factor interaction cannot be tested in the example just discussed concerning the times required to carry out a task, it is worth briefly discussing the meaning of this interaction. This can be done in terms of changes in two factor interactions.

The two factor interactions are measures of the way that the main effect of one factor changes with the levels of a second factor. Hence, for instance, the machine × operator interaction sum of squares is the part of the total sum of squares that is accounted for by allowing the effect of machines to vary from operator to operator. In the same way, the machine × operator × time of day interaction can be thought of as measuring the extent to which one of the two factor interactions changes with the third factor. Thus, the machine × operator × time of day sum of squares can be thought of as the part of the total sum of squares that is accounted for by allowing the machine × operator interaction to be different for the two times of day. Or, it can also be thought of equally well as the part of the total sum of squares that is accounted for by allowing the machine × time of day interaction to vary from operator to operator, or as the part of the total sum of squares that is accounted for by allowing the operator × time of day interaction to vary from machine to machine.

Higher order interactions can be understood by a natural generalization of these ideas. Therefore, the four factor interaction between factors A, B, C and D can be thought of as measuring the extent to which the A × B × C interaction changes with the levels of factor D, the extent to which the A × B × D interaction changes with the levels of factor C, etc. One of the implications of this is that if an interaction exists then all the lower order interactions must also exist. For example, the existence of the A × B × C interaction indicates that the A × B interaction must exist for at least some levels of factor C in order to vary with the levels of C.

7.7 Blocking

In the terminology of experimental design, a *block* is a set of experimental units that are more uniform than experimental units in general. When such blocks are available they can be used as a means of reducing the experimental error variance and thereby making experiments more sensitive than they would otherwise be. The important principle involved is that treatment comparisons made within blocks should be more precise than those made with treatments in different blocks.

The simplest experimental design that embodies this principle is the *randomized complete block experiment*, in which each of the treatments of interest is used in several blocks. The adjective 'randomized' is used to indicate that the assignment of the treatments to the experimental units is made at random within each block. The adjective 'complete', which is sometimes omitted, refers to the fact that all treatments are used in each block. *Randomized incomplete block experiments* are discussed briefly later in this section.

For example, suppose that three teaching methods are to be compared in 12 classes, with the assessment being based on a score for the average class achievement on a certain task after three months of teaching. An experimental design without blocking would involve allocating each of the teaching methods to four classes at random. This is a valid design, but no attempt is made to compare the teaching methods in similar classes. A better design would be one which uses each of the treatments in four schools. The design might then take the form shown in Table 7.10. Here, the different ordering of the letters a to c in the different schools is used to indicate that the allocation of teaching methods is randomly assigned to the three classes within schools. This is a randomized complete block experiment, with the schools being the blocks.

One of the standard assumptions about the effects of blocks is that these effects do not interact with the effects of other factors. Therefore, in the experiment on teaching methods it would be usual to assume that there is no school × teaching method interaction. In other words, aside from random variation, the differences between teaching methods are the same in all schools. On this basis, the experiment could be analysed by a two factor analysis of variance without replication, as indicated in Table 7.11. An F-ratio for the effect of schools could also be calculated and tested for significance if this was desired, but it would be the significance of differences between teaching methods that would be the prime concern.

It sometimes happens that the blocks that are available are not large enough to include all the treatments of interest. In that case it is desirable to allocate the treatments to blocks so as to produce a *balanced incomplete block experiment*, where the description 'balanced' is used to indicate that the effects of all treatments, and their differences, are estimated with the same precision.

A key requirement is that every pair of treatments occurs together the same number of times. Hence, to compare four teaching methods (a, b, c and d) in three classes from each of four schools, a balanced incomplete block design is as shown in Table 7.12. Here, each teaching method occurs with each other method in three schools, and four schools are required to produce a balanced design because one teaching method is omitted from each school.

Usually, the choice of a balanced incomplete block design for an experiment is not as straightforward as it is here, since the 'obvious' design may require far too many blocks. However, specialist texts on experimental design indicate various ways of constructing experiments with relatively few observations.

Another aspect of the use of blocking in experiments is concerned with what is called *confounding*. This involves the choosing

Table 7.10. *A design for a randomized complete block experiment in which teaching methods a, b and c are used in four schools*

School				
	1	b	c	a
	2	c	a	b
	3	a	b	c
	4	b	c	a

Table 7.11. *Analysis of variance table for a randomized block experiment comparing three teaching methods in four schools*

Source of variation	Sum of squares	df	Mean square	F
Teaching methods	SSM	2	MSM	MSM/MSE
Schools (blocks)	SSB	3	MSB	
Error	SSE	6	MSE	
Total	SST	11		

Table 7.12. *A balanced incomplete block experiment in which four teaching methods a, b, c and d are used in three classes from each of four schools*

School				
	1	a	b	c
	2	a	b	d
	3	a	c	d
	4	b	c	d

of an experimental design so that any differences between the blocks in an experiment correspond exactly with the effects of one or more high order interactions which it is believed are negligible. In other words, the effects of blocks are confounded with the effects of interactions. This is done in order to use the increased precision that can be expected from making comparisons between treatments within blocks without having to replicate an experiment an unnecessary number of times. In effect, combinations of observations that are being 'wasted' on the estimation of interactions that do not exist are used instead to allow for differences between blocks.

7.8 Latin squares

The *Latin square* is another useful concept in experimental design, since it provides a simple way to examine the effects of three factors with a small number of observations, providing that it is reasonable to assume that these effects do not interact, and the factors all have the same number of levels.

As an example, suppose that it is desirable to compare four teaching methods in terms of a measure of the mean performance of classes after several months of teaching. It is thought that the size of a school and the town where the school is located may have an influence on results, so it is decided that the teaching methods should be tried in several sizes of school, and in several towns. A factorial design is possible for the experiment, but this may require too many classes to be tested. Thus, testing the four teaching methods in four sizes of school in four towns would involve using $4 \times 4 \times 4 = 64$ classes. A Latin square design with the same factor levels is shown in Table 7.13. What makes this design valuable is that, although there are only 16 observations, each teaching method is used once in each town and also once in each size of school. Also, one school of each size comes from each town. As a result, the effects of school sizes and towns average out when comparing the mean results for the teaching methods; the effects of the teaching methods and the towns average out when comparing the mean results for different sizes of school; and the effects of teaching methods and sizes of schools average out when comparing the mean results for different towns.

Analysis of variance can be used to analyse a Latin square experiment like this. The sums of squares accounted for by the three factors can be determined by multiple regression as discussed later in Section 7.14, but it is also possible to use the simple equation

$$\text{SSF} = \sum_{i=1}^{n} T_i^2/n - (T/n)^2,$$

where SSF is the sum of squares for a particular factor F, n is the number of levels of the factors, T_i is the total of the observations

Table 7.13. *A Latin square experiment to compare four teaching methods (a, b, c, d) in schools with four sizes in four towns*

		Size of School			
		1	2	3	4
Town	1	a	b	c	d
	2	b	c	d	a
	3	c	d	a	b
	4	d	a	b	c

at level i of the factor, and $T = \sum T_i$ is the total of all observations. This sum of squares has $n - 1$ degrees of freedom, so that the analysis of variance table takes the form shown in Table 7.14.

Latin squares are sometimes used as a part of more complicated designs, and higher order squares involving more than three factors can also be constructed.

7.9 Nested factors

In the factorial experiments discussed earlier, the factors were *crossed*. In other words, all the levels of every factor were used with all the levels of every other factor. This differs from the situation with a *nested* or *hierarchic* factor, for which the levels are applied within the levels of another factor.

Example 7.4: Variation in nitrogen percentages in fertilizer

As an example of a nested experimental design, suppose that a study is carried out to investigate variation in the percentage of nitrogen in the fertilizer produced in a factory. First, five batches are chosen at random from the large number of batches produced in a year. Next, three bags are chosen at random from each batch. Finally, the nitrogen content is determined for two samples taken at random from each bag. The results obtained are then as shown in Table 7.15.

At first sight this might appear to be a 5×3 factorial experiment with two replicates and both factors with random effects, or a $5 \times 3 \times 2$ factorial experiment without replication, with all three

Table 7.14. *The analysis of variance table for a Latin square experiment with the three factors A, B and C, at n levels each*

Source of variation	Sum of squares	df	Mean square	F
Factor A	SSA	$n - 1$	MSA	MSA/MSE
Factor B	SSB	$n - 1$	MSB	MSB/MSE
Factor C	SSC	$n - 1$	MSC	MSC/MSE
Error	SSE	$n^2 - 3n + 2$	MSE	
Total	SST	$n^2 - 1$		

factors having random effects. However, it is important to notice here that the numbering of bags within batches is quite arbitrary. There is no reason at all why bags that happen to have the same number within a batch should have anything in common. Similarly, the numbering of samples from the bags is arbitrary.

For the analysis of variance, the nature of the sample factor can be recognized by regarding the two samples from each bag as being replicates, differing because of sampling variation only. However, the bag factor requires a special treatment that takes into account that it is a nested factor which comes from subsampling within the levels of the batch factor. What is required is to make the sum of squares associated with bags equal to the sum of squares for the main effect of this factor plus the sum of squares for the interaction of bags with samples, as shown in Table 7.16. To test for the effect of batches, the bags within batches mean square should be used as the denominator in the *F*-ratio, while to test for differences between bags within batches the samples within bags mean square should be used as the denominator in the *F*-ratio.

Hierarchic experiments like this can have more than three levels, and nested factors can be combined with crossed factors. Computer programs often allow factors to be defined as nested or crossed, and modify the analysis of variance accordingly.

7.10 Split-plot experiments in agricultural research

A split-plot experiment is a special type of nested design that is popular for agricultural research. In this setting, the experiment is

Table 7.15. *Results from a hierarchic experiment with three sources of variation. The observations are percentages of nitrogen from random samples taken from randomly chosen bags within randomly chosen batches*

Batch

		1			2			3			4			5	
Bag	1	2	3	1	2	3	1	2	3	1	2	3	1	2	3
Sample 1	63	60	63	60	57	61	59	64	65	57	57	65	55	55	59
2	63	62	63	61	57	61	57	63	64	56	59	65	55	54	58

Table 7.16. *Analysis of variance table for the data in Table 7.15*

Source of variation	Sum of squares	df	Mean square	F
Batches	154.20	4	38.55	2.21
Bags within batches	174.67	10	17.47	29.11[a]
Samples within bags	9.00	15	0.60	
Total	337.87	29		

[a] Significantly large at the 0.1% level.

carried out using several plots of ground, each of which is given a different level of one factor. Each plot is also split into several subplots for the levels of a second factor. There is a random allocation of factor levels both at the plot and subplot level. Therefore, a split-plot experiment is like a hierarchic experiment at two levels with treatment factors randomly allocated to the units at each level.

Example 7.5: The yields of different varieties of alfalfa

As an example, consider a simplified version of an experiment described by Snedecor and Cochran (1980, p. 326) that was conducted to study the yield of three varieties of alfalfa (Cossack, Ranger and Ladack) with four cutting dates (A, B, C and D). Part of the experiment was carried out in three blocks, each of which was set out as three split-plots. For example, block 1 was as shown in Figure 7.2. The order within the subplots was chosen at random. For blocks 2 and 3, the same treatments were used but in different random orders at the plot and subplot levels. The experimental results obtained from the whole experiment are shown in Table 7.17, in tenths of a ton per acre.

At first sight, this might appear to be a factorial experiment with two factors (variety of alfalfa at three levels, and cutting date at four levels), replicated in three blocks. However, this ignores the fact that the observations on the four cutting dates within one plot can be expected to be somewhat similar as a result of the individual characteristics of the plot. Or, as another way of looking at the situation, the experimental errors for subplots are nested within plots instead of being independent.

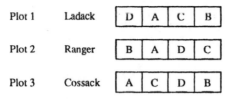

Figure 7.2. Block 1 of a split-plot experiment.

Snedecor and Cochran (1980, p. 325) describe the details of the calculations required for analysis of variance with a split-plot experiment. For the alfalfa example the analysis of variance table is provided in Table 7.18. An important point to note is the division of the table into two parts. The top part of the table shows sums of squares that can be calculated using the totals of the observations for the different plots. These provide a total of 8 degrees of freedom, reflecting the fact that there are 9 plots altogether. The bottom part of the table shows sums of squares based on observations within plots, where these account for 27 degrees of freedom. The total degrees of freedom for the whole experiment is 35, which is one less than the number of subplots. The plot level mean squares are tested against the variety × block interaction mean square, which is an estimate of the error variance at the plot level on the assumption that, in fact, this interaction does not exist. The subplot level mean squares are tested against the pooled mean square for the cutting date × block interaction and the cutting date × variety × block interaction, which is an estimate of the subplot level error on the assumption that these interactions do not exist. The use of the interaction mean squares as estimates of error variances is justifiable on the usual assumption that a block factor does not interact with other factors.

7.11 Other uses of the split-plot design

The split-plot design is sometimes used in non-agricultural areas of research, in which case the word 'plot' simply means a piece of relatively uniform raw material needed to carry out the experiment. For example, in an experiment on the effects of a carcinogen the 'plots' might be ten litters of five rats each, with a rat being regarded as a 'subplot'. Different litters could be randomly assigned to different levels of the carcinogen, and the five rats in each litter could be randomly chosen to be sacrificed at five

Table 7.17. *Results from a split-plot experiment, with three varieties of alfalfa as the plot level factor, and four cutting dates at the subplot level. Observations are yields in tenths of a ton per acre. (Snedecor and Cochran, 1980)*

Variety	Date	Block		
		1	2	3
Ladack	A	22	19	16
	B	16	13	12
	C	23	16	17
	D	22	20	18
Cossack	A	23	20	17
	B	14	13	19
	C	19	17	18
	D	23	18	20
Ranger	A	18	20	21
	B	15	15	18
	C	16	16	18
	D	16	17	20

different times to measure tumour levels. Then the carcinogen levels provide the plot level factor, and the sacrifice times provide the subplot level factor.

There are two reasons why the split-plot design may be an appropriate design for an experiment. First, it sometimes happens that it is convenient or necessary to apply some treatments to whole plots at the same time. Second, the design allows good comparisons between the levels of the factor that is applied at the subplot level, somewhat at the expense of the comparisons between the levels of the factor applied at the plot level since in general the comparisons made between subplots on the same plot will be less affected by experimental errors than comparisons made between plots.

The split-plot design can be generalized to allow split-split plot experiments, where sub-plots are split into sub-sub-plots and levels of a third factor allocated to these at random. Split-split-split plot experiments can also be considered, and in fact there is no limit to the way that plots can be divided and subdivided other than the need to maintain a certain minimum size for the units on which measurements are taken.

Table 7.18. *The form of analysis of variance table for the split-plot experiment with the data shown in Table 7.17*

Source of variation	Sum of squares	df	Mean square	F
Plot level comparisons				
Variety of alfalfa	5.17	2	2.58	0.16
Blocks	22.17	2	11.08	0.66
Plot level error				
Variety × Block	66.67	4	16.67	
Between plots total	94.00	8		
Subplot comparisons				
Date of cutting	118.97	3	39.66	14.32[a]
Date × Variety	23.94	6	3.99	1.44
Subplot level error				
Date × Block	21.61	6		
Date × Variety × Block	28.22	12	2.77	
Within plots total	192.74	27		
Overall total	286.74	35		

[a]Significant at the 0.1% level.

7.12 Repeated measures experiments

The description *repeated measures experiments* can be used as a label for all designs that involve taking several measurements on each experimental unit. Therefore, the category includes designs with nested factors and split-plot designs. Often, the reason for using these designs is that they allow better use of the experimental units available. For example, a psychology experiment that involves one factor at five levels and a second factor at six levels requires 90 subjects for a full factorial experiment replicated three times. However, with a repeated measures factor the levels of the first factor might be applied to five groups of three subjects each, and all the levels of the second factor given to each of the subjects. In that way the experiment can be carried out using 15 subjects only.

One special case of a repeated measures experiment is the *change-over experiment*, where each experimental unit is subjected to a series of treatments, with different orderings of these treatments being used on different groups of units. For example, some units might get the treatments A, B and C in the order ABC, other units might get the order BCA, others CAB, etc. with an observation being taken for each treatment on each experimental unit. The analysis of these designs may need to take into account the *carry-over effects* of treatments on the treatments that follow them. For more information see Koch *et al.* (1988).

Another special case of a repeated measures experiment is the *longitudinal study* where observations are taken in the same order on each experimental unit. The ordering is usually based on time, but it can also be based on location in space, or any other condition that produces an order that cannot be changed by the experimenter. Therefore, what differentiates a longitudinal study from a split-plot design is the fact that the conditions that are associated with the repeated measures cannot be randomly assigned. Longitudinal studies are so common that the description *repeated measures design* is sometimes taken to mean just these types of study.

There are various ways that the results of a longitudinal study can be analysed:

(a) The time trends in the results for one experimental unit can be characterized by summary variables calculated from the observations on that unit such as the mean or the difference between the last observation and the first observation. These summary variables can then be subjected to analysis of variance to see how they vary with the factors that describe groups (Mead, 1988, p. 409)

(b) A response function can be fitted to the observations on one experimental unit and the parameters subjected to an analysis of variance to see how they vary with the factors that describe groups (Mead, 1988, p. 414). The form of the response function used can then be as simple or complicated as necessary, depending on the nature of the data

(c) The observations for each experimental unit can be analysed by a *multivariate analysis of variance* which takes into account the correlations between observations made at different times (Winer, 1971, p. 232)

(d) The data can be analysed by an analysis of variance in essentially the same way as is done with a split-plot experiment

Example 7.6: Plasma fluoride concentrations for baby rats

An example of a longitudinal study that was discussed by Koch *et al.* (1988) was concerned with plasma fluoride concentrations in groups of litters of baby rats. There were two factors varied between these groups (age in days, and dose in micrograms per gram of body weight) and one within-group or repeated measures factor (minutes after the injection). The results for the experiment are shown in Table 7.19, with each observation consisting of the average of the natural logarithms of plasma fluoride concentrations for a pair of baby rats from the same litter.

A split-plot type of analysis of variance gives the results that are shown in Table 7.20. The analysis is in two parts. First, the sum of squares for the 18 mean values for litters is partitioned into sums of squares for age, dose and the age × dose interaction, with 1, 2 and 2 degrees of freedom, respectively, and a residual sum of squares (litter within groups) with 12 degrees of freedom. The litters are treated as a random effects factor that is nested within age and dose, so that the sums of squares for all the interactions between this factor and the other factors, and the sum of squares for litters combine to provide the error sum of squares. The mean squares for age, dose and age × dose are all tested against the residual mean square. The only significant effect is for the dose factor.

The second part of the analysis is for variation within litters. There are 54 observations altogether, and hence a total of 53 degrees of freedom for the analysis of variance. Of these, 17 account for differences between litters, and 36 for differences within litters. In the analysis of variance the sum of squares within litters is partitioned into sums of squares for time, time × age, time × dose, time × age × dose, with 2, 2, 4 and 4 degrees of freedom, respectively, and a residual with 24 degrees of freedom. The residual mean square provides the denominator for all the *F*-tests on within litter effects. The effect of time and the time × dose interaction prove to be significant.

7.13 The assumption of compound symmetry

The analysis of variance on data from repeated measures experiments has proved popular, particularly for experiments in

Table 7.19. *Average logarithms of plasma fluoride concentrations from a longitudinal study on plasma fluoride levels of baby rats after they received injections of fluoride at different doses (in µg per gram of body weight). (Koch et al., 1988)*

Age of rats (days)	Dose (µg)	Litter	Minutes after injection		
			15	30	60
6	0.50	1	4.1	3.9	3.3
		2	5.1	4.0	3.2
		3	5.8	5.8	4.4
	0.25	4	4.8	3.4	2.3
		5	3.9	3.5	2.6
		6	5.2	4.8	3.7
	0.10	7	3.3	2.2	1.6
		8	3.4	2.9	1.8
		9	3.7	3.8	2.2
11	0.50	10	5.1	3.5	1.9
		11	5.6	4.6	3.4
		12	5.9	5.0	3.2
	0.25	13	3.9	2.3	1.6
		14	6.5	4.0	2.6
		15	5.2	4.6	2.7
	0.10	16	2.8	2.0	1.8
		17	4.3	3.3	1.9
		18	3.8	3.6	2.6

psychology, to a large extent because of the influence of the book by Winer (1971). It certainly is a relatively straightforward approach. However, it does require the assumption of compound symmetry, which is questionable with longitudinal studies. What this assumption means is that the correlation between the repeated observations on one experimental unit is the same for all pairs of these observations. For example, in the case of the experiment on rats that has been described in Example 7.6, the correlation between the observations for a litter at 15 minutes and 30 minutes is assumed to be the same as the correlation between the results for 15 minutes and the results for 60 minutes. This is questionable, since in many situations there is a tendency for observations that are close in time to be more similar than ones that are far apart in time.

With split-plot experiments the assumption of compound symmetry is justified by the random allocation of treatment levels to

Table 7.20. *Repeated measures analysis of variance on the plasma fluoride concentration data shown in Table 7.19*

Source of variation	Sum of squares	df	Mean square	F
Between litter analysis				
Age of rats	0.01	1	0.01	0.01
Dose	21.24	2	10.62	7.14[a]
Age × Dose	0.25	2	0.12	0.08
Between litter error	17.84	12	1.49	
Between litters total	39.34	17		
Within litter analysis				
Time	35.27	2	17.63	146.92[b]
Time × Age	1.54	2	0.77	6.42[a]
Time × Dose	0.89	4	0.22	1.83
Time × Age × Dose	1.01	4	0.25	2.08
Within litter error	2.78	24	0.12	
Within litters total	41.49	36		
Overall total	80.83	53		

[a] Significant at the 1% level.
[b] Significant at the 0.1% level.

subplots within plots, but with longitudinal experiments it is advisable to check the assumption with a formal test. Some computer programs allow this as an option, or carry out a test automatically. If the assumption appears not to hold then it is possible to reduce the degrees of freedom in the analysis of variance table to allow for this using a factor provided by Greenhouse and Geisser (1959). Again, this is available as an option in some computer programs.

Koch *et al*. show that the assumption of compound symmetry is, in fact, realistic with the rat data used in Example 7.6 so that a repeated measures analysis of variance is justified in this case.

7.14 Analysis of variance by multiple regression

There are a number of standard computer programs available for carrying out the analysis of variance calculations needed for the various experimental designs that have been described in this chapter, and generally the researcher will find that it is best to use one of these to analyse any experiment that involves more than a few observations. However, it is useful to understand how multiple regression can be used to carry out the calculations since this method can be used as a last resort if an alternative method is not available. Also, a regression model can be thought of as the justification for the analysis of variance. In fact, the method that is about to be described has been used several times already. For example, this is the way that seasonal effect were handled in Case Study 4 concerning the loss of sales due to a fire in a hardware store. It is also the method that was suggested for accounting for the effects of different factors in Exercise 2 of Chapter 4.

The basic idea is that the effects of factors can be taken into account in a regression analysis by using 'dummy' variables to represent these effects. For example, consider again the example that has been used before of four teaching methods being compared in four towns in schools with four different sizes (Table 7.13). In this case, if the effects of different teaching methods and different sizes of schools are ignored then a regression model that allows for the effects of towns is

$$Y = \beta_0 + \beta_1 X_1 + \beta_2 X_2 + \beta_3 X_3 + \varepsilon,$$

where $X_i = 1$ for an observation from the ith town, or otherwise is zero. In effect, this implies that the mean of the observations for town 1 is $\beta_0 + \beta_1$, the mean of the observations for town 2 is $\beta_0 + \beta_2$, the mean of the observations for town 3 is $\beta_0 + \beta_3$, and the mean of the observations for town 4 is β_0. In other words, the regression coefficients β_1, β_2 and β_3 measure the differences between town 1, 2 and 3 and town 4, which can be thought of as the 'standard' town.

With this regression model the extra sum of squares accounted for by the variables X_1 to X_3, with three degrees of freedom, is the part of the total sum of squares that is accounted for by the effects of towns. If it is significantly large then there is evidence that this factor has an effect. It is generally true that $n - 1$ dummy variables can be used to account for the main effect of a factor with n levels, which explains why there are $n - 1$ degrees of freedom for the factor in the analysis of variance table.

The mean value of observations can be made to vary with the size of the school as well as the towns, by introducing three additional dummy variables, X_4, X_5 and X_6 where $X_{i+3} = 1$ for an observation from a school of size i, or is otherwise zero. The regression model then becomes

$$Y = \beta_0 + \beta_1 X_1 + \beta_2 X_2 + \beta_3 X_3 + \beta_4 X_4 + \beta_5 X_5 + \beta_6 X_6 + \varepsilon.$$

This implies that the effect of school size, which is added to any town effects, is β_4 for schools of size 1, β_5 for schools of size 2, β_6 for schools of size 3, and zero for schools of size 4. Therefore, schools of size 4 become the standard with which schools of other sizes are compared.

Finally, the effects of different teaching methods can also be allowed for by introducing three more dummy variables, X_7, X_8 and X_9, where $X_{i+6} = 1$ for teaching method i, or is otherwise zero. The regression model then becomes

$$Y = \beta_0 + \beta_1 X_1 + \beta_2 X_2 + \beta_3 X_3 + \beta_4 X_4 + \beta_5 X_5 + \beta_6 X_6$$
$$+ \beta_7 X_7 + \beta_8 X_8 + \beta_9 X_9 + \varepsilon.$$

This implies that the effect of teaching methods, which is in addition to any effects of towns and school sizes, is β_7 for teaching method 1, β_8 for teaching method 2, β_9 for teaching method 3, and zero for teaching method 4. The standard teaching method to which the other teaching methods are compared is therefore teaching method 4.

There is no particular reason why town 4, school size 4 and teaching method 4 should be chosen as the ones that do not have associated regression coefficients. Other choices would serve equally well.

The values of the X variables for the regression model depend on the study design that is used. For example, suppose that the design is the Latin square shown in Table 7.13. There are 16 observations for which the values of the nine X variables are as shown in Table 7.21. An array of values of X variables like this is sometimes called the *design matrix*, since it accounts for the effects of factors according to the experimental design that has been used.

As mentioned before, it is appropriate to assess the significance of a factor in terms of the extra sum of squares accounted for by all the dummy variables for that factor taken together. Hence for the example being considered the analysis of variance table takes the form shown in Table 7.22. Since this is a Latin square design, the extra sums of squares accounted for by the three factors are the same irrespective of the order in which the factors are considered. However, this is not necessarily the case and the sum of squares for a factor may depend on which other factors were

Table 7.21. Regression variables for the Latin square experiment with the design shown in Table 7.13

Observations	Row	Column	Town			Size			Method		
			1	2	3	1	2	3	a	b	c
			X_1	X_2	X_3	X_4	X_5	X_6	X_7	X_8	X_9
1	1	1	1	0	0	1	0	0	1	0	0
2	1	2	1	0	0	0	1	0	0	1	0
3	1	3	1	0	0	0	0	1	0	0	1
4	1	4	1	0	0	0	0	0	0	0	0
5	2	1	0	1	0	1	0	0	0	1	0
6	2	2	0	1	0	0	1	0	0	0	1
7	2	3	0	1	0	0	0	1	0	0	0
8	2	4	0	1	0	0	0	0	1	0	0
9	3	1	0	0	1	1	0	0	0	0	1
10	3	2	0	0	1	0	1	0	0	0	0
11	3	3	0	0	1	0	0	1	1	0	0
12	3	4	0	0	1	0	0	0	0	1	0
13	4	1	0	0	0	1	0	0	0	0	0
14	4	2	0	0	0	0	1	0	1	0	0
15	4	3	0	0	0	0	0	1	0	1	0
16	4	4	0	0	0	0	0	0	0	0	1

Table 7.22. *An analysis of variance for an experiment on comparing teaching methods based on the extra sum of squares principle*

Size|Town indicates the variation accounted for by Size in addition to the Town; and Method|Size, Town indicates the variation accounted for by Method in addition to the Size and Town.

Source of variation	SS	df	MS	F
Town	SSA	3	MSA	MSA/MSE
Size|Town	SSB	3	MSB	MSB/MSE
Method|Size, Town	SSC	3	MSC	MSC/MSE
Residual	SSE	6	MSE	
	SST	15		

added into the model earlier. It is for this reason that generally the appropriate sum of squares for assessing the effect of the methods of teaching would be the extra sum of squares for this factor after allowing for the effects of towns and school sizes.

The Latin square experimental design is used when interactions between factors can be assumed to be negligible. Therefore, in this example it is not necessary to consider making up dummy variables to account for interactions. In other situations this does become necessary, and can be done by introducing variables that are products of the dummy variables used to account for the main effects of factors.

Therefore, suppose for some reason that it is necessary to make up dummy variables to allow for an interaction between the town and the size of the schools. The first of these dummy variables would then be the product of the X_1 and X_4 from Table 7.21. This would be 1 for observations in town 1 on schools of size 1, but otherwise 0. The second dummy variable would be the product of X_1 and X_5, which is 1 for observations in town 1 on schools of size 2, but otherwise 0. The last dummy variable would be the product of X_3 and X_6, which is 1 for observations in town 3 on schools of size 3. There are nine products of this type between the dummy variables that allow for differences between towns (X_1 to X_3) and the dummy variables that allow for differences between schools of different sizes (X_4 to X_6), and hence it requires nine dummy variables to allow for the interaction between these two factors.

This method for constructing dummy variables to allow for an interaction works because it has the effect of permitting the differences between towns to vary with the size of school being considered. For example, if the product of X_1 and X_4 is included as a predictor variable in a regression equation in addition to variables X_1 to X_6 then it allows schools of size 1 in town 1 to have a mean level that is different from what is obtained from a regression that includes X_1 to X_6 only.

More generally, if the main effect of a factor with I levels is allowed for using $I - 1$ dummy variables and the main effect of another factor with J levels is allowed for using $J - 1$ dummy variables then the $(I - 1)(J - 1)$ products of these dummy variables will allow for the interaction. This is one explanation of why there are $(I - 1)(J - 1)$ degrees of freedom for the interaction in an analysis of variance table.

The principle of multiplying dummy variables for the main effects of factors in order to obtain dummy variables for interactions also applies to three factor and higher order interactions. However, this is an extension that does not need to be considered here.

7.15 Ancillary analyses

Although analysis of variance provides a basic summary of the results of a designed experiment, and is a convenient method for assessing the effects of different factors and interactions, it should be only a part of a full analysis. Additional consideration should be given to checking the validity of the model being used and examining the magnitude of any effects that seem to be present.

Since the model used for analysis of variance is just a special type of multiple regression model, residual plots can be used to see if there is any evidence of the error variance changing with different factor combinations, or whether the distribution of errors appears to be normal. The constancy of error variances can also be checked with plots such as those in Figure 7.1.

The magnitude of effects can be seen by comparing mean values for different factor levels or different combinations of factor levels. This comparison can either be done informally, for example by plotting means against factor levels with the standard errors of the means indicated, or in terms of tests for significant differences. If tests are performed then an important consideration is that if several tests are carried out at the same time then the probability of getting at least one significant result can be quite large even when there are no real effects at all. This has led to the development of a number of *multiple comparison techniques* that are designed to control the probability of declaring any result significant by mistake. More information about these techniques is provided by Miller (1985) and Hochberg and Tamhane (1987).

7.16 Summary and further reading

The purpose of this chapter has been to provide a review of the most important aspects of the modern theory of experimental design and analysis. The topics covered have been factorial experiments, blocking, Latin squares, split-plot and other repeated measures designs, and the use of analysis of variance and multiple regression. The discussion has been broad rather than deep, and those interested in more details should consult a specialist text such as that of Mead (1988), Montgomery (1984) or Snedecor and Cochran (1980).

Exercises

(1) With a suitable computer program, or otherwise, use the data in Tables 7.1, 7.4, 7.8, 7.15, 7.17 and 7.19 to obtain the analyses of variance shown in Tables 7.3, 7.7, 7.9, 7.16, 7.18 and 7.20. In all cases make appropriate residual plots to check the assumptions being made if these have not already been provided in this chapter.

(2) Mead (1988, p. 410) describes a repeated measures experiment carried out on 27 rats. The rats were divided at random into three groups with sizes of 10, 7 and 10, and each group was given a different treatment. Treatment 1 was a control, treatment 2 was thyroxin added to the drinking water, and treatment 3 was thiouracil added to the drinking water. The weights of all rats were recorded at the start of the experiment and then at weekly intervals for four weeks. The full data are shown in Table 7.23.

   (i) Plot the weight of each rat against time and comment on the apparent effects, if any, of adding thyroxin and thiouracil to the drinking water.

   (ii) Carry out an analysis of variance separately on the

Table 7.23. *A repeated measures experiment with three treatments on rats.*
(Mead, 1988)

	Rat	Week				
		0	1	2	3	4
Control	1	57	86	114	139	172
	2	60	93	123	146	177
	3	52	77	111	144	185
	4	49	67	100	129	164
	5	56	81	104	121	151
	6	46	70	102	131	153
	7	51	71	94	110	141
	8	63	91	112	130	154
	9	49	67	90	112	140
	10	57	82	110	139	169
Thyroxin	1	59	85	121	156	191
	2	54	71	90	110	138
	3	56	75	108	151	189
	4	59	85	116	148	177
	5	57	72	97	120	144
	6	52	73	97	116	140
	7	52	70	105	138	171
Thiouracil	1	61	86	109	120	129
	2	59	80	101	111	126
	3	53	79	100	106	133
	4	59	88	100	111	122
	5	51	75	101	123	140
	6	51	75	92	100	119
	7	56	78	95	103	109
	8	58	69	93	114	138
	9	46	61	78	90	107
	10	53	72	89	104	122

weights after 1, 2, 3 and 4 weeks, and the difference between the final weight and the initial weight. Comment on the results obtained.

(iii) Fit the quadratic response function

$$w = \beta_0 + \beta_1(t - 2) + \beta_2(t - 2)^2$$

to the observations for each rat, where w is the weight and t is the time in weeks. Then analyse the resulting estimates of the regression coefficients by analysis of variance to see how they vary with the different treatments. Comment on your results. (Note that the parameterization for the response function is chosen so that the product of the linear term $(t - 2)$ and the quadratic term $(t - 2)^2$ is zero. This makes the estimates of β_1 and β_2 uncorrelated.)

(iv) Why is it questionable to analyse these data as coming from a split-plot experiment?

CASE STUDY 7
An experiment on lockstitch seams

Although there has been interest in the mechanical behaviour and structure of seamed textiles for more than fifty years, most experimental work on the properties of seams have had a simple design with only one factor varied at a time. A notable exception is the experiment described by Laing (1987) and Laing and Pearshouse (1987) on lockstich seams (International Standards Association stitch type 301), which are commonly used in apparel, upholstery and for some industrial applications. This case study is concerned with a part of this experiment that was concerned with the identification of the crucial factors affecting the work required to rupture the first thread.

The first stage in the design of the experiment was the choice of the factors that would be varied. Five factors were considered to be relevant, these being:

(A) the balance ratio, which is the length of needle thread per stitch divided by the length of the bobbin thread
(B) the linear stitch density in stitches per centimetre
(C) the type of thread
(D) the type of substrate
(E) the number of substrate plies

The next stage in designing the experiment was the choice of the levels to use for each factor, which immediately introduced the potential problem that more observations would be required than was possible in practice. It was considered that at least three levels should be used for each factor, so that a full factorial experiment would require $3^5 = 243$ different factor combinations. However, this was quite out of the question taking into account the time and effort required to set up just one factor combination.

This problem was overcome by using an experimental design that is called a $\frac{1}{3}$ replicate of a 3^5 experiment. This is a design which uses only 81 of the 243 possible factor combinations for the full 3^5, but with these being chosen so as to make it possible to estimate main effects for all five factors, and all the two factor interactions. Thus, a considerably reduced number of observations was taken at the cost of not being able to investigate the higher order interactions.

There is a considerable literature on *fractional factorial designs* of this type, since the problem of a full factorial experiment requiring too many observations is fairly common. See Montgomery (1984, Chapter 11) for more details. The design used in the lockstitch experiment is shown in Table 7.24, the source being Cochran and Cox (1957, Plan 6A.19, p. 291).

The levels that were chosen for factors A to E were:

(A) balance ratio: 0.5, 1.0 or 1.5
(B) linear stitch density: 4, 6 or 8 stitches per cm
(C) thread type: mercerized cotton, spun polyester or continuous filament polyester
(D) substrate type: knitted 1×1 rib, knitted interlock or woven twill with elastomeric yarn
(E) number of substrate plies: 1, 2 or 4

These correspond to the levels 0, 1 and 2 in Table 7.24.

It was relatively easy to take several measures of the work to rupture the first thread once one of the combinations of factor levels was set up. An attempt was made, therefore, to take five replicate observations for each combination used. However, for various reasons valid observations could not always be taken, with the result that in the end the number of replications varied from combination to combination and no observations at all were obtained for a few combinations. A summary of the results obtained is shown in Table 7.25.

Because of the unequal numbers of replicates at different factor combinations, the relatively simple analysis of variance that is possible with the experiment with equal numbers of replicates at each factor combination had to be replaced with one based on fitting regression models that allow for the effects of factors and two factor interactions, along the lines discussed in Section 7.15.

Table 7.24. *The experimental design used for the lockstitch experiment, which is a 1/3 replicate of a 3^5 factorial experiment. (Cochran and Cox, 1957)*

The notation used is that 0, 1 and 2 indicate the three levels of a factor. Hence 00000 indicates an observation at the first level of all five factors, 10122 indicates the second level of factor A, the first level of factor B, the second level of factor C, and the third levels for factors D and E. The levels for factors A and B are indicated in the first column of the table while the other columns indicate the levels for the other three factors.

AB	CDE	CDE	CDE	CDE	CDE	CDE	CDE	CDE	CDE
00	000	201	102	120	021	222	111	012	210
10	122	020	221	212	110	011	200	101	002
20	211	112	010	001	202	100	022	220	121
01	110	011	212	200	101	002	221	122	020
11	202	100	001	022	220	121	010	211	112
21	021	222	120	111	012	210	102	000	201
02	220	121	022	101	211	112	001	202	100
12	012	210	111	102	000	201	120	021	222
22	101	002	200	221	122	020	212	110	011

The computer package GENSTAT 5 (Genstat 5 Committee, 1987) was used for this purpose.

A plot of the standard deviations for different factor combinations against their corresponding means shows a clear indication that the standard deviation for experimental errors increased with the mean. However, a logarithmic transformation was found to overcome this problem.

The analysis of variance table using base 10 logarithms is shown in Table 7.26. Here, the sum of squares for each factor and interaction is the extra sum of squares accounted for in the model when the dummy regression variables for the term are added to the model after the terms shown above it in the analysis of variance table. For example, the sum of squares for the number of plies is the extra sums of squares accounted for by the dummy variables for this factor after the dummy variables for the other four factors have already been included. All the factors are considered to have fixed effects, so that the error mean square is the appropriate denominator for all F-ratios. On this basis all the factors and two factor interactions are significant at the 0.1% level.

Table 7.25. *Summary of the results for the experiment relating the work at the first stitch break (n = number of replicate observations available; Mean = mean of the replicate observations in millijoules; SD = standard deviation of the replicate observations). (Laing, 1987; Laing and Pearshouse, 1987)*

	Factor					Factor					Factor			
	levels	n	Mean	SD		levels	n	Mean	SD		levels	n	Mean	SD
1	00000	4	17.8	4.3	28	00120	5	84.5	12.5	55	00011	3	52.1	9.5
2	10122	0	—	—	29	10212	5	747.0	130.0	56	10200	5	306.1	31.9
3	20211	3	295.2	38.0	30	20001	5	92.0	10.0	57	20022	0	—	—
4	01110	5	35.4	5.2	31	01200	4	186.5	36.9	58	01221	3	4002.0	455.8
5	11202	5	722.0	116.0	32	11022	0	—	—	59	11010	3	19.8	2.1
6	21021	5	37.1	5.3	33	21111	5	64.1	15.9	60	21102	5	427.5	34.2
7	02220	4	766.0	158.0	34	02010	5	12.8	0.7	61	02001	5	69.8	7.1
8	12012	5	594.0	170.0	35	12102	2	801.6	41.5	62	12120	2	3550.0	1210.9
9	22101	5	250.1	29.9	36	22221	0	—	—	63	22212	5	478.4	9.18
10	00201	5	306.8	42.3	37	00021	3	24.4	9.9	64	00012	4	26.8	6.2
11	10020	5	54.3	9.6	38	10110	4	72.2	18.9	65	10101	5	203.2	27.7
12	20112	5	260.6	48.4	39	20202	5	1196.9	81.1	66	20220	2	1718.0	525.0
13	01011	4	17.3	1.4	40	01101	4	183.9	13.3	67	01122	0	—	—
14	11100	5	161.1	12.2	41	11220	5	2265.0	631.0	68	11211	5	495.7	62.2
15	21222	0	—	—	42	21012	3	138.4	46.8	69	21000	4	93.6	9.5
16	02121	1	550.3	—	43	02211	3	294.9	42.0	70	02202	5	686.0	194.0
17	12210	3	96.4	17.6	44	12000	3	73.6	3.7	71	12021	0	—	—
18	22002	4	319.9	36.4	45	22122	0	—	—	72	22110	5	53.6	5.0
19	00102	4	331.1	43.6	46	00222	0	—	—	73	00210	4	45.4	11.9
20	10221	0	—	—	47	10011	4	53.4	5.0	74	10002	4	123.5	41.0

No.	code				No.	code				No.	code			
21	20010	4	22.0	2.3	48	20100	3	203.1	28.7	75	20121	4	1272.0	757.0
22	01212	3	887.2	46.6	49	01002	5	125.2	59.2	76	01020	5	52.9	9.7
23	11001	2	249.1	5.8	50	11121	0	—	—	77	11112	5	436.4	99.0
24	21120	4	844.0	161.0	51	21210	4	75.1	16.2	78	21201	4	452.4	76.9
25	02022	0	—	—	52	02112	5	765.0	209.0	79	02100	4	146.5	14.5
26	12111	4	80.3	15.8	53	12201	4	392.7	60.2	80	12222	0	—	—
27	22200	2	281.2	0.9	54	22020	4	59.3	15.2	81	22011	5	47.3	3.3

The interaction sum of squares for the substrates and the number of plies (D × E) has only three degrees of freedom since it so happens that no observations are available for one of the six possible combinations for these two factors (woven twill with four plies). This obviously makes it impossible to fit a regression model that accounts for the effect of woven twill to be different for four plies from what it is for other numbers of plies. However, the GENSTAT program automatically checks for this type of problem and adjusts the analysis accordingly.

A full analysis of the results required the consideration of the factors and interactions in terms of the mean levels of work at different factor levels. Laing (1987) and Laing and Pearshouse (1987) should be consulted for more details concerning these matters which will not be considered further here. However, before leaving the Case Study two general comments about the experiment are in order.

First, the experiment might be considered to be rather unsatisfactory since an experimental design was chosen and then it was found that it was not possible to gather all the required data. As a result, the sums of squares in the analysis of variance table depend on the order in which the factors and interactions are added in to the regression model. However, missing data would have been a problem with any experimental design and under the circumstances it was better to use a good design to gather the data rather than to use no design at all. The design used was such that if there had been no missing data then the sums of squares would not have changed with the order of entering terms into the regression model and by using it the ordering effects caused by missing data were minimized. In fact, doing the analysis with different orders for entering terms makes very little difference to the sums of squares.

The second comment that can be made concerns the assumption that three factor and higher order interactions are negligible, which is inherent in the use of the 1/3 replicate of a 3^5 experiment. Obviously it would have been better to avoid this assumption, but this was not possible within the constraints of the resources available for the experiment. It is, of course, possible that the results of the experiment are misleading because of the existence of a high order interaction, but this seems unlikely since it is generally true that high order interactions are of less practical importance than low order interactions. Furthermore, in the present example, the main effects of the five factors on their own account for 76.9% of the total sum of squares, and the two factor

Table 7.26. *Analysis of variance for the results from the experiment on the work to first stitch break.*

The sums of squares for the factors and their interactions are the extra sums of squares accounted for when dummy variables for these terms are added in to a regression model after the terms shown higher in the table.

Source of variation	SS	df	MS	F^a
A (balance ratio)	4.50	2	2.25	103.58
+B (linear stitch density)	1.32	2	0.66	30.37
+C (thread type)	35.84	2	17.92	825.42
+D (substrate type)	9.56	2	4.78	220.09
+E (number of substrate plies)	19.36	2	9.68	445.81
+A × B	3.17	4	0.79	36.47
+A × C	1.07	4	0.27	12.34
+A × D	1.05	4	0.26	12.04
+A × E	0.77	4	0.19	8.92
+B × C	1.84	4	0.46	21.24
+B × D	0.65	4	0.16	7.53
+B × E	0.88	4	0.22	10.12
+C × D	4.43	4	1.11	51.05
+C × E	0.87	4	0.22	10.06
+D × E	1.57	3	0.52	24.18
Error	4.93	227	0.022	
Total	91.81	276		

[a] All significantly large at the 0.1% level.

interactions account for a further 17.8%. This leaves only about 5.3% to be accounted for by the higher order interactions, of which many are possible. There is, therefore, little scope for these higher order interactions to have important effects.

8

Some special types of data

8.1 Introduction

Although many of the standard statistical methods were developed for normally distributed data with a constant error variance, anyone who does much data analysis soon discovers that real data are often not so well behaved. For example, it is common to find that a set of observations contains a few values that are very large relative to the majority of values, although there is no reason to believe that these extreme values are not genuine. Another common situation is that a high proportion of data values is zero, particularly in cases where these values are counts of the number of times that a certain event occurs.

There are five options available for handling non-normal data:

(a) The non-normality can be ignored, on the grounds that many standard methods of analysis such as the analysis of variance and linear regression are known to be 'robust' to the assumption of normality, particularly with large data sets

(b) The data can be transformed, as discussed in Section 7.4 in the context of the analysis of variance. For example each observation can be replaced by its logarithm, its square root or its reciprocal. One possibility involves using a general power transformation, whereby the observation x is replaced by

$$x' = \begin{cases} (x^\tau - 1)/\tau, & \tau \neq 0, \\ \log_e (x), & \tau = 0, \end{cases}$$

with the parameter τ chosen to satisfy some criterion of normality. This type of very flexible transformation was suggested by Box and Cox (1964), and is discussed further by Madansky (1988, p. 158)

(c) It may be possible to replace an analysis based on the normal distribution with a non-parametric analysis that makes no particular assumptions about the distribution of data. There are many possibilities here, and the researcher will find one or more non-parametric counterparts for most of the standard methods based on the assumption of normally distributed data. Non-parametric methods are reviewed by Gibbons (1982), who lists a number of books on the topic

(d) A standard analysis can be carried out, but the significance level for the data can be determined by a computer intensive procedure, instead of from the usual statistical tables. For example, the F-ratio from an analysis of variance can be calculated in order to compare the mean values of several samples. The significance level of the F-ratio can then be assessed by comparing it with the distribution of F-values that is obtained by randomly allocating the observed data values to samples. Procedures of this type, which are called *randomization tests*, are discussed further in Chapter 9

(e) A method of analysis can be used which recognizes that because of the special nature of the data they will have some particular known non-normal distribution

The first part of this chapter is concerned primarily with the last of these possibilities, concentrating on situations where there are count or proportion data. With count data, the Poisson distribution takes over from the normal distribution the role of being the standard distribution that can be assumed to apply in the absence of evidence to the contrary. A number of methods for analysing count data are therefore available, based on the assumption that these data have a Poisson distribution. With proportion data, what is observed is the proportion of times that a certain event (a 'success') occurs when there have been N opportunities for this event to occur. In this case the standard distribution that can be assumed for the count of the number of successes is the binomial distribution with N trials and a probability π of a success at each trial. Again, methods have been developed specifically for handling data from distribution.

Another type of data that requires some attention comes from survival studies, where these involve either observing survival times for the items or subjects being studied, or observing the proportions surviving for certain specified periods of time. In this case, special data analysis methods are required, since survival times tend to have distinctly non-normal distributions. A brief introduction to these methods is provided in Section 8.9.

Many of the models for data that are considered in this chapter can be considered to fall within a general category of generalized linear models. These have the characteristic that the expected value of an observation is given by a function of a linear combination of some explanatory variables, while the deviations from expected values have one of a number of possible distributions. A powerful approach to data analysis, which is discussed in Section 8.10, involves modelling data by making an intelligent choice from the many options available for a generalized linear model.

Finally, the chapter concludes with a mention of multivariate statistical methods, which are designed to analyse several related variables at the same time. Many of these methods are obvious generalizations of standard univariate methods, but others involve new concepts. Researchers need to be aware of these techniques because it is possible to have patterns in data that are not clear until the effects of several variables are considered together.

8.2 The analysis of count data

With count data, what is recorded is the number of cases that fall within certain categories. The simplest situation is where these categories relate to one variable only. For example, the records in a factory might show that there were the following numbers of accidents last year on different days of the week: Monday, 25; Tuesday, 15; Wednesday, 14; Thursday, 10; Friday, 21. It is then interesting to determine whether there is any evidence that the probability of an accident varies according to the day of the week.

A slightly more complicated situation occurs when there are two variables involved in the categories. An example of a situation of this type is provided in Table 8.1, which shows the number of deaths from tuberculosis according to the nature of the disease and the sex of the sufferer. Here, there might be some interest in knowing whether there is any evidence that males and females differ in their susceptibility to the two forms of tuberculosis. A two way table of counts, possibly with more than two categories for one or both of the two variables being considered, is sometimes called a *contingency table*.

An example where categories depend on three variables is shown in Table 8.2. These data, which were used as an example by

Table 8.1. *Cases of deaths from tuberculosis classified according to the nature of the disease and the sex of the sufferer. Original data from Everitt (1977)*

	Males	Female	Total
TB of respiratory system	3534	1319	4853
Other forms of TB	270	252	522
Total	3804	1571	5375

Table 8.2. *A group of 1330 patients classified according to their blood pressure levels, their serum cholesterol levels, and the presence or absence of heart disease. (Ku and Kullbach, 1974)*

	Blood pressure (mmHg)	Serum cholesterol (mg/100 ml)				Total
		< 200	200–219	220–259	260+	
Heart disease	< 127	2	3	3	4	12
	127–146	3	2	1	3	9
	147–166	8	11	6	6	31
	167+	7	12	11	11	41
No heart disease	< 127	117	121	47	22	307
	127–146	85	98	43	20	246
	147–166	119	209	68	43	439
	167+	67	99	46	33	245
Total		408	555	225	142	1330

Ku and Kullback (1974), involve 1330 patients classified according to the presence or absence of heart disease, the level of blood pressure and the level of serum cholesterol. In this case there might be interest in questions such as: is the presence or absence of heart disease related to the levels of blood pressure and serum cholesterol?

8.3 Chi-squared tests on count data

Chi-squared tests provide a simple way to answer many questions relating to count data with one or two variables of classification since all that is necessary to carry out these tests is the ability to calculate a set of expected frequencies with which the observed frequencies can be compared. Given these expected frequencies, the Pearson chi-squared statistic X_P^2 can be determined from the equation

$$X_P^2 = \sum (O_i - E_i)^2 / E_i,$$

where O_i denotes the ith observed frequency, E_i denotes the corresponding expected frequency, and the summation is over all the frequencies involved. By its nature, this statistic will be large in situations where the observed and expected frequencies are very different, and it will be small when the observed and expected frequencies are similar. A value of zero can occur only if all the observed frequencies are exactly equal to their expected values. Thus the X_P^2 statistic is an objective measure of the agreement between the observed and expected frequencies.

The statistic X_P^2 will approximately follow a chi-squared distribution if the items are classified independently, the expected frequencies are all 'large' and they are determined for the correct model. Therefore, the procedure for a chi-squared test involves comparing the observed X_P^2 value with the percentage points of the chi-squared distribution that are found in statistical tables. If the observed value exceeds the 5% point then this is usually regarded as evidence that the observed frequencies do not agree well with the expected frequencies.

The assumptions needed for the use of the chi-squared distribution require some amplification. The independence requirement means that the classification of each item is unrelated to the classification of any other item. For example, for the tuberculosis data, this assumption would not be valid if for some reason the data included the count for a batch of patients from a hospital where they had to be males with tuberculosis of the respiratory system.

The requirement that the expected frequencies should be 'large' is sometimes taken to mean that they should be all at least five. However, there is evidence to suggest that in practice this rule can be relaxed providing that the average frequency is greater than two for a test at the 5% level and greater than four for a test at the 1% level (Rayner and Best, 1989, p. 23).

In using a table of percentage points of the chi-squared distribution, it is necessary to determine the degrees of freedom that apply, where this is the number of expected frequencies that have to be determined independently before all the expected frequencies are fixed. In simple cases with one or two variables of classification the degrees of freedom can be determined easily from this definition. In more complicated situation a useful rule is that the degrees of freedom are given by the formula

$$df = n - q,$$

where n is the total number of frequencies and q is the number of parameters that have to be estimated in order to calculate the expected frequencies. It is helpful to remember that if the model being tested is correct then the mean value of X_P^2 is equal to the degrees of freedom. Therefore, there is no need to consult tables to see whether a value of X_P^2 is significantly large if this value is less than or equal to the degrees of freedom.

The Pearson chi-squared statistic is not the only possible measure of the agreement between observed and expected frequencies. An alternative, is the log-likelihood chi-squared statistic

$$X_L^2 = \sum 2O_i \log_e (O_i/E_i),$$

where the summation is over the n frequencies. This will be approximately equal to X_P^2 whenever the observed and expected frequencies are not very small, and the differences between observed and expected frequencies are not very large. The discussion above on the need for expected frequencies to be 'large', and the remarks on the determination of degrees of freedom apply equally well to X_P^2 and X_L^2. Sometimes X_L^2 is called the *deviance*, particularly in the context of log-linear modelling.

Example 8.1: Testing whether the probability of an accident varies with the days of the week

As a simple example of a chi-squared test, consider the data given earlier on the numbers of accidents in a factory last year on different days of the week (Monday, 25; Tuesday, 15; Wednesday, 14; Thursday, 10; Friday, 21). The total number of accidents is 85. Therefore, on the hypothesis that an accident is equally likely to occur on any day of the week the expected frequency is $85/5 = 17$ accidents for each day. There are four degrees of freedom since once 17 accidents are allocated to each of the days Monday to

Thursday it is fixed that the remaining 17 accidents must be allocated to Friday.

With these expected frequencies, the Pearson chi-squared statistic is

$$X_P^2 = \{(25 - 17)^2/17\} + \{(15 - 17)^2/17\} + \{(14 - 17)^2/17\}$$
$$+ \{(10 - 17)^2/17\} + \{(21 - 17)^2/17\}$$
$$= 8.35.$$

Chi-squared tables show that the probability of a value this large occurring by chance is between 0.1 and 0.05, so that there is no clear evidence that accidents are more likely to occur on some days of the week than others. The log-likelihood chi-square statistic is

$$X_L^2 = 2\{25 \cdot \log_e (25/17) + 15 \cdot \log_e (15/17) + 14 \cdot \log_e(14/17)$$
$$+ 10 \cdot \log_e (10/17) + 21 \cdot \log_e (21/17)\}$$
$$= 8.35,$$

again with four degrees of freedom. This is the same as X_P^2 to two decimal places so that the significance level is the same.

Example 8.2 Testing for an association between sex and the classification of cases of tuberculosis

Consider now the question of whether the data shown in Table 8.1 suggest that the classification of cases of tuberculosis into those of the respiratory system and others is related to the sex of the patient. One way to answer this involves calculating expected frequencies on the assumption that the two classifications are independent, so that the probability that tuberculosis is of the respiratory system is the same for males and females. The observed and expected frequencies can then be compared using X_P^2 or X_L^2.

Consider first the expected frequency of males with tuberculosis of the respiratory system. To calculate this, note that the overall proportion of cases of tuberculosis in the respiratory system is $4853/5375 = 0.9029$. Therefore, assuming that the probability of this type of tuberculosis is the same for males and females, the expected frequency is $3804 \times 4853/5357 = 3804 \times 0.9029 = 3434.6$, which is the column total times the row total divided by the overall total from Table 8.1.

Once one frequency has been calculated the other expected frequencies can be determined from the row and column totals in Table 8.1. Thus, the expected number of males with other forms of tuberculosis is $3804 - 3434.6 = 369.4$ (since the total number of males is 3804), the expected number of females with tuberculosis of the respiratory system is $4853 - 3434.6 = 1418.4$ (since the total number of cases of this type of disease is 4853), and the expected number of females with other forms of tuberculosis is $1571 - 1418.4 = 152.6$ (since the total number of females is 1571). The four expected frequencies are therefore as shown in Table 8.3, with those in parentheses being derived from the row and column totals. The fact that all the expected frequencies are fixed once one is determined means that there is one degree of freedom for determining these frequencies.

With the calculated expected frequencies, Pearson's chi-squared statistic is

$$X_P^2 = \{(3534 - 3434.6)^2/3434.6\} + \{(1319 - 1418.4)^2/1418.4\}$$
$$+ \{(270 - 369.4)^2/369.4\} + \{(252 - 152.6)^2/152.6\}$$
$$= 101.34,$$

which is very highly significantly large when compared to the percentage points of the chi-squared distribution with one degree of freedom. Therefore, there is very strong evidence that the basis of the calculation of the expected frequencies is not correct. In other words, the classifications based on the type of tuberculosis and the sex of the patient do not seem to be independent.

The log-likelihood chi-squared statistic is

$$X_L^2 = 2\{3534 \cdot \log_e (3534/3434.6) + 1319 \cdot \log_e (1319/1418.4)$$
$$+ 270 \cdot \log_e (270/369.4) + 252 \log_e (252/152.6)\}$$
$$= 93.53.$$

This is smaller than X_P^2, but is still highly significantly large.

Before leaving this example, there are two general points that should be mentioned. First, when doing calculations for a 2×2 table as in this example it is common to make use of what is called *Yates' correction*, with the idea of improving the chi-squared approximation for the significance level of the data. This correction, which is usually associated with X_P^2 rather than X_L^2, involves moving each of the observed frequencies by an amount $\frac{1}{2}$ towards the corresponding expected frequency before calculating the test

Table 8.3. *Expected frequencies to compare with the expected frequencies in Table 8.1*

	Males	Female	Total
TB of respiratory systems	3434.6	(1418.4)	4853
Other forms of TB	(369.4)	(152.6)	522
Total	3804	1571	5375

statistic. Thus X_P^2 is changed to $\sum(|E_i - O_i| - \frac{1}{2})^2/E_i$. With large observed and expected frequencies this modification has very little effect, but with small frequencies it may reduce the significance level substantially.

It was originally thought that Yates' correction would always improve the chi-squared approximation for a 2×2 table. However, later research showed that this is not the case so that the value of using it is debatable. For a further discussion on this matter, including a description of *Fisher's exact test* for small frequencies, see Madansky (1988, p. 256).

The second general comment that can be made is that the test for the independence of the row and column variables used in this example can be generalized in an obvious way for contingency tables with R rows and C columns. The expected frequency to compare with any observed frequency is the row total times the column total divided by the overall total, and it will be found that once these frequencies have been calculated for $R - 1$ rows and $C - 1$ columns the remaining expected frequencies are fixed by the row and column totals. Therefore, there are $(R - 1) \times (C - 1)$ degrees of freedom for the chi-squared statistics X_P^2 and X_L^2.

8.4 McNemar's test for correlated proportions

It is important to realize that the chi-squared test used in the last example is not appropriate for all 2×2 tables. One example where it does not apply is where subjects are matched on a number of variables such as age, sex, duration of illness, etc. and one subject in each pair (preferably chosen at random) gets some treatment while the other is an untreated control. Each pair is then classified according to the outcome for the two patients. In a situation like this the pair is really the experimental unit, rather than the subject, and the usual chi-squared test is not appropriate for testing for a treatment effect. Instead, the appropriate test is McNemar's test for correlated proportions (McNemar, 1955), which is illustrated by the following example.

Example 8.3: Comparison of control and treated pollution sites

Suppose that an experiment is carried out to assess the value of a new treatment on some sites with oil pollution. This is done by making up pairs of sites that are initially similar in the level of pollution, and then choosing one site from each pair for the new treatment. After a period of time the sites are inspected and categorized as 'improved' or 'unchanged' in terms of the degree of pollution damage, with the results shown in Table 8.4.

The usual chi-squared test can be applied here. It tests whether the probability of improvement of the treated site is independent of the improvement of its matched site. However, this test is not of much interest since the whole point of matching the sites was to find pairs with similar probabilities of improvement in the absence of the treatment. Hence the usual chi-squared test just examines whether the matching was successful. What is really of interest is to know whether there was any tendency for either the treated or the untreated site to improve in those pairs where only one of the sites improved. In other words, is 12 (the number of times that only the untreated site improved) significantly different from 18 (the number of times that only the treated site improved)?

It is expected that the frequencies of the two types of discrepant pairs will be equal if the treatment has no effect. With a total of 30 discrepant pairs, this gives an expected frequency of 15 for each of the two types and the Pearson chi-squared statistic is

$$X_P^2 = \sum (O_i - E_i)^2 / E_i$$
$$= \{(12 - 15)^2 / 15\} + \{(18 - 15)^2 / 15\}$$
$$= 1.20.$$

There is one degree of freedom, since once the expected frequency of one of the discrepant pairs is fixed the other must be the difference between this number and 30. Comparison with chi-squared tables shows that the result is not at all significant, so that there is no evidence of a treatment effect.

Table 8.4. *The improvement of polluted sites in a matched pair experiment*

	Treated site		Total
	Unchanged	Improved	
Untreated site			
Unchanged	2	18	20
Improved	12	18	30
Total	14	36	50

The message to draw from this example is the need to make sure that the chi-squared test that is employed really does answer the question of interest, and not just a trivial question of no real importance.

8.5 Log-linear models

With multiple regression (Section 4.4) the model assumed is

$$Y = \beta_0 + \beta_1 X_1 + \beta_2 X_2 +, \ldots, + \beta_p X_p + \varepsilon,$$

where Y is a dependent variable, the X's are explanatory variables, and the error ε is normally distributed with mean zero and a constant variance. A log-linear model is similar but the dependent variable Y is a count that is assumed to be given by the equation

$$Y = \exp(\beta_0 + \beta_1 X_1 + \beta_2 X_2 +, \ldots, + \beta_p X_p) + \varepsilon.$$

The X variables are still thought of as accounting for variation in Y and ε is still a random error with mean zero. However, the errors are such that Y has a Poisson distribution instead of a normal distribution. There are two reasons for using this type of model with count data in preference to the standard multiple regression model. First, the use of the exponential function ensures that negative expected counts cannot occur. Second, the discrete Poisson distribution is more appropriate than the continuous normal distribution for count data.

The log-linear model can be written in the alternative form

$$Y = \exp(\beta_0) \cdot \exp(\beta_1 X_1) \cdot \exp(\beta_2 X_2), \ldots, \exp(\beta_p X_p) + \varepsilon.$$

This emphasizes that the effects of the different regression variables are assumed to operate multiplicatively rather than additively. That is to say, there is a basic frequency $\exp(\beta_0)$, which is modified by being multiplied by the factors $\exp(\beta_1 X_1)$, $\exp(\beta_2 X_2)$, ..., $\exp(\beta_p X_p)$ to account for the effects of the regression variables $X_1, X_2, \ldots, X_p$, respectively.

Fitting a log-linear model involves finding the values of the β parameters so as to make the log-likelihood chi-squared value as small as possible. This is more complicated than fitting a multiple regression and usually requires iterative calculations. Computer programs for log-linear modelling often allow counts to depend on both quantitative variables and factors, with the factors being accounted for by dummy variables in the manner that has been discussed in Section 7.14.

Regression modelling of count data does not necessarily have to be done with a log-linear model. If the counts being analysed are all reasonably large (say five or more) then it may well be reasonable to treat them as being approximately normally distributed. If, in addition, the counts do not vary greatly then it will be reasonable to regard the variances of the counts to be more or less constant. It follows that it is valid to use a multiple linear regression model to analyse the data rather than a log-linear model. This is the argument that can be used to justify using linear regression for analysing road death statistics in Example 6.1 and Exercise 1 in Chapter 6.

In assessing a log-linear model for a set of data there are four aspects of the fit that can be considered:

(a) The goodness of fit of the model can be measured by one or both of the log-likelihood and Pearson chi-squared statistics defined above ($X_L^2 = 2\sum O_i \log_e(O_i/E_i)$ and $X_P^2 = \sum(O_i - E_i)^2/E_i$), with the degrees of freedom being $n - 1 - p$, where n is the total number of frequencies and p is the number of regression variables. If the chi-squared statistics are significantly large in comparison with tables of percentage points of the chi-squared distribution then there is evidence that the model being considered does not fit the data

(b) The residuals $O_i - E_i$ can be studied to see whether there are some observed frequencies that are fitted particularly badly by the model. Since the standard deviation of O_i is approximately $\sqrt{E_i}$, the ith standardized residuals can be defined to be

$$R_i = (O_i - E_i)/\sqrt{E_i}.$$

Then, one simple way to detect a poor fit is to isolate the residuals that are more than two standard deviations from zero, so that $|R_i| \geqslant 2$. These residuals are significantly large at approximately the 5% level

(c) The most important regression variables can be determined by comparing the estimated β values with their standard errors. Any estimate that is more than two standard errors from zero, which is shown by

$$|(\text{Estimate})/(\text{Standard Error})| > 2,$$

is significantly different from zero at approximately the 5% level

(d) The improvement in the fit that is obtained by adding one or more extra X variables into the model can be assessed by considering the reduction in the log-likelihood chi-squared value (the 'deviance') that is obtained through using the extra variables. The significance of this reduction can be determined by comparing it with the percentage points of the chi-squared distribution using the number of extra X variables involved as degrees of freedom. A significantly large reduction indicates that the extra X variables make a useful contribution to the model. This method of assessing the value of X variables, which is sometimes called the *analysis of deviance*, is a generalization of the extra sum of squares principle that is used with multiple regression (Section 4.5)

The following example shows how these four ways of looking at the fit of a model are used in practice.

Example 8.4: Levels of church attendance related to religion and age

The data in Table 8.5 come from Knoke and Burke (1980), and show the level of church attendance related to religion and age for 1591 subjects in a social survey. Here a log-linear model can be used to see how the counts in the different cells of the table depend on religion, age, and the level of church attendance. One way to do this involves fitting a series of models that become more

Table 8.5. *Church attendance related to religion and age from a sample survey carried out in 1972. (Knoke and Burke, 1980)*

| Religion | Age | Church attendance | | | Total |
		Low	Medium	High	
Non-Catholic	Young	322	122	141	585
Non-Catholic	Old	250	152	194	596
Catholic	Young	88	45	106	239
Catholic	Old	28	24	119	171
Total		688	343	560	1591

and more complicated, to see what level of complication is needed to get a good fit to the data.

Model 1 assumes that the three factors religion, age and church attendance operate independently. This requires a dummy variable for religion (0 for non-Catholics, 1 for Catholic), a dummy variable for age (0 for young, 1 for old), and two dummy variables for church attendance. The first church attendance variable is 1 for low attendance and 0 otherwise. The second church attendance variable is 1 for medium attendance and 0 otherwise. Table 8.6 shows the values of the regression variables for the 12 counts for this model.

The model can be estimated by any of the available computer programs for log-linear modelling. For this example a modified version of a program published by Rindskopf (1987) was used. The log-likelihood chi-squared of the model is $X_L^2 = 150.86$ and the Pearson chi-squared is $X_P^2 = 141.03$. With $n - p - 1 = 12 - 4 - 1 = 7$ degrees of freedom both these values show that the model is a poor fit. Part (A) of Table 8.7 shows the observed and expected frequencies for the fitted model. The poor fit is indicated by the fact that seven of the standardized residuals are outside the range ± 2. Part (B) of Table 8.7 shows the estimated parameter values with their standard errors. The ratios of the parameter estimates to their standard errors indicate that the effects of religion and attendance levels are highly significant, but the effect of age is not.

Since the independence model does not appear to be appropriate, a more complicated model involving interactions between the factors must be considered. It may be recalled from section 7.14 that dummy variables for interactions can be set up by

Table 8.6. *Regression variables for a log-linear model of the data in Table 8.5 (Model 1: independent effects of religion, age and church attendance)*

Y	X_1	X_2	X_3	X_4
322	0	0	1	0
250	0	1	1	0
88	1	0	1	0
28	1	1	1	0
124	0	0	0	1
152	0	1	0	1
45	1	0	0	1
24	1	1	0	1
141	0	0	0	0
194	0	1	0	0
106	1	0	0	0
119	1	1	0	0

multiplying together the dummy variables for the main effects of factors. Therefore, an interaction between religion and age can be allowed for by including the variable $X_5 = X_1 \cdot X_2$ in the log-linear model. The effect of religion (X_1) is then allowed to vary with age (X_2). *Model 2*, which includes this interaction term fits hardly any better than *Model 1*. Goodness of fit statistics are $X_L^2 = 141.65$ and $X_P^2 = 144.33$, both with six degrees of freedom.

Model 3, which can be considered next, allows for an interaction of attendance with religion and attendance with age, in addition to an interaction between religion and age. To allow for a religion by church attendance interaction, the two variables $X_6 = X_1 \cdot X_3$ and $X_7 = X_1 \cdot X_4$ can be introduced, and to allow for church attendance to depend on age, the two variables $X_8 = X_2 \cdot X_3$ and $X_9 = X_2 \cdot X_4$, can also be introduced. Table 8.8 shows the values of all the X variables that are then being used.

The goodness of fit statistics for *Model 3* are $X_L^2 = 7.25$ and $X_P^2 = 7.16$, both with two degrees of freedom. Hence this model fits the data much better than *Model 1* and *Model 2*, although the goodness of fit statistics are still significantly large at the 5% level. Part (A) of Table 8.9 shows that the standardized residuals are all well within the range ± 2, while part (B) of the table shows that all the estimated coefficients are more than two standard errors from zero, with the exception of the coefficients of X_1 and X_4.

The last five parameters are the most interesting ones for the

Table 8.7. *Details of log-linear Model 1, allowing for independent effects of religion, age, and level of church attendance, when it is fitted to the data of Table 8.6*

(A) *Observed and expected frequencies*

Case	Observed	Expected	Standardized residual	Case	Observed	Expected	Standardized residual
1	322	264.9	3.51[a]	2	250	246.0	0.25
3	88	91.8	-0.40	4	28	85.3	-6.20[a]
5	124	132.8	-0.77	6	152	123.4	2.58[a]
7	45	46.0	-0.15	8	24	42.8	-2.87[a]
9	141	215.6	-5.08[a]	10	194	200.2	-0.44
11	106	74.7	3.62[a]	12	119	69.4	5.95[a]

[a]Outside the range ±2.

(B) *Parameter estimates*

Beta	Estimate	SE	Ratio	Interpretation of parameter
0	5.3736	—	—	Constant term
1	-1.0597	0.0573	-18.49	The overall effect of religion
2	-0.0741	0.0501	-1.48	The overall effect of age
3	0.2059	0.0569	3.62	The low attendance frequency
4	-0.4844	0.0684	-7.08	The medium attendance frequency

Table 8.8. *Regression variables for a log-linear Model 3 for the data in Table 8.5, allowing for an interaction between religion and church attendance and between age and church attendance*

Y	X_1	X_2	X_3	X_4	X_5	X_6	X_7	X_8	X_9
322	0	0	1	0	0	0	0	0	0
250	0	1	1	0	0	0	0	1	0
88	1	0	1	0	0	1	0	0	0
28	1	1	1	0	1	1	0	1	0
124	0	0	0	1	0	0	0	0	0
152	0	1	0	1	0	0	0	0	1
45	1	0	0	1	0	0	1	0	0
24	1	1	0	1	1	0	1	0	1
141	0	0	0	0	0	0	0	0	0
194	0	1	0	0	0	0	0	0	0
106	1	0	0	0	0	0	0	'0	0
119	1	1	0	0	1	0	0	0	0

interpretation of the data. From the estimated coefficient of X_5 (−0.53) it seems that there are a relatively small number of old Catholics. From the estimated coefficients of X_6 and X_7 (−1.30 and −1.03) it seems that there are relatively small numbers of low and medium attendance Catholics. From the estimated coefficients of X_8 and X_9 (−0.76 and −0.31) it seems that there are relatively small numbers of low and medium attendance older people. In other words, the data suggest that Catholics tend to be younger than the average age of people attending church, and that high church attendance is more likely with Catholics and older people.

It would be possible to consider a *Model 4* which allows for a three factor interaction between religion, age and church attendance. In other words, the levels of church attendance could be allowed to be different for the four classes young non-Catholics, old non-Catholics, young Catholics and old Catholics. However, this model is *saturated* in the sense that it must fit the data perfectly since it has as many parameters as frequencies. Therefore, *Model 4* is not very informative. Nevertheless, since the model without the three factor interaction has chi-squared goodness of fit statistics that are significantly large, it follows that three factor interaction terms do make a significant contribution towards accounting for the variance in the data.

The *analysis of deviance* for the models that have been fitted to the church attendance data is summarized in Table 8.10. It can be

Table 8.9. *Details of the log-linear Model 3 fitted to the data in Table 8.8*

(A) Observed and expected frequencies

Case	Observed	Expected	Standardized residual	Case	Observed	Expected	Standardized residual
1	322	329.05	−0.39	2	250	242.95	0.45
3	88	80.95	0.78	4	28	35.05	−1.19
5	124	127.90	−0.34	6	152	148.10	0.32
7	45	41.10	0.61	8	24	27.90	−0.74
9	141	130.05	0.96	10	194	204.95	−0.76
11	106	116.95	−1.01	12	119	108.05	1.05

(B) Parameter estimates

Beta	Estimate	SE	Ratio	Interpretation of parameter
0	4.8679	—	—	Constant term
1	−0.1062	0.1087	−0.98	The overall effect of religion
2	0.4548	0.0996	4.57	The overall effect of age
3	0.9283	0.0955	9.72	The low attendance frequency
4	−0.0167	0.1143	−0.15	The medium attendance frequency
5	−0.5339	0.1221	−4.37	Religion by age
6	−1.2961	0.1368	−9.48	Low attendance by religion
7	−1.0291	0.1614	−6.38	Medium attendance by religion
8	−0.7581	0.1204	−6.30	Low attendance by age
9	−0.3082	0.1408	−2.19	Medium attendance by age

Table 8.10. *Analysis of deviance for the models fitted to the church attendance data*

Fitted Model	$X_L{}^2$	df	Difference $X_L{}^2$	df
Model 1: factors with independent effects	150.86^c	7		
			9.21^b	1
Model 2: as for *Model 1* plus a religion × age interaction	141.65^c	6		
			134.40^c	4
Model 3: as for *Model 2* plus religion × church attendance and age × church attendance interactions	7.25^a	2		
			7.25^a	2
Model 4: saturated model with all possible effects	0.00	0		

^{a}Significantly large at the 5% level.
^{b}Significantly large at the 1% level.
^{c}Significantly large at the 0.1% level.

seen that the independence model has a very poor fit ($X_L^2 = 150.86$); there is a highly significant improvement in the fit when a religion by age interaction is added ($X_L^2 = 9.21$); a further very highly significant improvement when religion by church attendance and age by church attendance interactions are added ($X_L^2 = 134.40$); and yet a further significant improvement if the saturated model is fitted ($X_L^2 = 7.25$).

8.6 Extraneous variance

It is not uncommon to find that only the uninformative saturated model fits a set of data when the counts in different cells are in the hundreds or more. Often this just reflects the fact that few models are perfect, so that a significant lack of fit can be expected with very large data sets. However, an alternative explanation is that the observed frequencies do not follow a Poisson distribution. If the latter explanation is correct then the variance of an observed count may exceed its expected value, so that there is what is called *extraneous variance* present.

Extraneous variance occurs when the individuals being classified are not providing independent data. For example, in the context of Example 8.4 on church attendance it could be that some of the people surveyed were husbands and wives who tended to be in exactly the same categories for age, religion and church attendance. Then the effect of this would be to raise the variance of each of the data counts above what is expected for a sample of independent subjects.

One way of taking into account extraneous variance involves assuming that the variances of all the data counts are multiplied by the same *heterogeneity factor*, H, which can be estimated by either $\hat{H}_L = X_L^2/(n - p - 1)$ or $\hat{H}_P = X_P^2/(n - p - 1)$. Then, the variances of the estimated coefficients of the X variables in the log-linear model can be adjusted for extraneous variance by multiplying them by $\hat{H}_L$ or $\hat{H}_P$. McCullagh and Nelder (1989) suggest that $\hat{H}_P$ is best for this purpose.

As an example, of the adjustment, consider the estimate of the coefficient for the overall effect of age that is shown in Table 8.9. This estimate is 0.4548, with associated variance (the standard error squared) of $0.0996^2 = 0.00992$. Pearson's chi-squared value for the fitted model is 7.16 with 2 degrees of freedom, so that the estimated heterogeneity factor is $\hat{H}_P = 7.16/2 = 3.58$. Hence, the variance adjusted for extraneous variance is $0.00992 \times 3.58 = 0.0355$, and the adjusted standard error is $\sqrt{0.0355} = 0.188$.

The possibility of extraneous variance being present with many data sets has led some statisticians to propose that this correction to the variances of the coefficients of X values should be used whenever goodness of fit statistics exceed their degrees of freedom. However, it is important to distinguish between cases where extraneous variance may genuinely exist and cases where the log-linear model being considered is simply wrong. Unfortunately, the situation will often be that the data analyst does not know which of the two situations is the correct one.

8.7 Using base rates

Occasions do arise where there is a good reason to believe that expected counts will be proportional to some known constants in the absence of any effects of the predictor variables used in a log-linear model. For example, the number of accidents in a factory in one month can be expected to be proportional to the number of working days in the month, although it may depend also on other variables such as the season and the amount of output produced. In cases like this, it is desirable to estimate the coefficients of the predictor variables after making an allowance for the expected base rates. The following example shows how this can be done.

Example 8.5: Relating numbers of accidents to working days and the output produced

Suppose that the numbers of accidents per month in a factory are as shown in Table 8.11 for a period of six months. Here a reasonable model for the number of accidents in the absence of any production effects is

$$Y_i = \exp(\beta_0)W_i + \varepsilon_i,$$

where Y_i is the number of accidents in month i, for which the number of working days is W_i, and ε_i is a random 'error'. The effect of production can be added to the model by changing it to

$$Y_i = \exp(\beta_0 + \beta_i P_i)W_i + \varepsilon_i,$$

where P_i is the production in month i. Finally, the effect of the different working days can be included in the exponential term by rewriting the equation as

$$Y_i = \exp\{\beta_0 + \log_e(W_i) + \beta_i P_i\} + \varepsilon_i.$$

On this basis, the appropriate adjustment to allow for inherently different base rates for the number of accidents in different months involves adding the $\log_e(W_i)$ terms into the argument of the exponential function. In effect, $\log_e(W_i)$ is treated as a predictor variable with a known coefficient of exactly one. This type of adjustment is allowed in some computer programs for fitting log-linear models, with the quantity $\log_e(W_i)$ sometimes being called the *offset*.

The computer program published by Rindskopf (1987) that was used to do the calculations for Example 8.4 allows for base rates. Using the program, the estimated equation for the expected number of accidents in a month with W working days and a production of P is

$$\hat{Y} = \exp\{-1.418 + \log_e(W) + 0.063P\},$$

with the standard error of the estimated coefficient of P being 0.066, and goodness of fit statistics being $X_P^2 = 5.71$ and

Table 8.11. *Accidents in a factory in a six-month period, with the number of working days per month and a measure of the total production in each month*

Number of accidents (Y)	Working days in month (W)	Production in month (P)
5	20	98
10	21	130
7	16	80
12	23	134
8	20	89
17	22	112

$X_L^2 = 5.51$, with four degrees of freedom. Since the goodness of fit statistics are not significantly large in comparison to the percentage points of the chi-squared distribution the model is a good fit to the data. However, the estimated coefficient of P is not significantly different from zero at the 5% level since the ratio of this estimate to its standard error is well inside the range ± 2.

8.8 The analysis of proportion data

Consider again the data in Table 8.1 on the number of deaths from tuberculosis according to the nature of the disease and the sex of the sufferer. This can be treated as an example of proportion data; interest being in whether the proportion of males with tuberculosis of the respiratory system $(3534/3804 = 0.929)$ is significantly different from that of females $(1319/1571 = 0.840)$.

Another example where the critical information can be thought of in terms of proportions is provided by the data shown in Table 8.12, which come from Everitt (1977, p. 30). Here, the proportions are for the incidence of tics in samples of maladjusted children of different ages and sexes, and there might be interest in whether the proportions vary significantly with these factors.

In many cases, proportion data can be treated as count data and analysed by chi-squared tests, as described in Section 8.3. It just happens that the variable of particular interest has two categories. In fact Example 8.2 provides an analysis of the tuberculosis data that gives an answer to the question of whether males and females have the same probability of having tuberculosis of the respiratory system, given that they have some form of tuberculosis. In more

Table 8.12. *Results of a survey of maladjusted children to determine the incidence of tics. (Everitt, 1977)*

Age range	Sex	Number with tics	Total	Proportion
5–9	Boys	13	70	0.186
	Girls	3	26	0.115
10–12	Boys	26	82	0.317
	Girls	11	40	0.275
13–15	Boys	15	71	0.211
	Girls	2	29	0.069

complicated cases, a log-linear model can be considered, and again it does not matter that there happens to be two categories for the variable of particular interest.

However, frequently the researcher is naturally led to think of the proportion of cases within a certain category as being the dependent variable in the data, and attempts to account for the variation in this proportion in terms of the other variables that have been recorded. This leads to the idea of modelling the data using a *logistic regression model*.

The general framework for this type of model is that there are m groups to be compared, with group i consisting of n_i subjects, of which Y_i exhibit a positive response (a 'success') and $n_i - Y_i$ exhibit a negative response (a 'failure'). The individuals in group i are described by values X_{i1}, X_{i2}, ..., X_{ip} for variables X_1 to X_p, and the assumption is made that the probability of a success for an individual in group i is given by

$$\pi_i = \frac{\exp{(\beta_0 + \beta_1 X_{i1} + \beta_2 X_{i2} +, \ldots, + \beta_p X_{ip})}}{1 + \exp{(\beta_0 + \beta_1 X_{i1} + \beta_2 X_{i2} +, \ldots, + \beta_p X_{ip})}}$$

where the X variables take into account the effects of quantitative variables or factors. This probability must apply to all individuals in the group, irrespective of the successes or failures of the other individuals in that or any other group. The probability of a failure is $1 - \pi_i$.

The function that is being used here to relate the probability of a success to the X variables is a called a logistic function, which explains why fitting this model is called logistic regression. This form of function forces the estimated probabilities to lie within the range zero to one, which is why it is more sensible than a linear regression model that does not embody this constraint.

Logistic regression, like log-linear modelling, requires iterative calculations to be carried out by a computer program. Assessing the fit of models also involves essentially the same four procedures as with log-linear models:

(a) The goodness of fit can be measured by the log-likelihood chi-squared statistic (the deviance)

$$X^2_L = 2\sum_{i=1}^{m} Y_i \log_e [Y_i/(n_i\hat{\pi}_i)]$$
$$+ (n_i - Y_i)\log_e[(n_i - Y_i)/\{n_i(1 - \hat{\pi}_i)\}],$$

and the Pearson chi-squared statistic

$$X^2_P = \sum_{i=1}^{m} (Y_i - n_i\hat{\pi}_i)^2/\{n_i\hat{\pi}_i(1 - \hat{\pi}_i)\},$$

where $\hat{\pi}_i$ is the estimated probability of a 'success' for the ith group. The degrees of freedom are $m - p - 1$ for both statistics, where m is the total number of groups and p is the number of regression variables

(b) The residuals, $Y_i - n_i\hat{\pi}_i$, can be studied to see whether there are some observed frequencies that are fitted particularly badly by the model. Here $\hat{\pi}_i$ is the estimated probability of a success in group i according to the fitted logistic regression equation. The standard deviation of Y_i is estimated by $\sqrt{\{n_i\hat{\pi}_i(1 - \hat{\pi}_i)\}}$, so that standardized residuals are given by

$$R_i = (Y_i - n_i\hat{\pi}_i)/\sqrt{\{n_i\hat{\pi}_i(1 - \pi_i)\}}.$$

These residuals are significantly different from zero at approximately the 5% level when they are outside the range ± 2

(c) The important regression variables can be determined by comparing the estimated β values with their standard errors. Any estimate that is more than two standard errors from zero, so that

$$|(\text{Estimate})/(\text{Standard Error})| > 2,$$

is significantly different from zero at approximately the 5% level

(d) An analysis of deviance can be carried out to see whether the reduction in X^2_L due to adding one or more X variables to the model is significantly large

A further parallel with the situation for log-linear models is that cases arise where a particular model is believed to be appropriate for a set of data, but goodness of fit statistics indicate a lack of fit. Then, one possibility is that the model is indeed correct, but the sample proportions are displaying extraneous variance caused, for example, by some dependence in the responses of the experimental units in the same groups. If this is the case, and the proportional increase in variance is the same for each group, then the extent to which variances exceed those expected from the binomial distribution (the heterogeneity factor, H) can be estimated by $\hat{H}_P = X_P^2/(N - p - 1)$. The alternative estimator $\hat{H}_L = X_L^2/(N - p - 1)$ is also possible, but is not recommended (McCullagh and Nelder, 1989, p. 128).

The estimated heterogeneity factor can be used to correct the variances of the estimated coefficients of X variables in the logistic regression to allow for the extraneous variance by multiplying the variance of each coefficient by $\hat{H}_P$. However, as with log-linear modelling, this type of correction is only appropriate when there are good grounds for believing that lack of fit is due to increased error variances rather than to the model being wrong.

The logistic function is just one of a number of functions that are used to relate the probability of a 'success' to regression variables. There are alternatives that are also frequently used. First, there is the *probit model* for which the probability of a 'success' is given by the equation

$$\pi = \phi(\beta_0 + \beta_1 X_1 + \beta_2 X_2 +, \ldots, + \beta_p X_p),$$

where $\phi(x)$ is the integral from minus infinity to x for the standard normal distribution. Second, there is the *double exponential model* for which the probability of a 'success' is given by

$$\pi = \exp\{ - \exp(\beta_0 + \beta_1 X_1 + \beta_2 X_2 +, \ldots, + \beta_p X_p)\}.$$

The probit model was the first one to be used for handling proportions data because of its relationship to the normal distribution. Early applications included the estimation of LD50 doses of insecticides (the dose that will kill 50% of insects) from experiments that involved trying a range of doses on different groups of insects. In the past there has been some controversy about the relative merits of the logistic and probit models for applications of this type. However, it is now generally accepted that for most sets of data the results obtained from an analysis on proportion data do not depend strongly on the choice of the model, so that the logistic model will be satisfactory for the majority of applications.

The double exponential model is often used for analysing survival data, with the X variables accounting for variables that might influence the probability of survival such as, for example, blood pressure and age. This model, which is called the *proportional hazards model* in this context, is appropriate because in many situations changing the survival time will only change the constant β_0, and not the coefficients of the X variables. This makes it possible to analyse data for cases with a variety of survival periods in a very straightforward way.

Finally, it should be realized that if the proportions to be analysed are all from samples with about the same sizes which are reasonably large, and none of these proportions are close to zero, then it is realistic to consider fitting multiple linear regression models to the data. This is because the sample proportions will be approximately normally distributed with a fairly constant variance so that the assumptions required for linear regression will be met.

Example 8.6: The incidence of maladjusted children with tics.

This example concerns the data on the incidence of maladjusted children with tics that are shown in Table 8.12. There are two potential variables for predicting the probability of a child having tics: age, which can be taken as the centre of each age range (7, 11 or 14), and sex, which can be coded as 0 for boys and 1 for girls.

The logistic regression equation,

$$\pi = \exp(\beta_0)/\{1 + \exp(\beta_0)\},$$

gives a 'null model' in this situation, since it says that the probability of a child having tics is the same for boys and girls of both sexes. It will be called *Model 0*. The estimate of β_0, that minimizes the log-likelihood chi-squared value can be shown in this case to be the value which makes π equal to P, the overall observed proportion of children with tics. In other words, the estimate of β_0, is the value $\hat{\beta}_0$, that satisfies the equation

$$P = \exp(\hat{\beta}_0)/\{1 + \exp(\hat{\beta}_0)\},$$

so that

$$\hat{\beta}_0 = \log_e\{P/(1 - P)\}.$$

The corresponding log-likelihood and Pearson chi-squared values, which are found by putting $\hat{\pi}_i = P$ for all i, are $X_L^2 = 12.12$ and

259

$X_P^2 = 11.23$. These both have five degrees of freedom since there are six proportions and one parameter is being estimated. The statistics are significantly large at the 5% level in comparison with the percentage points of the chi-squared distribution so that there is evidence that the null model is not appropriate.

There are a number of models that can be considered to relate the probability of tics to the age and sex of the children. One possibility is what will be called *Model 1*, with

$$\hat{\pi} = \frac{\exp(\beta_0 + \beta_1 \text{Age} + \beta_2 \text{Sex})}{1 + \exp(\beta_0 + \beta_1 \text{Age} + \beta_2 \text{Sex})}$$

This has data as set out in Table 8.13. The fitted equation is

$$\hat{\pi} = \frac{\exp(-1.30 + 0.014 \text{Age} - 0.458 \text{Sex})}{1 + \exp(-1.30 + 0.014 \text{Age} - 0.458 \text{Sex})}$$

where the standard error for the coefficient of the Age variable is 0.049 and the standard error for the coefficient of the Sex variable is 0.316. Neither of the coefficients is more than two standard errors from zero. The goodness of fit statistics, $X_L^2 = 9.87$ and $X_P^2 = 9.78$, both with three degrees of freedom, are significantly large at the 5% level. Therefore, *Model 1* does not seem to fit the data well.

The data proportions suggest that a model which allows the probability of having tics to be highest for the middle age-group may be more realistic than *Model 1*. This can be allowed for by including the variable Age^2, taking the values 49, 121 and 196 for the three age-groups, in a model that can be called *Model 2*. Fitting this model reduces the goodness of fit statistics to $X_L^2 = 1.65$ and $X_P^2 = 1.54$, with two degrees of freedom. The fit is now very good.

The fitted logistic regression equation for *Model 2* is

$$\hat{\pi} = \frac{\exp(-8.00 + 1.39 \text{Age} - 0.51 \text{Sex} - 0.066 \text{Age}^2)}{1 + \exp(-8.00 + 1.39 \text{Age} - 0.51 \text{Sex} - 0.066 \text{Age}^2)}$$

The standard errors for the coefficients of Age, Sex and Age^2 are 0.48, 0.32 and 0.023, respectively. Therefore, the estimates of the coefficients Age and Age^2 are both about 2.8 standard errors from zero, and are significant at the 5% level. The estimated coefficient of Sex is only 1.6 standard errors from zero, which suggests that a difference between the incidence of tics for the two sexes is not clearly established.

At this point, it seems that a *Model 3* with Age and Age^2

Table 8.13. *Logistic regression data from the data shown in Table 8.12*

Y	Total	Age	Sex
13	70	7	0
3	26	7	1
26	82	11	0
11	40	11	1
15	71	14	0
2	29	14	1

included, but no allowance for the sex of the children, may be appropriate. When this is fitted the estimated logistic regression equation becomes

$$\hat{\pi} = \frac{\exp(-7.87 + 1.39\,\text{Age} - 0.064\,\text{Age}^2)}{1 + \exp(-7.87 + 1.39\,\text{Age} - 0.064\,\text{Age}^2)}$$

Here the estimated standard errors for the coefficients of Age and Age^2 are 0.48 and 0.023, respectively, so that the estimates of both coefficients are still about 2.8 standard errors from zero. The goodness of fit statistics are $X_L^2 = 4.35$ and $X_p^2 = 3.85$, with three degrees of freedom, so that the model is a good fit. Therefore, this model seems satisfactory for the data.

The standardized residuals for *Model 3* are shown in Table 8.14. These are all within the range ± 2, but it is disturbing to see that they are all positive for boys and all negative for girls. This suggests that a model that includes the Sex variable may be more satisfactory even though the coefficient of the Sex variable is not significantly different from zero.

The improvement in moving from the null model to a model with the Age variable only, to the model with Age and Age^2, and finally to the model with Age, Age^2 and Sex, is shown by the analysis of deviance provided in Table 8.15. This gives a useful summary of the relative goodness of fit of the different models.

8.9 Survival data

Survival data occur in many areas of science and technology. For example, medical researchers are obviously concerned with the survival of patients after surgical operations and other treatments,

Table 8.14. *Observed frequencies, expected frequencies, and standardized residuals from the logistic regression model fitted to the data in Table 8.12, for Model 3 with the inclusion of Age and Age^2 variables to predict the incidence of tics. (Frequencies are for those with tics)*

Age range	Boys			Girls		
	Ob-served	Ex-pected	Standard-ized residual	Ob-served	Ex-pected	Standard-ized residual
5–9	13	11.7	0.43	3	4.3	−0.70
10–12	26	24.9	0.27	11	12.1	−0.39
13–15	15	12.1	0.92	2	4.9	−1.45

Table 8.15. *Analysis of deviance for the data on the incidence of tics*

Fitted Model	X_L^2	df	Difference X_L^2	df
Constant probability of tics	12.16[a]	5		
			0.08	1
Age effect only	12.08[a]	4		
			7.73[b]	1
+ Age^2	4.35	3		
			2.70	1
+ Sex	1.65	2		

[a]Significantly large at the 5% level.
[b]Significantly large at the 1% level.

while industrial engineers are interested in questions concerning the length of time that systems operate before a breakdown.

As was mentioned in the first section of this chapter, there are two types of survival data that are commonly collected: times of death, and numbers surviving different amounts of time. For the first type of data special methods of analysis have been developed because survival times are often not well approximated by normal distributions, and it is common to find that a study is terminated before all individuals are dead. Therefore, methods of analysis that cater for non-normal and censored data are required. Here 'censored' means that all that is known is that the survival time for an individual exceeds a known amount.

A typical study in the medical area is described by Andersen and Vaeth (1988). In the period 1964–75, 205 cancer patients had radical surgery. At the end of the follow-up period (1 January 1978), 57 of the patients were dead, and there was interest in seeing how survival was related to the sex of the patient, the tumour thickness, and whether ulceration was present. Because of the limited follow-up period, the time of death is censored for most patients, with the amount of censoring being greatest for the patients that received their operation towards the end of 1975.

A study involving the recording of proportions surviving different amounts of time is described by Manly (1985, p. 122). This concerned the survival of snails in an unheated room over a period of about eight months. On 29 September 1968, the snails were placed in the room without food, and the size of each snail was recorded. Then, on six subsequent occasions the survivors were counted. This made it possible to know how many of each size of snail survived to each of the recording times. An analysis was based on the assumption that the proportional hazards survival function

$$\pi(t) = \exp\{-\exp(\beta_0 + \beta_1 X_1 + \beta_2 X_2 + \ldots, + \beta_p X_p)t\},$$

applied, where $\pi(t)$ is the probability of survival for a time t, and the X variables accounted for the effect of size. What makes this model particularly useful is the fact that the survival function can be rewritten as

$$\pi(t) = \exp[-\exp\{\beta_0 + \log_e(t) + \beta_1 X_1 + \beta_2 X_2 + \ldots,$$
$$+ \beta_p X_p\}].$$

This shows that if the model is correct then changing the survival time simply changes the term $\beta_0 + \log_e(t)$, without affecting the other β coefficients. This is a particularly simple way to allow for the passage of time.

8.10 Generalized linear modelling

Multiple regression, log-linear, logistic, proportional hazards and probit models all fall within a class of what are called generalized linear models (Nelder and Wedderburn, 1972). These models have the property that the observations to be accounted for by some explanatory variables $X_1, X_2, \ldots, X_p$ take the form

$$Y = f(\beta_0 + \beta_1 X_1 + \beta_2 X_2 + \ldots, + \beta_p X_p) + \varepsilon,$$

where $f(z)$ is one of several possible functions, and ε is an error term from one of several distributions. For example:

(a) If $f(z) = z$, and ε is normally distributed then the model is just a multiple regression

(b) If $f(z) = \exp(z)$ and the Y values are Poisson-distributed counts then there is a log-linear model

(c) If $f(z) = \exp(z)/\{1 + \exp(z)\}$ and Y is a proportion then there is a logistic regression model

Generalized linear models can be fitted by a special computer program called GLIM (Payne, 1987). This allows eight possible choices for the function $f(z)$, including those that give multiple regression, log-linear, logistic, probit or proportional hazards models. These can be combined with the assumption that the distribution of the data is normal, gamma, binomial or Poisson, except that some combinations of $f(z)$ functions and errors are not permitted. The GENSTAT program (Genstat 5 Committee, 1987) also incorporates the facility to fit generalized linear models.

8.11 Multivariate data

Multivariate analysis is the area of statistics that is concerned with the methods for simultaneous analysis of several correlated variables. Usually the variables in question are thought of as being of equal importance, at least initially, and they are not just a set of variables that is being used to account for the variation in some other variable. In this sense techniques like multiple regression, log-linear modelling, and logistic regression are univariate rather than multivariate methods although several variables are being used.

To make this distinction clearer it is useful to consider an example of a truly multivariate situation. Suppose, therefore, that an educational researcher is interested in studying the effectiveness of a new style of teaching English to 12-year-old children. There are 20 classes available, each with different teachers, and the new style of teaching is randomly allocated to ten of these. The other ten classes continue with the standard teaching method. After a suitable period of time, the researcher tests all the children on their English ability, and gets scores for ten variables for each child, such as comprehension (X_1), spelling (X_2), reading (X_3), etc. Then she wants to know which, if any, of these variables show significant differences between the classes taught in different ways.

One way to approach the analysis of an experiment like this would be to analyse each of the variables in turn, and indeed this would be a reasonable first step. However, it ignores the fact that the results for the ten variables are likely to show high positive correlations, since the children that have a high score on one variable are likely also to have high scores on the other nine variables. In other words, the ten analyses on the individual variables may not be at all independent. Therefore, it will be difficult to know the extent to which the ten tests together provide evidence of a difference between the effect of the standard and new methods of teaching.

Another problem is that if ten tests are carried out on the same set of data using (say) a 5% level of significance then the probability of at least one significant result occuring by chance will be higher than 0.05. If the tests are independent then the probability of no significant results is 0.95^{10}. Hence, the probability of at least one significant result is $1 - 0.95^{10} = 0.40$. With tests on positively correlated variables the probability of at least one significant result by chance will not be this high, but it may still be high enough to cause the researcher to worry whether some significant results are due to chance rather than a real difference between the teaching methods.

In a situation like this there are three ways that an overall comparison of the two teaching methods can be made:

(a) An index of achievement can be constructed from the values of the ten individual variables for each child. For example, the sum of all the variables might be calculated. This single variable can then be analysed. This approach has the advantage of simplicity, but the disadvantage that the positive effects of some variables may be masked by the negative effects of others

(b) The ten variables can be tested individually, but with the significance level used for each test adjusted so that the probability of declaring any test result significant by chance is suitably small. This can be achieved by using the *Bonferroni inequality*, which says that if m tests are carried out at the $100(\alpha/m)\%$ level then the probability of one or more significant results by chance is α or less. Therefore, if ten tests are each carried out at the 0.5% level, the probability of any of them being declared significant is 0.05 when there are no real effects in the data

(c) A suitable multivariate test can be used. This has the advantage of making the appropriate allowance for the correlations between the variables being considered, and the disadvantage that the calculations required may be rather more complicated than what is required for approaches (a) and (b)

There are multivariate extensions of many of the standard univariate tests. For example, the pooled two sample t-test generalizes to the T^2-test, and analysis of variance generalizes to multivariate analysis of variances. In addition, there are a number of multivariate techniques that have no univariate counterpart. Examples are factor analysis, which attempts to account for the variation in a set of p variables in terms of a smaller number of unobservable factors, and multidimensional scaling, which attempts to produce a graphical representation showing how sample units are related, starting from a matrix of distances between these units.

8.12 Summary and further reading

This chapter has been a review of methods for handling various special types of data for which standard methods of analysis based on the normal distribution may not be appropriate. Particular attention has been given to count and proportion data, including discussions of the uses of log-linear and logistic regression type models. Briefer coverage is given of the analysis of data from survival studies, generalized linear models and multivariate methods.

Those interested in reading more about the analysis of count data in general and log-linear modelling in particular should consult one of the introductory texts of the subject, such as those of Everitt (1977), Knoke and Burke (1980), and Upton (1978). The first and last of these texts also discuss logistic regression.

For more information about the analysis of survival data, the review article by Anderson and Vaeth (1988) will be found to be useful. Also, Cox and Oakes (1984) give an introduction to technical details, while Manly (1985, Chapter 5) and Deddens and Koch (1988) discuss the analysis of data on proportions surviving for different amounts of time.

A comprehensive guide to the theory and applications of generalized linear models is provided by McCullagh and Nelder (1989), while Aitkin *et al.* (1989) and Healy (1988) give introductory accounts. Lindsey (1989) concentrates on using GLIM to model count data.

Those interested in learning more about multivariate methods may find the introductory text provided by Manly (1986) to be useful. More comprehensive treatments of the theory are given by Chatfield and Collins (1980) and Harris (1985).

Exercises

(1) This exercise concerns an experiment carried out on New Guinea school children, and reported by Manly and Shannon (1974). In this experiment, individual school children were given a box with five switches and shown that a light on the side of the box could be turned on with at least one combination of switches. Then they were asked to try to turn on the light and work out how the switches work. After a fixed amount of time had elapsed the children were asked to turn on the light and explain the function of each switch. Their responses were rated from A (able to turn on the light and explain the effect of each switch) to D (unable to turn on the light or explain the effect of any switch). This procedure is analogous to the first chemical experiment of Inhelder and Piaget (1958), which was designed to determine the extent to which children are able to think logically. Four primary schools and two high schools were visited, in two areas of New Guinea. The children tested in the primary schools were in standard 5 or standard 6 while the children tested in high schools were in form 1 or form 2. Because of the nature of the New Guinea school system, the children in one class can have wide differences in their ages. Table 8.16 shows the number of children reaching different levels of solution in each of these schools.

(i) Fit a log-linear model to the data allowing for differences between response levels (A to D), between areas (Madang and Wewak) and between types of school (rural primary school, urban primary school, and urban high school). Do this either by setting up appropriate 0–1 dummy variables or by using a computer program that sets these up automatically.

267

Table 8.16. *Results of giving New Guinean school children a problem to solve, with solutions classified from A (complete) to D (very incomplete). (Manly and Shannon, 1974)*

The values shown in the table are the counts of numbers achieving the different levels of solution in different schools.

School	Area	Urban or rural	Children reaching solution level				
			A	B	C	D	Total
Tusbah High School	Madang	urban	7	12	6	17	42
Kreer Primary School	Wewak	urban	7	6	1	18	32
Passam Primary School	Wewak	rural	2	7	3	28	40
Kusbah Primary School	Madang	urban	3	10	6	19	38
Gum Primary School	Madang	rural	2	6	6	19	33
Brandi High School	Wewak	urban	23	12	9	38	82

(ii) Add an allowance for an interaction between the response level and the type of school to the model in (i) and see whether this significantly improves the fit.

(iii) Add an allowance for an interaction between the response level and the area to the model in (ii) and see whether this significantly improves the fit.

(iv) Examine the standardized residuals from the fit of the model in (iii).

(v) Comment on the following assertions:

    (a) Wewak children are not as advanced as Madang children at the same school level in terms of logical thinking

    (b) Urban children are more advanced than rural children in terms of logical thinking

    (c) High school children are only slightly more advanced than primary school children at logical thinking

(2) Reexamine the data from Exercise (1) by fitting logistic regression models for the probability of the school children being able to achieve a level A solution to the problem.

(3) After a severe storm on 1 February 1898, a number of moribund sparrows were taken to the biological laboratory at Brown University, Rhode Island. Subsequently, about half the birds died and Hermon Bumpus used this as an opportunity to study whether the deaths were random, or were the result of natural selection in favour of birds of a certain size. Bumpus took eight morphological measurements on each bird, and published his full set of data (Bumpus, 1898). Table 8.17 shows these data for five measurements on the females only.

(i) Compare the distribution of each measurement for the survivors and the non-survivors and comment on any apparent differences.

(ii) Fit a logistic regression model which gives the probability of surviving as a function of the five variables. Remove variables from the model if this seems appropriate.

(iii) Report your conclusions from your analysis.

The location of prehistoric Maya sites

Case Study 3 was concerned with the location of prehistoric settlement sites in north east Thailand, and, in particular, with the question of whether these appear to be randomly located in the Khorat Basin. It was concluded from an analysis of quadrat counts and nearest neighbour distances that large sites could have been randomly located, but small sites are clustered to some extent. Generally in studies like this it can be expected that there is a non-random distribution of sites as a result of there being a non-random distribution of resources within the study region. This leads the researcher naturally to the consideration of whether the probability of a site occurring in a particular area can be related to the characteristics of that area.

The present case study is an example of this type. It concerns the location of prehistoric Maya sites within the Corozal District of Belize in Central America. The investigator was Green (1973) who discusses the proposition that 'sites were located so as to minimize the effort expended in acquiring scarce resources'.

Green divided the study area into 151 squares each with 2.5 km sides. Thirteen variables were then measured on each square, related to soil types, vegetation types, distance to navigable water, the distance to Santa Rita (a possible prehistoric commercial and political centre), and the number of sites in neighbouring squares. One or two sites were known to exist on 29 of the squares, giving 34 sites in total. Green's data are shown in Table 8.18. Column 2 gives the number of sites in the squares and columns 3 to 14 give the first 12 of Green's 13 variables, labelled v_1 to v_{12}. The other variable recorded by Green (the number of sites in neighbouring squares) is not considered here, since it is not a fixed characteristic of squares in the same way as the other variables.

Green used multiple linear regression to relate the number of sites in a square to the other variables. Since the nature of the dependent variable means that the regression residuals cannot be normally distributed, this analysis is somewhat questionable. Therefore, a different approach will be adopted here, with logistic regression being used to estimate a function that gives the probability of a square containing at least one site.

Before considering logistic regression, it is useful to compare the distribution of each of the variables in Table 8.18 for the squares

Table 8.17. *Measurements (in mm) on 49 female sparrows picked up after a severe storm. (Bumpus, 1898)*

Bird	Total length	Alar extent	Length beak & head	Length humerus	Length keel of sternum	Survived
1	156	245	31.6	18.5	20.5	yes
2	154	240	30.4	17.9	19.6	yes
3	153	240	31.0	18.4	20.6	yes
4	153	236	30.9	17.7	20.2	yes
5	155	243	31.5	18.6	20.3	yes
6	163	247	32.0	19.0	20.9	yes
7	157	238	30.9	18.4	20.2	yes
8	155	239	32.8	18.6	21.2	yes
9	164	248	32.7	19.1	21.1	yes
10	158	238	31.0	18.8	22.0	yes
11	158	240	31.3	18.6	22.0	yes
12	160	244	31.1	18.6	20.5	yes
13	161	246	32.3	19.3	21.8	yes
14	157	245	32.0	19.1	20.0	yes
15	157	235	31.5	18.1	19.8	yes
16	156	237	30.9	18.0	20.3	yes
17	158	244	31.4	18.5	21.6	yes
18	153	238	30.5	18.2	20.9	yes
19	155	236	30.3	18.5	20.1	yes
20	163	246	32.5	18.6	21.9	yes
21	159	236	31.5	18.0	21.5	yes
22	155	240	31.4	18.0	20.7	no
23	156	240	31.5	18.2	20.6	no
24	160	242	32.6	18.8	21.7	no
25	152	232	30.3	17.2	19.8	no
26	160	250	31.7	18.8	22.5	no
27	155	237	31.0	18.5	20.0	no
28	157	245	32.2	19.5	21.4	no
29	165	245	33.1	19.8	22.7	no
30	153	231	30.1	17.3	19.8	no
31	162	239	30.3	18.0	23.1	no
32	162	243	31.6	18.8	21.3	no
33	159	245	31.8	18.5	21.7	no
34	159	247	30.9	18.1	19.0	no
35	155	243	30.9	18.5	21.3	no
36	162	252	31.9	19.1	22.2	no
37	152	230	30.4	17.3	18.6	no
38	159	242	30.8	18.2	20.5	no

Table 8.17. *(continued)*

Bird	Total length	Alar extent	Length beak & head	Length humerus	Length keel of sternum	Survived
39	155	238	31.2	17.9	19.3	no
40	163	249	33.4	19.5	22.8	no
41	163	242	31.0	18.1	20.7	no
42	156	237	31.7	18.2	20.3	no
43	159	238	31.5	18.4	20.3	no
44	161	245	32.1	19.1	20.8	no
45	155	235	30.7	17.7	19.6	no
46	162	247	31.9	19.1	20.4	no
47	153	237	30.6	18.6	20.4	no
48	162	245	32.5	18.5	21.1	no
49	164	248	32.3	18.8	20.9	no

with sites and the squares without sites. This is shown in Figure 8.1, which displays histograms of the percentages of squares with different characteristics, separately for squares with sites and squares without sites. It can be seen that the distributions are fairly similar except for variables v_1 (the percentage of soils under conditions of constant lime enrichment), v_5 (the percentage of deciduous seasonal broadleaf forest), v_6 (the percentage of high and low marsh forest, herbaceous marsh and swamp), and v_{12} (the distance to Santa Rita). In particular, the squares with sites tend to have a relatively high percentage of soil with constant lime enrichment, a relatively high percentage of deciduous seasonal broadleaf forest, a relatively low percentage of high and low marsh forest or herbaceous marsh and swamp, and to be relatively close to Santa Rita.

The computer program SOLO (BMDP, 1989) was used to fit various logistic regression models of the form

$$\pi = \frac{\exp(\beta_0 + \beta_1 v_1 + \beta_2 v_2 +, \ldots, + \beta_p v_p)}{1 + \exp(\beta_0 + \beta_1 v_1 + \beta_2 v_2 +, \ldots, + \beta_p v_p)}$$

to the data, where π denotes the probability of a square having at least one site and the v variables are the measured characteristics on the square.

First, an attempt was made to include all 12 variables from

Table 8.18 in the equation. This failed because of computational problems, probably due to relationships between the variables which mean that at least one of these variables is essentially redundant. This is a problem of multicolinearity that was mentioned in Section 4.5 in the context of multiple regression. There are various techniques available for handling this problem in the logistic regression context (Marx and Smith, 1990), of which the simplest is to reduce the number of variables being considered.

The problem was avoided in the present case by doing a stepwise logistic regression using the computer program SOLO, whereby variables are added one at a time into the logistic regression equation until the improvement in fit obtained by adding any further variables is only of minor importance. This resulted in the selection of variables v_1, v_2, v_4 and v_6 as being the important ones to include in the equation. Of course, only v_1 and v_6 show obvious differences between the squares with sites and the squares without sites (Figure 8.1) so that the effects for v_2 and v_4 must be being hidden to some extent by the effects for v_1 and v_6.

The variables chosen by the stepwise selection procedure are percentages of soils and percentages of vegetation types in the squares. Therefore, it was considered appropriate to fit a final logistic regression equation including all the soil variables (v_1 to v_4) and all the vegetation variables (v_5 to v_8) on the assumption that it was soil type and vegetation type generally that influenced the choice of site. The equation obtained has the coefficients that are shown in Table 8.19.

In this equation, only v_2 and v_6 have coefficients that are significantly different from zero at the 5% level when the ratio of these coefficients to their standard errors are compared with the percentage points of the standard normal distribution. However, the reduction in the log-likelihood statistic X_L^2 that is obtained by fitting the model to the data is 26.95 with 8 degrees of freedom. This is significantly large at the 0.1% level in comparison with the critical points for the chi-squared distribution. Hence, there is clear evidence that the equation has some predictive power.

Finally, it is interesting to make a comparison of the distribution of estimated probabilities of a square possessing a site for the 29 squares with at least one site and the 122 squares without a site. This gives some idea of the extent to which squares were in fact selected for use. Figure 8.2 provides this comparison. It shows the percentages of the 29 squares for which the fitted logistic regression equation gives an estimated probability in each of the ranges

273

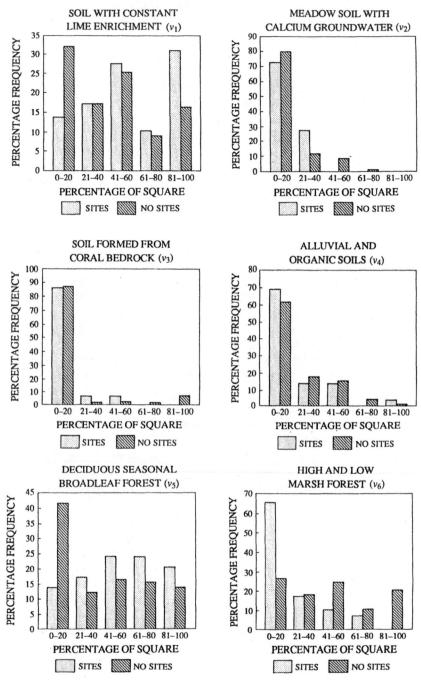

Figure 8.1. Comparison of the distribution of variables for squares with and without prehistoric sites. The vertical scales are the percentages of squares (either the 29 with sites or the 122 without

274

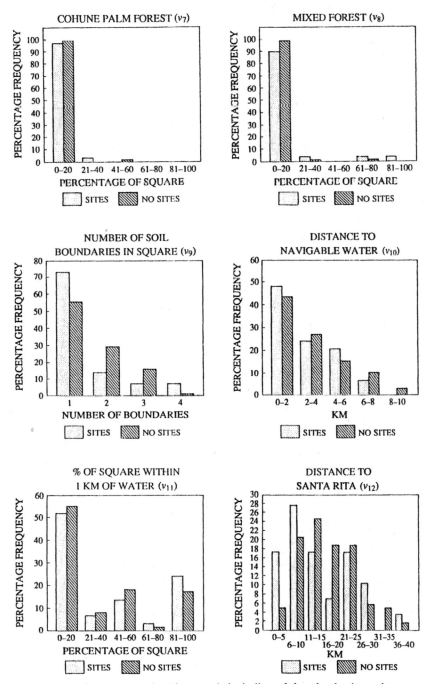

sites) that possess the characteristic indicated by the horizontal
scale. The graphs shown are for the distributions of variables v_1 to
v_{12} that are described in Table 8.18.

Table 8.18. *Data on 151 squares with 2.5 km sides in the Corozal District of northern British Honduras (Belize). (Green, 1973)*

Variables are: v_1 = percentage of soils with constant lime enrichment; v_2 = percentage meadow soil with calcium groundwater; v_3 = percentage soil formed from coral bedrock under conditions of constant lime enrichment; v_4 = percentage alluvial and organic soils adjacent to rivers and saline organic soil at the coast; v_5 = percentage deciduous seasonal broadleaf forest; v_6 = percentage high and low marsh forest, herbaceous marsh and swamp; v_7 = percentage cohune palm forest; v_8 = percentage mixed forest composed of types listed for v_5 and v_7; v_9 = number of soil boundaries in square; v_{10} = distance to navigable water (km); v_{11} = percentage of square within 1 km of navigable water; v_{12} = distance to the site of Santa Rita (km); Sites = number of sites in the square.

Sites		Soil percentages				Vegetation percentages					Other variables		
		v_1	v_2	v_3	v_4	v_5	v_6	v_7	v_8	v_9	v_{10}	v_{11}	v_{12}
1	0	40	30	0	30	0	25	0	0	1	0.5	30	15.0
2	0	20	0	0	10	10	90	0	0	2	0.5	50	13.0
3	0	5	0	0	50	20	50	0	0	2	0.5	40	12.5
4	0	30	0	0	30	0	60	0	0	1	0.0	40	10.0
5	0	40	20	0	20	0	95	0	0	3	1.3	30	13.8
6	0	60	20	0	5	0	100	0	0	4	2.8	0	11.5
7	0	90	0	0	10	0	100	0	0	3	2.5	0	9.0
8	0	100	0	0	0	20	80	0	0	3	2.5	0	7.5
9	0	0	0	0	10	40	60	0	0	2	1.3	50	8.8
10	2	15	0	0	20	25	10	0	0	0	0.0	50	9.0
11	0	20	0	0	10	5	50	0	0	1	0.5	40	10.0
12	0	0	0	0	50	5	60	0	0	1	0.5	50	11.0
13	0	10	0	0	30	30	60	0	0	2	3.8	20	7.0
14	0	40	0	0	20	50	10	0	0	1	2.3	50	7.0

No.													
15	7.5	0	3.0	1	0	0	20	80	40	0	0	10	0
16	8.8	0	3.0	0	0	0	0	100	0	0	0	60	0
17	12.5	45	0.3	0	0	0	60	5	0	0	0	45	0
18	10.3	45	2.0	0	0	0	0	100	0	0	0	100	1
19	12.5	100	0.0	0	0	0	50	20	60	0	0	20	0
20	15.0	50	0.3	0	0	0	75	0	80	0	0	0	0
21	14.8	50	0.5	0	0	0	50	0	50	0	0	0	0
22	16.3	50	0.0	0	0	0	100	0	60	0	10	30	0
23	14.8	20	2.5	2	0	0	50	0	50	0	0	0	0
24	16.5	50	0.0	0	0	0	100	0	30	0	20	50	0
25	15.0	?	2.5	3	0	0	100	10	80	0	15	5	0
26	12.5	?	2.5	1	0	0	90	50	0	0	40	60	0
27	10.0	?	4.0	2	0	0	50	90	0	0	40	60	0
28	7.5	?	7.8	2	0	0	10	0	0	0	5	94	0
29	6.3	?	10.0	2	0	0	100	25	20	0	0	80	0
30	11.0	?	3.0	1	0	0	75	75	0	50	50	50	0
31	9.8	?	5.2	3	0	0	25	10	0	75	40	10	0
32	6.5	?	7.5	3	0	0	90	15	0	0	12	12	0
33	4.0	?	5.3	2	0	0	85	80	0	10	50	50	0
34	11.3	?	5.0	2	0	0	20	100	0	100	40	50	0
35	9.8	0	7.3	3	0	0	0	100	0	100	0	0	1
36	6.3	0	7.0	0	0	0	0	50	0	0	0	0	0
37	4.8	0	3.8	0	0	0	50	50	0	20	30	70	0
38	11.5	0	4.5	2	0	0	50	100	0	100	40	40	0
39	10.0	0	8.8	2	0	0	0	100	0	50	0	0	0
40	7.5	0	6.3	0	0	0					25	25	0
41	5.2	0	3.8	1	0	0							1

Table 8.18. (continued)

Sites	Soil percentages				Vegetation percentages				Other variables			
	v_1	v_2	v_3	v_4	v_5	v_6	v_7	v_8	v_9	v_{10}	v_{11}	v_{12}
42	0	40	40	0	20	80	20	0	0	3	2.0	0	4.0
43	0	90	0	0	10	100	0	0	0	1	5.0	0	3.8
44	0	100	0	0	0	100	0	0	0	0	3.8	0	5.0
45	0	100	0	0	0	90	10	0	0	0	2.5	25	7.6
46	1	10	0	0	90	100	0	0	0	2	3.5	0	2.5
47	1	80	0	0	20	100	0	0	0	1	2.8	5	0.0
48	0	60	0	0	30	80	0	0	0	1	1.3	50	3.0
49	0	40	0	0	0	0	30	0	0	0	0.0	100	5.3
50	2	50	0	0	50	100	0	0	0	1	2.0	50	2.0
51	2	50	0	0	0	40	0	0	0	0	0.0	100	1.3
52	1	30	30	0	20	30	60	0	0	2	1.3	50	4.0
53	0	20	20	0	40	0	100	0	0	2	1.0	50	17.6
54	0	20	80	0	0	0	100	0	0	1	3.0	0	15.2
55	0	0	10	0	60	0	75	0	0	1	0.3	50	21.3
56	0	0	50	0	30	0	75	0	0	2	2.8	20	18.8
57	0	50	50	0	0	30	70	0	0	2	5.5	80	16.3
58	0	0	0	0	60	0	60	0	0	0	0.0	50	24.0
59	0	20	20	0	60	0	100	0	0	2	2.5	20	21.5
60	1	90	10	0	0	70	30	0	0	1	5.0	0	20.0
61	0	100	0	0	0	100	0	0	0	0	6.3	0	17.6
62	0	15	15	0	30	0	40	0	0	2	1.0	50	25.2
63	1	100	0	0	0	25	75	0	0	0	3.0	0	23.8

64	21.4	0	5.5	0	0	0	10	90	5	0	0	95	1
65	20.0	0	8.0	0	0	0	10	90	5	0	0	95	0
66	12.6	0	6.0	1	0	0	50	50	0	0	40	60	1
67	11.0		8.5	3	0	0	40	50	10	10	60	30	0
68	9.0		3.0	1	0	0	0	100	50	50	0	50	1
69	7.5	25	1.3	1	0	0	40	60	10	0	30	60	1
70	14.8		7.5	4	0	0	20	80	2	0	8	90	1
71	11.5	40	4.8	3	0	0	40	60	40	30	30	30	1
72	11.0		1.8	2	0	0	25	75	33	33	33	33	1
73	9.8	100	0.0	1	0	0	100	0	40	0	10	20	0
74	16.0		5.3	2	0	0	60	40	50	0	0	50	0
75	14.8		2.5	1	0	0	50	50	12	0	12	75	0
76	13.0	100	0.5	2	0	0	60	40	25	0	0	75	0
77	11.5	100	0.0	1	0	0	100	0	50	0	0	30	0
78	17.5		5.0	2	0	0	95	5	30	0	10	50	0
79	17.3		2.5	3	0	0	40	60	0	0	0	100	0
80	15.0	100	0.0	1	0	0	80	20	50	0	0	50	0
81	14.9	100	0.3	2	0	0	100	0	90	0	0	10	0
82	6.3	100	0.8	1	0	0	85	0	20	0	30	30	0
83	6.3	80	0.0	3	0	0	75	0	20	0	20	20	0
84	7.5	100	0.5	3	0	0	25	50	0	0	0	90	1
85	8.7	100	0.0	0	0	0	5	30	0	0	0	30	0
86	8.8	100	1.0	0	0	0	80	20	50	0	30	20	2
87	8.8	100	0.0	4	0	0	50	50	10	0	30	50	0
88	-8.9	100	1.8	1	0	0	10	70	0	0	0	80	0
89	10.0	100	0.8	0	0	0	0	50	0	0	0	80	1
90	11.3	50	1.3	3	0	0	15	80	25	0	10	60	0

Table 8.18. (continued)

Sites	Soil percentages			Vegetation percentages						Other variables		
	v_1	v_2	v_3	v_4	v_5	v_6	v_7	v_8	v_9	v_{10}	v_{11}	v_{12}
91	0	50	0	0	0	75	0	0	0	0	0.0	100	11.3
92	0	70	0	0	0	75	0	0	0	0	0.0	100	11.5
93	0	100	0	0	0	85	15	0	0	0	2.5	0	13.3
94	0	60	30	0	0	40	60	0	0	3	2.5	25	13.3
95	0	80	20	0	0	50	50	0	0	1	0.0	100	13.8
96	0	100	0	0	0	100	0	0	0	0	2.5	40	14.5
97	0	100	0	0	0	95	5	0	0	0	5.0	0	15.0
98	0	0	0	0	60	0	50	0	0	2	0.3	45	34.0
99	0	30	20	0	30	0	60	0	40	3	1.3	45	32.5
100	0	15	0	0	35	20	30	0	0	0	0.0	50	40.0
101	1	40	0	0	45	70	20	0	0	2	1.3	50	37.8
102	0	30	0	0	45	20	40	0	20	3	0.0	100	35.2
103	0	60	10	0	30	10	65	5	20	3	1.3	20	33.8
104	0	40	20	0	40	0	25	0	75	3	1.0	60	27.0
105	1	100	0	0	0	70	0	0	30	0	3.0	0	25.0
106	1	100	0	0	0	40	60	0	0	2	6.0	0	23.5
107	0	80	10	0	10	40	60	0	0	2	8.0	0	21.4
108	1	90	0	0	10	10	0	0	90	0	1.3	75	28.8
109	1	100	0	0	0	20	10	0	70	0	3.0	0	26.5
110	0	30	50	0	20	10	90	0	0	2	6.0	0	25.0
111	0	60	40	0	0	50	50	0	0	1	5.3	0	23.3
112	0	100	0	0	0	80	10	0	10	0	2.5	0	33.0

113	1	60	0	0	40	60	10	30	0	1	4.8	0	28.4
114	0	50	50	0	0	0	100	0	0	2	7.0	0	27.0
115	0	60	30	0	10	25	75	50	0	3	4.5	0	25.5
116	0	40	0	0	60	30	20	50	0	1	5.0	0	31.5
117	0	30	0	0	70	0	50	0	0	2	7.5	0	30.3
118	0	50	20	0	30	25	100	0	0	3	6.0	0	29.0
119	0	50	50	0	0	50	75	0	0	1	6.5	0	27.5
120	0	90	10	0	0	60	50	0	0	1	5.5	0	20.2
121	0	100	0	0	50	70	40	0	0	0	3.0	100	18.5
122	0	50	0	0	80	0	30	0	0	1	0.0	100	17.5
123	1	10	10	0	0	30	100	0	0	2	0.3	0	17.4
124	0	50	50	0	25	80	70	0	0	2	3.8	90	22.0
125	0	75	0	0	60	0	20	0	0	1	1.3	90	20.5
126	0	40	0	0	10	75	100	0	0	2	0.3	20	20.0
127	0	90	10	0	55	30	25	0	0	2	3.5	30	19.0
128	0	45	45	0	80	10	70	0	0	2	2.3	100	23.8
129	0	20	35	0	20	70	90	0	0	2	0.3	10	22.8
130	0	80	0	0	0	90	30	0	0	2	2.8	0	22.3
131	0	100	0	0	25	50	0	0	0	0	5.0	50	21.3
132	0	75	0	0	40	50	50	0	0	2	1.0	100	26.3
133	0	60	5	0	60	60	50	0	0	2	0.3	0	25.0
134	0	40	0	0	40	70	40	0	0	1	2.8	30	24.0
135	0	60	0	0	10	75	15	0	0	1	5.0	100	23.8
136	0	90	10	0	0	30	25	0	0	1	2.0	20	16.3
137	0	50	0	5	0	70	20	0	0	0	0.0	0	16.3
138	0	70	0	30	0	100	30	0	0	1	2.0	0	17.0
139	0	60	0	40	0	0	0	0	0	1	4.8	0	17.5

Table 8.18. (continued)

Sites	Soil percentages				Vegetation percentages					Other variables		
	v_1	v_2	v_3	v_4	v_5	v_6	v_7	v_8	v_9	v_{10}	v_{11}	v_{12}
140 2	50	0	0	0	50	0	0	0	0	0.0	100	19.0
141 0	30	0	50	0	60	40	0	0	1	1.3	60	19.0
142 0	5	0	95	0	80	20	0	0	1	3.8	0	19.0
143 0	10	0	90	0	70	30	0	0	1	6.3	0	19.5
144 0	50	0	0	0	15	30	0	0	0	0.0	100	21.3
145 0	20	0	80	0	50	50	0	0	1	2.8	0	21.3
146 0	0	0	100	0	90	10	0	0	0	5.3	0	22.0
147 0	0	0	100	0	75	25	0	0	0	7.5	0	22.0
148 0	90	0	10	0	60	30	10	0	1	1.3	20	23.8
149 0	0	0	100	0	80	10	10	0	0	3.8	0	23.8
150 0	0	0	100	0	60	40	0	0	0	6.3	0	23.8
151 0	0	40	60	40	50	50	0	0	1	8.3	0	23.9

Table 8.19. *Coefficients of variables in a fitted logistic equation including all the soil percentage and vegetation percentage variables*

The 'Ratio' shown is the coefficient divided by the standard error. This can be tested for significance by comparison to tables of the standard normal distribution.

Variable	Parameter estimate	SE	Ratio
Constant	−2.476	1.483	1.67
v_1, % soils with constant lime enrichment	0.035	0.020	1.79
v_2, % meadow soil etc.	0.050	0.022	2.28[a]
v_3, % soil with coral bedrock etc.	0.015	0.021	0.73
v_4, % alluvial and organic soils etc.	0.035	0.019	1.81
v_5, % deciduous seasonal broadleaf forest	−0.013	0.020	0.66
v_6, % high and low marsh forest	−0.052	0.021	2.41[a]
v_7, % cohune palm forest	−0.013	0.039	0.35
v_8, % mixed deciduous and cohune palm forest	0.005	0.021	0.20

[a] Significantly different from zero at 5% level.

0–0.1, 0.1–0.2, and so on up to 0.7–0.8. The corresponding percentages for the 122 squares without sites are also shown, and it can be seen clearly that the probabilities of a site tend to be distinctly higher for the squares with sites than they are for the squares without sites. In fact, about 58% of the squares without a site on them have probabilities of a site estimated to be within the range 0–0.1, whereas only about 13% of the squares possessing one or more sites had an estimated probability this low.

To some extent the comparison made in Figure 8.2 is biased by the fact that the logistic regression equation was estimated in such a way as to maximize the difference between squares with and without sites. However, the differences observed in this figure seem to be much larger than the differences that are likely to have occurred purely by chance. This is indicated by Figure 8.3, which shows the result of estimating probabilities of squares having sites when the data analysed were obtained by randomly choosing 29 of the 151 squares to have sites. In other words, Figure 8.3 is a demonstration of what can be expected if in fact all squares have the same probability of being used.

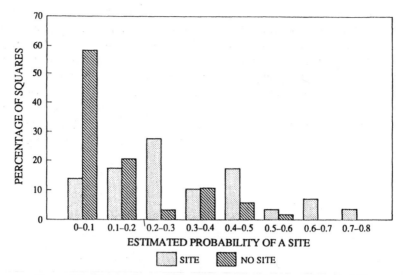

Figure 8.2. Comparison of the distribution of estimated probabilities of a square possessing a site for 29 squares with at least one site and 122 squares without a site.

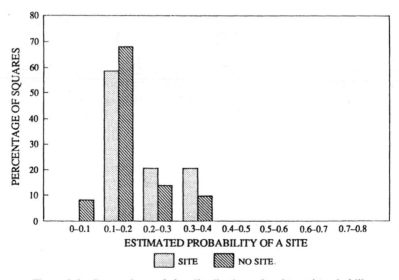

Figure 8.3. Comparison of the distribution of estimated probabilities of a square possessing a site when a logistic regression function is estimated for data with 29 randomly allocated 'sites'.

Since Figure 8.3 shows quite a small difference between the probabilities of use calculated for the 29 squares randomly allocated 'sites' and the remaining 122 squares, it seems that the differences that are displayed in Figure 8.2 are likely to be meaningful rather than just a bias resulting from the estimation process. It can be noted also that with random data none of the coefficients in the estimated logistic regression equation were significantly different from zero at the 5% level, and the equation does not account for the presence of sites in any significant way.

9

Computer intensive statistics

9.1 Introduction

For the average researcher, one of the most obvious results of the increasing availability of computers in the last 30 years has been the remarkable improvements in the ease with which standard statistical calculations can be carried out. In 1960, a complex analysis of variance would probably have to have been done on a mechanical calculator, which was not a task to be undertaken lightly. Doing a multiple regression on a large set of data with many predictor variables was not really practical for most researchers, and the iterative fitting of a log-linear or logistic model was quite out of the question. However, nowadays there are many programs available to do standard statistical calculations, including sophisticated packages like BMDP, SPSSX, SAS, and MINITAB. As a result, multiple regression analysis is commonplace, and models that require iterative fitting are being used more and more.

Still, computer intensive statistical methods are not yet commonly used, where this label refers to a body of analyses that can be characterized by the way that they generally require very many more arithmetical calculations than are needed by a standard analysis. For example, to carry out a regular t-test to see whether the means $\bar{X}_1$ and $\bar{X}_2$ of two independent samples are significantly different, the statistic

$$t = (\bar{X}_1 - \bar{X}_2)/\{s_p\sqrt{(1/n_1 + 1/n_2)}\}$$

can be calculated, where s_p is the pooled within-sample standard deviation, and n_1 and n_2 are the two sample sizes. This value is then compared with the tabulated critical values of the t-distribution with $n_1 + n_2 - 2$ degrees of freedom to see whether it is significantly different from zero. A computer intensive alternative with the same objective as the t-test involves comparing the observed t-statistic with the distribution of values that is found by generating on a computer another 5000 t-statistics by some process that produces alternative values that might have occurred if, in

286

fact, the two samples have been taken from distributions with the same mean. For the moment, there is no need to go into the question of which method might be used to generate the 5000 other t-values. Either randomization or bootstrapping could be used, as described below. The important point is that, instead of calculating one t-value and using a table to assess the significance of a sample mean difference, it might be considered better to multiply the calculations by 5000 in order to assess the significance of the observed t-value in comparison with a computer generated empirical distribution.

There are basically two reasons why a computer intensive analysis might be better than some more standard alternative. First, the standard alternative might require assumptions that are questionable for the data at hand. For example, it is often the case that the data are supposed to be normally distributed but this is clearly doubtful. Second, computer intensive methods are generally more flexible in their use of test statistics. For example, these methods make it just as easy to compare the difference between two sample medians as it is to compare two sample means. More generally, it can be said that computer intensive methods can be tailored to specific questions to a far greater extent than is possible with more standard methods, with the price that is paid for this facility being an enormous increase in the amount of computation that is required.

The four computer intensive methods that are considered in this chapter are:

(a) *Randomization methods:* which can be used to test hypotheses and (under certain conditions) to determine confidence limits for parameters. Randomization testing involves determining the significance level of a test statistic calculated from an observed set of data by comparing the statistic with the distribution of values that is obtained by randomly reordering the data values in some sense. Randomization confidence limits for a parameter are given by the range of values of that parameter for which randomization testing gives a non-significant result

(b) *Monte Carlo methods:* which can also be used to test hypotheses and construct confidence intervals. Testing still involves comparing an observed test statistic with values obtained by sampling a distribution. However, in this case the distribution sampled need not arise from simply reordering the observed data values. Rather, the distribution is of the test statistics generated by a computer model for the situation being studied. Confidence intervals can be based directly on the variation in parameter estimates observed in data generated from the model.

(c) *Jackknifing:* which is a means of removing the bias from an estimator and approximating the standard error by making estimation procedures analogous to the estimation of a population mean from a simple random sample.

(d) *Bootstrapping:* which involves resampling the data values in a random sample to approximate the distribution that would be obtained by resampling the population that the sample came from in the first place.

Randomization methods have a long history. The basic approach was suggested by Fisher (1935, 1936), and developed further by Pitman (1937*a,b,c*) and others around the same time, although it was hardly a practical method of data analysis in those days. Monte Carlo methods are of more recent origin, having grown up at the same time as computers. Jackknifing was suggested by Tukey in 1958, and was an area of some research interest for about 20 years from then on. Bootstrapping was first suggested as a general procedure by Efron (1979), and was soon recognized to be more general and potentially more useful than jackknifing.

9.2 Randomization tests

Many hypotheses of interest in science can be regarded as alternatives to null hypotheses of randomness. That is to say, the hypothesis under investigation suggests that there will be a tendency for a certain type of pattern to appear in data whereas the null hypothesis says that if this pattern is present then this is purely due to chance since the observations are in a random order.

With randomization testing, a statistic S is chosen to measure the extent to which data show the pattern in question. The value s_0 of S for the observed data is then compared with the distribution of S that is obtained by randomly reordering the data. The argument made is that if the null hypothesis is true then all possible orders for the data were equally likely to have occurred. The observed data order is then just one of the equally likely orders, and s_0 should appear as a typical value from the randomization distribution of S. If this does not seem to be the case (so that s_0 is 'significant') then the null hypothesis is discredited to some extent and, by implication, the alternative hypothesis is considered more reasonable.

The significance level of s_0 (the p-value) is the proportion or percentage of values that are as extreme or more extreme than this value in the randomization distribution. This can be interpreted in the same way as for conventional tests of significance: if it is less than 5% then this provides some evidence that the null hypothesis is not true, if it is less than 1% then it provides strong evidence that the null hypothesis is not true, and if it is less than 0.1% then it provides very strong evidence that the null hypothesis is not true.

In some situations it is possible to determine the randomization distribution of the test statistic exactly by systematically enumerating all possible orders for the data being considered. More commonly, however, the number of possibilities is huge, so that it is more practical to sample the randomization distribution by calculating the test statistic for a large number of randomly ordered sets of data. In fact, there is usually nothing much to be gained from a complete enumeration. Taking a large sample from the randomization distribution can be expected to give essentially the same result, and avoids the problem of finding a systematic way of working through all possible orders. Furthermore, as noted by Dwass (1957), the significance level of a randomization test is 'exact' even when the randomization distribution is only sampled, since if the null hypothesis is true the probability of a result significant at the α level is α or less.

Example 9.1: Disk bead counts related to age at the Khok Phanom Di burial site

Randomization tests are most useful when the validity of standard tests is debatable. An example of this comes from a study of the contents of different graves at the Khok Phanom Di excavation site in Thailand, in relationship to factors such as the sex, age at death and time of death of the body.

A typical question is whether there is any evidence that the number of disk beads varies according to whether the body was under or over 21 years of age. According to information provided by Professor Charles Higham of the University of Otago, there were $n_1 = 93$ burials where the body was under 21 years of age at death. For 71 of these burials, there were no disk beads, while the counts for the other 22 were: 2, 2, 3, 9, 12, 16, 41, 50, 56, 73, 120, 189, 250, 269, 610, 626, 690, 730, 1043, 7845, 12 247, 17 786. This gives a mean count for these children and juveniles of $\bar{x}_1 = 458.8$, with a standard deviation of $s_1 = 2357.5$. There were $n_2 = 60$ burials where the body was 21 years or over at the time of death. Of these, there were 35 with no disk beads, and 25 had the following counts: 3, 3, 8, 11, 14, 59, 93, 105, 220, 224, 327, 330, 330, 542, 859, 866, 1260, 1294, 1500, 1588, 1600, 9969, 39 000, 56 200, 120 787. This gives a mean count for adults of $\bar{x}_2 = 3953.2$, with standard deviation $s_2 = 17 680.5$.

The mean and standard deviation for adults are nearly 10 times as large as the corresponding statistics for children and juveniles, mainly because of the three highest adult counts. A large sample test to compare the two means that does not assume equal standard deviations in the populations being sampled involves calculating

$$z = (\bar{x}_1 - \bar{x}_2)/\sqrt{(s_1^2/n_1 + s_2^2/n_2)},$$

which is the difference between the two means divided by the estimated standard error of this difference. If the null hypothesis that the samples come from populations with the same mean value is true, then z should approximately be a random value from the standard normal distribution. Since the observed value of z is 1.52, the difference between the sample means is not significantly different from zero at the 5% level. On the other hand, the probability of a variance ratio as large as the observed $F = s_2^2/s_1^2 = 56.2$ is zero to six decimal places in comparison with percentage points of the F-distribution with 59 and 92 degrees of freedom.

The test for comparing the two sample means relies on the central limit theorem to ensure that the two means have a normal distribution. With sample sizes of 93 and 60 this would be reasonable, except that the observed distributions of counts are so far from normal. The F-test is well known to be sensitive to non-normal data, so that little credibility can be given to the very highly significant result.

Both tests are questionable on the grounds that they assume that the two groups being compared are random samples from populations. However, it is difficult to imagine what these populations are, since the data are from all graves found at the burial site, and therefore constitute all the graves of interest. The 'populations' being assumed must therefore be from hypothetical graves that might have been observed if history had somehow been different from what it actually was.

These difficulties are overcome by randomization testing. For this, the null hypothesis is that the counts of disk beads and the age of death of a body were completely unrelated, so that all possible allocations of the disk bead counts to the two groups of burials were equally likely to have occurred. The number of possible allocations of the 153 disk bead counts to one group of 93 children and juveniles and a second group of 60 adults is the number of combinations of 153 things taken 93 at a time, which is about 10^{45}. In effect, many of these will be the same because the majority of counts are just zero. However, it is clearly unrealistic to attempt to enumerate the exact randomization distribution.

For this example, the alternative to a complete enumeration of the randomization distribution that was used involved approximately the randomization distribution with 5000 values from this distribution. A computer program was written to allocate randomly 93 of the observed bead counts to 'young' graves and the remaining 60 bead counts to 'adult' graves. This was repeated a total of 4999 times. For each allocation, the mean difference in disk bead counts, $D = \bar{x}_1 - \bar{x}_2$, and the variance ratio, $F = \text{Max}(s_1^2/s_2^2, s_2^2/s_1^2)$, were calculated. If the null hypothesis is true then the actual historic allocation provides another random allocation, making a sample of 5000 from the randomization distribution in all. It was found that 2.9% of these 5000 allocations provided a D value as far from zero as the value of -3494.4 seen with the real data. Hence, there is some evidence that the allocation of disk beads was not random. In fact, it seems to have been made in favour of the adults. On the other hand, it was found that for 14.9% of the 5000 randomizations the F-ratio was as large or larger than the observed value of 56.2. Therefore, there is no evidence that the observed variance ratio is too large to be attributed to chance.

It is interesting that the randomization tests have produced quite opposite outcomes to those that were obtained by the more conventional tests. The z-score test found no significant difference between the observed sample means but the randomization test indicates that they are significantly different at the 5% level. The observed variance comes out very highly significant using the F-distribution, but not at all significant by a randomization test. There is surely no doubt that the randomization tests are the ones that can be relied on since the justification for these tests (the null hypothesis that disk bead counts were effectively allocated at random) is quite clear and strong, whereas the justification for the other tests is weak because of the assumptions that have to be made about distributions.

With well-behaved data it is usually found that the significance level from a randomization test is almost the same as the significance level from a classical test that is testing the same null hypothesis. In that respect, this example on counts of disk beads is not altogether typical.

9.3 Determining the number of randomizations required

As mentioned earlier, the results of Dwass (1957) show that a randomization test using random allocations of the data to determine significance levels is exact in the sense that the probability of a significant result at the $100\alpha\%$ level is α or less when the null hypothesis is true. This is true for any number of randomizations. Nevertheless, it might be argued that determining a significance level by randomizing the data is unsatisfactory, since the estimated significance level depends on the random allocations that happen to be made.

This objection can be answered by determining whether the sampling variation in the estimated significance level is likely to affect conclusions. This can be done by calculating a confidence interval for the significance level that would be obtained from an infinite number of random allocations. This is straightforward, since the estimated significance level from N randomizations, p say, will be distributed as a binomial proportion with standard error $\mathrm{SE}(p) = \surd\{\pi(1 - \pi)/N\} \approx \surd\{p(1 - p)/N\}$, where π is the probability of obtaining a more extreme result than that observed in the real data (i.e. π is the significance level that would be obtained from an infinite number of random allocations). Also, the central limit theorem ensures that p will be approximately normally distributed for large enough values of N.

In Example 9.1 there were 5000 randomizations (including the observed data order) and the estimated significance level for the observed difference between two mean counts of disk beads was 2.9%. Hence, a 99% confidence interval for the true randomization significance level is $0.029 \pm \{2.58 \times \surd(0.029 \times 0.971/5000)\}$, or 0.023 to 0.035 (2.3% to 3.5%), where 2.58 is the value that is exceeded with probability 0.005 for the standard normal distribution. Clearly, sampling errors in determining the significance level are of no consequence in this case. For the variance ratio the estimated significance level was 14.9%. Here the 99% confidence limits for the significance level that would be obtained from an infinite number of randomizations are 0.136 to 0.162 (13.6% to 16.2%). Again, the sampling error in estimating the significance level has no material effect on conclusions.

In general, the consideration of the confidence intervals that will be obtained from randomization suggests that to estimate a significance level of about 5% requires a minimum of 1000 randomizations, and to estimate a significance level of about 1% requires a minimum of 5000 randomizations (Manly, 1991, Section 3.3). However, there is one reservation that must be stressed in using these guidelines. If the researcher insists on results being either significant at the 5% level or not significant at all, then difficulties will arise in borderline situations. For example, if the true significance level is 4.9% then even if 100 000 randomizations are made there will still be quite a high chance of wrongly declaring the result to be significant at the 5% level.

9.4 Confidence limits by randomization

It is possible to determine confidence limits for a parameter using a randomization argument. In essence, a 95% confidence interval is the range of values of the parameter for which the results of a randomization test are not significant at the 5% level, a 99% confidence interval is the range of values of the parameter for which the results of a randomization test are not significant at the 1% level, and so on.

For example, a 95% significance level for the difference between two population means can be determined as follows from samples from the distributions, on the assumption that the only difference between the two populations is in the means:

(a) Take a trial value δ for the difference between the two population means

(b) Subtract δ from all the data values in the first sample. Note that if δ is the correct difference between the population means then this will produce two samples from exactly the same distribution

(c) Carry out a randomization test to see whether the two sample means are significantly different at the 5% level on a two-tailed test

(d) Repeat steps (a) to (c) so as to determine δ_1, a low value of δ that gives a randomization test result that is just significant at the 5% level, and δ_2, a high value of δ that also gives a randomization test result that is significant at the 5% level

The interval δ_1 to δ_2 is the required 95% confidence interval for the difference in the two population means.

Since randomization tests are computer intensive, finding confidence intervals by randomization is extremely computer intensive because this involves repeating a significance test many times in order to find the limits on a parameter that are borderline between being significant and not significant at a certain level. This is presumably one reason why such limits have not seen much use in the past.

9.5 Monte Carlo tests

With a Monte Carlo test the significance of an observed test statistic is assessed by comparing it with a sample of test statistics obtained by generating random data using some assumed model. For example, Besag and Diggle (1977) discuss tests to see whether points appear to be distributed randomly in space within a given region. In this case one reasonable test statistic is the mean of the distance from each point to its nearest neighbour, with high values indicating a tendency for points to be regularly spaced and low values indicating a certain amount of clustering. Then the significance of an observed statistic can be evaluated by comparing it with the distribution of values obtained when the points are placed in random positions over the study region.

The generation of one set of data for a Monte Carlo test may need considerably more calculations than are involved in randomly reordering a sample of observed values. For this reason it is not uncommon to find that the number of random test statistics generated for a Monte Carlo test is rather small. In an extreme case, a test at the 5% level of significance might involve comparing the observed test statistic with only 19 other values. This low number of randomly generated values can be justified on the grounds that the exactness of randomization tests with any number of random data permutations (Dwass, 1957) applies equally well with Monte Carlo tests (Barnard, 1963). Nevertheless, a large number of random values of the test statistic is always desirable to avoid inferences being strongly dependent on the properties of a small sample.

Monte Carlo methods can also be used to calculate confidence limits for population parameters. Essentially the idea is to use computer generated data to determine the amount of variation to be expected in sample statistics.

Example 9.2: Testing for spatial randomness in the position of albatross nests

This example concerns a set of data on the location of 22 albatross nests that has already been the subject of Exercise 2 in Chapter 3. Figure 9.1 shows the positions of the nests in a 42 m by 60 m rectangular region on the Otago Peninsular in New Zealand. There seems to be a tendency for the nests to be clustered, and the question that will be addressed in this example is whether this type of pattern is likely to have occurred if in fact each nest is at a random position. To be more specific, the null model to be tested states that each of the points was equally likely to occur anywhere within the square, independent of all the other points.

There are many different test statistics that could be used to summarize the data, and there is no reason why more than one should not be used at the same time. Here, what will be considered are a set of nearest neighbour statistics. The first, g_1, is the mean of the distances between nests and their nearest neighbour. Since there are 22 nests there are 22 distances to be averaged. The second statistic, g_2, is the mean of the distances between nests and their second nearest neighbours. Again this is an average of 22 distances, one for each nest. More generally, the ith statistic to be considered is g_i, the mean distance between nests and their ith nearest neighbours, for i from 1 to 10. Stopping with the tenth nearest neighbour is arbitrary, but will serve for the purpose of this example.

The statistics g_1 to g_{10} for the 22 nests are shown in the first row of Table 9.1. To assess their significance, 4999 random sets of data were generated by allocating 22 points to random positions within a 42 by 60 rectangle. For each of the generated sets of data the g statistics were calculated. The generated sets plus the data actually observed then provided 5000 of each of the ten g statistics with which to approximate their distribution for randomly placed points.

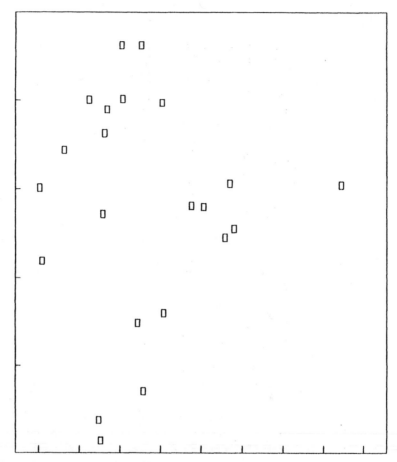

Figure 9.1. The position of 22 albatross nests in a region of size 42 m by 60 m on the Otago Peninsular, New Zealand.

On this basis, the lower and upper tail significance levels can be determined for each of the g statistics, as shown in the second and third rows of the table. Here, the lower tail significance level for the observed value of g_i is the proportion of the 5000 values of g_i that are less than or equal to the observed value. Similarly, the upper tail significance level for the observed value of g_i is the percentage of the 5000 g_i values that are greater than or equal to the observed value.

It seems from the results shown in Table 9.1 that there is some evidence that the distribution of albatross nests is not random

Table 9.1. *Nearest neighbour statistics for 22 albatross nests, with their estimated lower and upper tail significance levels as determined by approximating the distribution for randomly placed nests by the observed nests and 4999 randomly positioned sets of 22 nests*

	g_1	g_2	g_3	g_4	g_5	g_6	g_7	g_8	g_9	g_{10}
Observed	4.00	6.45	7.84	9.03	12.13	13.60	15.34	16.89	17.53	18.47
Lower % significance level	8.56	9.32	2.84	0.96	20.30	20.70	29.12	33.72	19.98	16.30
Upper % significance level	91.46	90.70	97.18	99.06	79.72	79.32	70.90	66.30	80.04	83.72

because of the rather low mean distances between nests and their third and fourth nearest neighbours. On two-tailed tests g_3 and g_4 are significantly far from the centre of the generated distributions at about the 5.6% and 1.9% levels, respectively when the lower significance levels are doubled to take into account the possibility of a result as extreme as that observed in the opposite tail of the distribution.

The evidence against the null hypothesis of random locations for nests is not that great because 10 statistics are being considered at the same time. This means that the chance of getting one or more of the statistics significant at the 5% level by chance alone is rather higher than 0.05. In fact, as has been noted in Section 8.11, the Bonferroni inequality says that if m tests are being made at the same time then the level of significance that is required for each test should be $(5/m)\%$ in order to have a probability of 0.05 or less of declaring any test result significant when the null hypothesis is true. This suggests that a reasonable level of significance to use with the nearest neighbour statistics for the albatross nest data is $(5/10)\% = 0.5\%$. On this basis, there is no real evidence of non-randomness obtained using these statistics.

9.6 Jackknifing

In ordinary usage the word 'jackknife' describes a large pocket knife, which does not seem to have much to do with statistics. However, these knives often have a multitude of small pull-out tools, so that the owner is able to tackle many small tasks without having to look for something better. It is for this reason that Tukey (1958) gave the name 'jackknife' to a general approach that he proposed for testing hypotheses and calculating confidence intervals in situations where no better methods are easily used.

One way of justifying this approach is to think in terms of what is usually done when estimating a mean value, but from an unusual point of view. Suppose, then, that a random sample of n values $X_1, X_2, \ldots, X_n$ is taken and the sample mean

$$\bar{X} = \sum_{i=1}^{n} X_i/n$$

is used to estimate the mean of the population. Next, suppose that the sample mean is calculated with the jth observation missed out, to give

$$\bar{X}_{-j} = \left(\sum_{i=1}^{n} X_i - X_j\right)/(n-1). \tag{9.1}$$

Then the last two equations can be solved for X_j to give

$$X_j = n\bar{X} - (n-1)\bar{X}_{-j}.$$

Therefore, it is possible to determine the sample value X_j from the overall mean and the mean with X_j removed.

Obviously, this is not a useful result if the sample values are known in the first place. However, it is potentially useful in situations where the parameter being estimated is something other than a sample mean. Thus, in a general situation, suppose that a parameter Θ is estimated by some function of the n sample values $\hat{\Theta}(X_1, X_2, \ldots, X_n)$, written as $\hat{\Theta}$ for short. With X_j removed this becomes the 'partial estimate' $\hat{\Theta}_{-j}$. Following equation (9.1), there are therefore the set of 'pseudo-values'

$$\hat{\Theta}_j^* = n\hat{\Theta} - (n-1)\hat{\Theta}_{-j}, \tag{9.2}$$

for $j = 1, 2, \ldots, n$, which play the same role as the values X_j in estimating a mean. The average of the pseudo-values

$$\hat{\Theta}^* = \sum_{j=1}^{n} \hat{\Theta}_j^*/n \tag{9.3}$$

is the jackknife estimate of Θ. Treating the pseudo-values as a random sample of independent estimates of Θ suggests that the variance of this jackknife estimate can be estimated by s^2/n, where s^2 is the sample variance of the pseudo-values. Going one step further suggests that an approximate $100(1-\alpha)\%$ confidence interval for Θ is given by $\hat{\Theta} \pm t_{100\alpha\%, n-1}s/\sqrt{n}$, where $t_{100\alpha\%, n-1}$ is the absolute value that is exceeded with probability α for the t distribution with $n-1$ degrees of freedom.

On the face of it this is a way of transforming many estimation problems into the problem of estimating a sample mean. All that is necessary is that the usual estimator of the parameter of interest is some function of n sample values. In reality, as might be expected, things are not quite as simple as that. In particular, the pseudo-values are likely to be correlated to some extent, so that the estimated variance of the jackknife estimator is biased upwards or downwards. Whether or not this is the case is difficult to predict theoretically. Usually therefore, the jackknife variance needs to be justified by numerical studies of a range of situations before it can be relied on.

Before the jackknife method was suggested as a general tool for inference by Tukey (1958), Quenouille (1956) had already pointed out that replacing an estimator by its jackknifed version has the effect of removing bias of order $1/n$. These early papers led to a keen interest in developing the theory of jackknife estimation from the mid 1960s through to the late 1970s. Review of early developments are provided by Gray and Schucany (1972) and Miller (1974) and a bibliography of 162 references has been produced by Parr and Schucany (1980). A more recent review is provided by Hinkley (1983).

Example 9.3: Comparing correlation matrices for morphological traits on an aphid

An example of the type of situation where jackknifing produces a solution to a non-standard problem is described by Riska (1985). As part of a study of geographical variation in correlations, samples of wingless stem mothers of the aphid *Pemphigus populacaulis* were taken from 33 localities in eastern North America, and measurements made on eight morphological traits. This allowed an 8×8 matrix to be constructed for each locality, where the ith row and jth column in the kth matrix was the sample correlation r_{ijk} between the ith and jth traits at the kth locality.

One of the questions of interest to Riska was whether there was any evidence that the correlations varied from locality to locality, for these correlations considered either individually or together. A test for the individual correlations could be made by recognizing that the transformation $z_{ijk} = \tanh^{-1}(r_{ijk})$ produces a variable that is approximately normally distributed with the variance $n_k - 3$, where n_k is the sample size for the kth locality. Therefore, the null hypothesis that the correlation between the ith and jth traits was constant at all localities can be tested by comparing the statistic

$$X_{ij}^2 = \sum_{k=1}^{33} (n_k - 3)(z_{ijk} - \bar{z}_{ij})^2,$$

with critical values of the chi-squared distribution with 32 degrees of freedom, where

$$\bar{z}_{ij} = \sum_{k=1}^{33} n_k z_{ijk} / \sum_{k=1}^{33} n_k$$

is the weighted average of the z_{ijk} values over the 33 localities. This test produces a very highly significant result for most of the 28 correlations between pairs of morphological traits.

A chi-squared variable with 32 degrees of freedom has the

expected value 32. Hence, on the null hypothesis that the correlation matrices are the same at all 33 localities, each of the X_{ij}^2 statistics has an expected value of 32 and the sum of all 28 X_{ij}^2 statistics has an expected value of $28 \times 32 = 896$. This suggests that a reasonable way to test whether the correlation matrices are the same at each locality involves seeing whether the sum of the X_{ij}^2 statistics divided by 896,

$$f = \sum_{i=2}^{8} \sum_{j=1}^{i-1} X_{ij}^2/896,$$

is significantly different from 1. If the X_{ij}^2 statistics had independent chi-squared distributions then f would approximately have an F-distribution with 896 and infinite degrees of freedom. Unfortunately, however, it is not realistic to assume that the X_{ij}^2 statistics have independent distributions. It is therefore not possible to test whether the observed value of f is significantly different from 1 using standard distribution theory.

Riska's solution to this problem was to use jackknifing on $\hat{\Theta} = \log(f)$, to see whether this is significantly different from 0. Presumably jackknifing was on $\log(f)$ rather than f to obtain a more normal distribution, although this is not stated in Riska's paper. The steps involved in jackknifing were as follows:

(a) The value of $\hat{\Theta}$ was calculated using the data from all localities. This is the 'full sample' estimate of Θ, the population mean of $\log(f)$.

(b) The 33 'partial estimates' $\hat{\Theta}_{-j}$ were calculated, where the jth of these is the estimate of Θ when the correlations for the jth locality are not included. Here, the degrees of freedom in the denominator of f were adjusted to $28 \times 31 = 868$, to reflect the loss of degrees of freedom from missing out one locality.

(c) The 33 'pseudo-values' $\hat{\Theta}_j^*$ were calculated using equation (9.2).

(d) The pseudo-values were treated as independent estimates of Θ. Their mean $\hat{\Theta}^*$ is the jackknife estimate of Θ, for which the standard error is estimated by $\hat{SE}(\hat{\Theta}^*) = s/\sqrt{33}$, where s^2 is the sample variance of the pseudo-values.

(e) The statistic $t = \hat{\Theta}^*/\hat{SE}(\hat{\Theta}^*)$ was compared with the t-distribution with 32 degrees of freedom to see whether its value is significantly greater than zero. A one-tailed test is required here because it is only large values of f, and

301

hence large values of $\Theta = \log(f)$ that indicate differences between the correlation matrices at different localities.

The final t-statistic from this procedure was found to be 6.7, which is very highly significant. Therefore, Riska concluded that there is very strong evidence that the population correlation matrices vary from locality to locality.

It must be stressed that this type of jackknife procedure may or may not work, depending on the circumstances. Riska was well aware of this, and carried out extensive simulations to assess the procedure for data of the type that he needed to analyse. If anything, he found that the procedure is conservative so that when tests are carried out using a nominal 5% level of significance the true probability of a significant result is between 0.02 and 0.045 when the null hypothesis is in fact true. On this basis, any significant results can be regarded as meaningful rather than some artefact of the jackknife procedure.

9.7 Bootstrapping

Efron (1979) pointed out that the jackknife can be regarded as an approximation to a more primitive method that he named the 'bootstrap' to reflect the fact that its use is analogous to someone pulling themselves up by their bootlaces. The basic idea is very simple. Suppose that a random sample of n values $X_1, X_2, \ldots, X_n$ is taken from a population and used to estimate some parameter Θ. Then the n observed values are regarded as the best indication of the population distribution of X. That is to say, the true population is approximated by an infinite population in which each of the observed X values is equally likely. The sampling variation in the estimator $\hat{\Theta}$ of Θ is assessed by taking random samples of size n, with replacement, from this approximate distribution.

The samples taken from the approximated distribution of X are called bootstrap samples, and each sample provides a bootstrap estimate of Θ. The simplest way to determine the distribution of these estimates is just to take a large number of random samples from the distribution of equally likely X values, although in some cases this distribution can be determined either theoretically or by a complete enumeration of all possibilities.

In many applications, it is the bias and the standard error of the estimator that are of particular interest. The bias is estimated as

302

the difference between the mean of the bootstrap estimates and the estimate from the original sample since the estimate from the original sample is the value of the parameter for the approximating distribution of X. The standard deviation of the bootstrap estimates is an immediate estimate of the standard error of the original estimate.

A more ambitious use of the bootstrap involves using it to determine an approximate confidence interval for a population parameter, or to test for a significant difference from a hypothetical value for this parameter. There are a number of ways that have been suggested for doing this, and the topic is generating a good deal of current research (DiCiccio and Romano, 1988).

Example 9.4: Estimating the density of points in a region

Solow (1989) suggested that the bootstrap provides a convenient method for approximating the sampling distributions of estimators related to the analysis of sparsely sampled spatial point patterns. As an example, he considered the estimation of the number of points per unit area in a region from data collected by T-square sampling (see Section 3.7). This is an application of bootstrapping which has great potential value since very little is known about the distribution theory for samples collected by T-square sampling except in the case where the points being studied have completely random positions.

Solow considered the estimator $\hat{D}' = m^2/(2\sqrt{2}\sum x_i \sum y_i)$ of the density of points over a region, where x_i is the distance from a randomly chosen position in the study region to the nearest object, and y_i is the distance from that object to the nearest second object in the direction away from the initial point (as shown in Figure 3.2), for $i = 1, 2, \ldots, m$ points. This estimator is an alternative to $\hat{D}^*$ given by equation (3.15), where both $\hat{D}'$ and $\hat{D}^*$ are intended to give valid results when objects are not randomly distributed.

Bootstrapping in this situation simply involves resampling the (x_i, y_i) pairs actually obtained, with replacement, to determine the bootstrap distribution of $\hat{D}'$. The standard deviation of this distribution is an immediate estimate of the standard error of $\hat{D}'$. In addition, a simple way to find a 95% confidence limit for the true density, which is called the 'percentile method' is simply to take the range of the central 95% of bootstrap estimates.

A sampling experiment carried out by Solow indicates that these procedures work quite well. He took the locations of 346 red oaks in a unit square region on Lansing Woods, Michigan as a model population. A sample of 25 equally-spaced points was then chosen as the starting point for 25 T-square samples, and $\hat{D}'$ calculated. This provided the estimated density of 305.3 trees over the whole of the study area with its unit area. The true sampling distribution of $\hat{D}'$ was then approximated by choosing 25 new equally-spaced starting points and estimating the density again, with this process being repeated 225 times. This resulted in 209 valid estimates and 16 failures because of T-square samples going outside the study region. A bootstrap distribution of $\hat{D}'$ was approximated by resampling the initial sample 209 times. This was found to match fairly well the distribution of $\hat{D}'$ found from genuine resampling. For example, the bootstrap standard deviation was 43.3 compared to the genuine resampling standard deviation of 36.5. Also, the bootstrap 95% confidence interval for the true density of 240 to 399 seems realistic, when it is remembered that the true density is 346.

In truth, one sampling experiment of this nature is not sufficient to provide confidence in the use of bootstrapping for density estimation from T-square sampling. However, it does indicate that this is a promising procedure for assessing sampling errors in a situation where the alternatives are not very satisfactory.

9.8 Summary and further reading

Four computer intensive methods have been reviewed in this chapter: randomization methods, Monte Carlo methods, jack-knifing, and bootstrapping. These methods are all potentially useful to the researcher for the analysis of grossly non-normal data, or to provide some analysis for data that would otherwise be very difficult to handle. A further discussion about randomization methods in the context of psychology is provided by Edgington (1987), and more details about all four methods with the emphasis on biological applications are provided by Manly (1991). See also Noreen (1989).

At the present time the major problem for the researcher wishing to use computer intensive methods is the need for special computer programs to carry out the calculations. It is possible to adapt some of the large standard statistical packages to do these calculations, but they are likely to be rather slow, and may produce an excessive amount of output from the repeated analyses. The code for FORTRAN programs for some of the simpler randomization tests are provided by Edgington (1987) and Manly (1991), while Noreen (1989) provides programs in BASIC, FORTRAN and PASCAL. A few special purpose computer programs are available commercially and interested researchers may find it worth obtaining a copy of StatXact (available from CYTEL Software Corporation, 137 Erie Street, Cambridge, MA 02139, USA) RESAMPLING STATS (available from 612 N. Jackson Street, Arlington, VA 22201, USA), or RT (available from the Centre for Applications of Statistics and Mathematics, University of Otago, P.O. Box 56, Dunedin, New Zealand, Fax: 64-3-479-8427).

Exercise

Case Study 8 was concerned with determining factors that affect the location of prehistoric Maya sites within the Corozal District of Belize in Central America. The approach used involved dividing the study area into 151 quadrats and characterizing each of these quadrats using 12 variables. Then logistic regression was used to relate the probability of at least one site being present by the values for the variables. The variables have very non-normal distributions (Figure 8.1) so that standard tests for differences between means and variances for quadrats with and without sites are of questionable validity. For this reason it is better to use randomization methods to carry out these tests. Carry out the tests using randomization and report your conclusions. Take into account the fact that 12 tests on mean values and 12 tests on sample variances are being made at the same time by using an appropriate level of significance for each test determined using Bonferroni's inequality.

CASE STUDY 9

The solar activity cycle in the past

One of the most interesting applications of randomization testing has been in the area of testing for periodicity in the times at which certain events have occurred in the past. This has been a controversial area because of the importance of some of the findings. For example, Raup and Sepkoski (1984) caused a considerable stir in the scientific world when they claimed, mainly on the basis of randomization testing, that there has been periodicity in biological extinction rates, with approximately 26 million years between times of peak extinctions. This claim was later refuted by others, since there are clearly some problems with the test procedure that Raup and Sepkoski used. However, the debate whether or not there is evidence of periodicity is still not completely settled (Manly, 1991, Chapter 9). What is clear is that, in principle, randomization testing offers an appropriate method for analysing data on the times of events that are hard to handle in any other way. As an example of the type of situation that arises in this area, this case study concentrates on the question of whether auroral displays in the past have exhibited an 11-year cycle associated with solar activity, such as is the case at the present time.

Stothers (1979) has catalogued mentions of unusual sky phenomena described as 'chasms', 'sky fire', 'night suns', 'blood rain', 'milk rain', 'beams', 'pillars', aurora-like 'torches', and aurora-like 'comets' in the works of some of the better known classical authors. His catalogue extends from 467 BC to 333 AD, but appears to be very incomplete except for the almost continually documented period from 223 to 91 BC, for which the source material is Livy's annalistic history of Rome. It seems that during that shorter period unusual sky phenomena were regarded as very serious religious matters related to the welfare of the state. Reports were carefully checked for accuracy because the rites that were needed to expiate these portents were expensive and time consuming. The years between 223 BC and 91 BC for which at least one of the unusual sky phenomena are recorded are shown in Table 9.2. There are 11 cases of 'sky fire', nine cases of 'night suns', 12 cases of 'blood rain', 14 cases of 'milk rain', and three cases of 'chasms'.

One approach to determining whether there is any evidence that events tended to occur according to a fixed cycle follows on from the work of Stothers (1979) and Rampino and Stothers (1984a,b). It involves examining the extent to which the times of events match the times given by the equation

$$t_n = t_0 + nP,$$

where t_n is the nth time at which the probability of an event being recorded is at a maximum, P is the period of a cycle, and $t_0 < P$ is the time origin. The procedure is as follows:

(a) A suitable range of trial periods (P) is set up
(b) For each trial P, a range of starting times (t_0) is tried, and for each (P,t_0) combination all of the observed events are assigned to their nearest t_n value. The fit of the model is then measured for each (P,t_0) combination by the residual standard deviation $s = \sqrt{(\sum d_i^2/N)}$, where d_i is the difference between the observed event time and the closest maximum, and the summation is over the N observed events. In this way, the best fitting value of t_0 is found for each trial period P. The corresponding minimum residual standard deviation, $s_{min}(P)$, is a measure of the goodness of fit obtained
(c) The significance level of $s_{min}(P)$ is estimated by repeating step (b) a large number of times with N events assigned to random times within the observation period. The estimated significance level for a trial period P is the proportion as $s_{min}(P)$ values obtained from all sets of data (random and real) that are less than or equal to the value for the real data

One of the useful properties of this procedure is that it is not upset by missing events because these make no contribution to the residual standard deviation.

The test was applied to the event times given in Table 9.2 separately for 'sky fire', 'night suns', 'blood rain' and 'milk rain'. Obviously the three cases of 'chasms' do not warrant a test. For each of the four events tested, the randomization distributions of the goodness of fit statistics $s_{min}(P)$ were approximated by 5000 values, consisting of the observed values and the values that were obtained from 4999 sets of data for which events were assigned to random times between 1 and 133. Trial periods P of from 2 to 20 years were considered. The significance level of an observed $s_{min}(P)$ was estimated as the percentage of the 5000 values that were as small or smaller than the observed value.

The results that were obtained from this procedure can be summarized as follows:

'Sky fire'
The only periods showing any unusually low goodness of fit statistics were for five years (significantly small at the 3.20% level) and for 18 years (significantly small at the 0.12% level).

Table 9.2. *Times of unusual sky phenomena from the works of classical authors. (Stothers, 1979)*

SF = 'sky fire', NS = 'night suns', X = 'chasms', BR = 'blood rain', and MR = 'milk rain'. Time is the year counting from 1 in 223 BC.

Year BC	Time	Category	Year BC	Time	Category
223	1	SF, NS	130	94	MR
217	7	X, SF	128	96	BR
214	10	BR	125	99	MR
209	15	MR	124	100	MR
206	18	NS	118	106	MR
204	20	NS	117	107	MR
200	24	SF	114	110	BR, MR
198	26	SF	113	111	SF, NS
197	27	NS	111	113	MR
183	41	BR	108	116	MR
181	43	BR	106	118	BR, MR
172	52	BR	104	120	BR, MR
169	55	SF	102	122	NS, BR
166	58	NS, BR	95	129	MR
163	61	SF, NS, MR	94	130	SF
162	62	SF	93	131	X, SF
147	77	SF	92	132	MR
134	90	NS, BR	91	133	X, BR

'Night suns'

The only period showing a significantly low goodness of fit statistic was for 10 years (significantly low at the 3.34% level).

'Blood rain'

The only period showing a significantly low goodness of fit statistic was for 11 years (significantly low at the 3.32% level).

'Milk rain'

No goodness of fit statistics were significantly low at the 5% level.

Although some significant results have been obtained, these should not be accepted at their face value without some consideration being given to the multiple testing that is inherent in the procedure being used. The problem is that since 19 periods (2–20 years) are being tested for each type of event it follows that the probability of getting a goodness of fit statistic that is significantly low at the 5% level with at least one of these periods must be considerably higher than 0.05. This raises the possibility that the 'significant' results that have been found are typical of what can be expected if, in fact, events occur at completely random times.

A common way round this problem involves requiring that results have a higher level of significance than 5% before they are regarded as being meaningful. For example, the Bonferroni inequality can be invoked. This says that if each of the 19 periods are tested at the $(5/19)\% = 0.26\%$ level then the probability of getting any of them significant by chance is less than 5%. On this basis, the only significant result is for an 18-year cycle with 'sky fire'. What is more, if all $19 \times 4 = 76$ tests are thought of as being carried out at the same time, then the Bonferroni inequality suggests that each test should be made at the $(5/76)\% = 0.07\%$ level. In that case nothing is significant.

Another way of looking at the problem of multiple testing is to ask what significance level to require for each period in order that only 5% of sets of data with random event times will provide one or more significant results. This significance level can then be obtained (at the expense of a considerable amount of computing) in the following way as part of the randomization testing of a set of observed event times:

(a) For each randomized set of data generated, find the significance level for each of the trial periods tested

(b) Again for each randomized set of data, find the period that has the most significant level

(c) Approximate the distribution of minimum significance levels by the values obtained from the randomized sets of data plus the minimum significance level obtained from the real event times that are being tested

(d) Regard the real set of data as having at least one significant period if the minimum significance level for this set of data is exceeded by 95% or more of the values in the approximating randomization distribution. Alternatively, think of the overall significance level of the real set of data as being the percentage of the approximating randomization distribution that is less than or equal to the minimum significance level for the real data

What this procedure does is to ensure that if, in fact, the real data have random event times then the probability of declaring any periods as significant is 0.05 or less. It is an example of a general procedure that was described by Manly *et al.* (1986) and Manly and McAlevey (1987) for handling multiple testing problems with randomization tests.

For 'sky fire' the minimum significance level is 0.12% for a period of 18 years. In comparison with the randomization distribution approximated by this value plus 4999 minimum significance levels for random sets of data, this is significantly low at the 1.62% level since 81 of the 5000 sets of data gave at least one period with a minimum significance level this low. Therefore, in this case there is some evidence of non-randomness. It is interesting to note that 54.7% of the 5000 sets of data gave at least one period with a significance level of 5% or less. This confirms quite clearly the need to allow for multiple testing.

For 'night suns' the minimum significance level for the observed data is 3.34% for a period of 10 years. This presents no real evidence of non-randomness since 41.72% of the randomized sets of data show at least one period that is this significant. The minimum significance level that is reached by only 5% of randomized sets of data is 0.36%.

For 'blood rain' the minimum significance level for the observed data is 3.32% for a period of 11 years. Again, there is no real evidence of significance since 42.20% of the randomized sets of data show at least one period that is this significant. The minimum significance level that is reached by only 5% of randomized sets of data is 0.34%.

Since there were no significant results for 'milk rain' ignoring the multiple testing problem, there is certainly no evidence of non-randomness if multiple testing is taken into account.

In summary, it can be said that this approach to handling multiple testing produces essentially the same result as the use of the Bonferroni inequality. The only evidence for periodicity in the times of any of the unusual sky phenomena is for an 18-year cycle in the records of 'sky fire'. However, even this is debatable given that results are being tested for four different phenomena at the same time.

This analysis is based on searching for evidence of any cycles with a length of from 2 to 20 years. That is not the same as considering whether there is any evidence for an 11-year cycle, which is what can be expected from the cycle of solar activity that exists today. In fact, there is little evidence of an 11-year cycle. For 'sky fire' and 'night suns' the goodness of fit statistics for models with this cycle length fitted to the observed event times are slightly larger than the averages obtained from random data. For 'blood rain' the goodness of fit statistic for the observed event times is significantly low at the 3.32% level for an 11-year cycle. For 'milk rain' the goodness of fit statistic for the observed event times is almost equal to the randomization mean. Therefore, there is only evidence for an 11-year cycle for the occurrences of one of the four unusual phenomena. Taking into account the fact that four series are being tested suggests that a significance level of $(5/4)\% = 1.25\%$ should be required for each series. On this basis, the evidence for an 11-year cycle evaporates completely.

10

Ethical considerations

10.1 Introduction

A dictionary definition of ethical behaviour is behaviour that is 'morally correct'. As such, it is inevitable that value judgements are involved in deciding whether a particular research study is or is not ethical. Also, it is inevitable that in some cases the decision will depend upon the cultural setting in which the study takes place and that it will sometimes happen that there is a conflict between different ethical principles. For these reasons, what is important is not so much to try to establish inflexible rules of ethics that researchers should follow, but instead to have some general guidelines about what to take into account when research plans are being assessed.

A number of professional bodies have devised codes of ethics for their members. To a large extent the present chapter is based on one of these, that is the International Statistical Institute's *declaration on professional ethics* (International Statistical Institute, 1986). This declaration recognizes four types of obligation that the statistician has in collecting and processing information: to society, to funders and employers, to colleagues, and to subjects. This chapter considers each of these obligations in turn, on the assumption that the ethical considerations that apply to a statistician involved in a research study apply equally well to researchers from other disciplines using statistical methods. Of course, some professions have their own codes of conduct that might incorporate principles that are not covered here.

10.2 Obligations to society

Most researchers would probably subscribe to the belief that in general the existence of high quality, reliable information about matters of importance is better than ignorance, although this may need to be tempered with an appropriate regard to the rights of

312

subjects from whom information is gained. On this basis, there is some obligation to improve statistical methods where possible, and to make the results of studies as widely known as possible.

It seems that problems about the publication of results of a study tend to arise when the uses of these results are not clarified before the study takes place. In that case, the researcher may suddenly find that there is pressure to keep results hidden, and there is a conflict between obligations to society and obligations to an employer. Clearly, the solution to this problem is for all parties to agree on a publication strategy before a study takes place.

Of course, the free publication of the results of a study means that there is the potential for these results to be misused by people who are unconnected with the study. However, once the principle is established that information should be shared as freely as possible, researchers can hardly be blamed for the misuse by others of the information that they obtain, although they may be able to take steps to minimize the chance of this happening.

It should go without saying that a researcher should always try to be objective in designing and analysing a study. Selective methods designed to produce a certain outcome should never be used. This is easier said than done in cases where the study is controversial and the researcher has a strongly held belief that he or she wants to have confirmed. In extreme cases it may be best to choose not to be involved at a professional level so as to avoid a conflict of interest that may lead to an unconscious bias.

10.3 Obligations to funders and employers

It is best to clarify in advance the respective obligations of the funder of a study and the researcher who carries out the study. If necessary, the researcher should make it clear that he or she intends to follow a particular code of ethics for the design, analysis and reporting of a study.

In some cases, the researcher will be provided with confidential information from the funder of a project. This information should not be divulged to others without permission. However, the statistical methods and analyses that are used to obtain published results should be open to scrutiny by professional colleagues.

The researcher has an obligation to the funder of a project to assess alternative research designs and analyses and to provide impartial advice about the method to be used, to the best of his or her ability. He or she should be frank about the limits of their expertise, and if necessary suggest that advice from another source should be obtained.

10.4 Obligations to colleagues

The confidence that the public has in a profession depends on how the members of that profession carry out their work. Therefore, researchers should be aware that poor practices on their part will reflect badly on all their professional colleagues. There is, therefore, an obligation to work towards maintaining and enhancing the public opinion of the profession as a whole.

In order to allow studies to be properly assessed by professional colleagues, adequate information must be made available about the methods used, within the limits of confidentiality requirements. On the other hand, when assessing the work of others, criticisms should be directed towards the methods rather than the individuals who selected or used those methods.

When a study involves participants from different disciplines, it is important for each participant to make his or her own ethical principles clear. The principles of each participant should then be respected and incorporated into a common consensus position.

10.5 Obligations to human subjects

A major consideration in studies that involve human subjects must be the potential for intrusion into the privacy of the subjects, which has to be balanced against the benefits that might be gained for society as a whole if the study takes place. It must be appreciated that subjects may perceive themselves to be harmed or threatened, even when there is no specific way that this occurs, because they feel that they have been 'used' against their will.

Wherever possible the principle of informed consent should apply. In other words, subjects should be told exactly why a study is taking place and the potential benefits from the study, and then invited to take part without any pressure being put on them to do so. They should also be allowed to withdraw freely at any time, and have their contribution to the study removed. Even when subjects are required to take part by the law, they should be provided with as much information as possible about the study.

If informed consent cannot be obtained before a study begins then the rights of the subjects should be safeguarded in whatever other ways are possible. If observations on subjects are made without their knowledge then researchers should consider the likely reaction of subjects if they were made aware of what was being done. The deception of subjects in order to gain information is very hard to justify even if this is only done temporarily.

Even when informed consent is obtained the researcher should do as much as possible to protect subjects from any harm resulting from their participation in a study, and to minimize disturbances to the subject. If the risks to subjects are considerable but the potential benefits from a study are large, then the researcher must consider very carefully whether the study should proceed. In these cases it will be best to seek advice from impartial colleagues.

Statistical studies are by their nature concerned with broad trends and averages rather than the results for individual subjects. Therefore, it is generally desirable to ensure that the records of individual subjects are kept confidential, whether or not this is promised to them. This includes considering whether the information that is published from the study is likely to make it possible to identify the results for specific individuals. This is particularly likely to happen, for example, if averages are presented for groups with different characteristics and some of the groups are very small, or if results for several attributes on each subject are presented so that it becomes clear which subject has a particular set of these.

There is another principle that applies to all studies, but most particularly to those that involve subjecting human subjects to inconvenience or stress. This is that the study should be large enough to give a high probability of providing clear evidence of any effects that are of practical importance, but should not be unnecessarily large. If this condition does not hold then the researcher may be wasting his or her own time, but in the past the principle has not always been used when studies are designed. For example, Armitage (1986) has pointed out that clinical trials of cancer treatments have often been too small to detect the levels of difference that can reasonably be expected to exist in practice.

To some extent, the determination of the sample sizes that are needed to detect effects of a plausible magnitude is often rather arbitrary since what constitutes a 'plausible magnitude' is debatable. Nevertheless, it is important to make some trial calculations in order to avoid carrying out a study that is either far too small or much too large. These calculations, which are called a *power analysis* are discussed further in Chapter 11.

10.6 Experiments on animals

For most people it is clear that the human subjects who are used in a research study have rights that must be respected. In fact, generally the obligations to these subjects that are covered in the previous section are largely a matter of common sense. It is, however, a different matter when it comes to studies that involve animals. On the one hand, it can be argued that researchers have no obligations towards animal subjects. On the other hand, it can be argued that animals do have rights, and that it is immoral to cause them any suffering at all.

Most researchers probably hold opinions that are somewhere between these extremes, and this is reflected in the type of declaration that institutions require before they allow animal experiments to be conducted within their jurisdiction. Typically, there are rules about how animals are acquired and cared for, and the steps that must be taken to minimize discomfort and pain. In addition, there may be a requirement that sample sizes are large enough to enable realistic levels of effects to be detected, but not so large as to cause any unnecessary suffering or sacrifice of animals. This is then the same requirement that was mentioned at the end of the last section concerning studies using human subjects. As noted at that point, it is discussed further in Chapter 11.

10.7 Summary and further reading

In this chapter the more important aspects of ethical questions have been reviewed. More information about these matters, with appropriate references, will be found in the International Statistical Institute's *Declaration on Professional Ethics* that was mentioned in Section 10.1 (International Statistical Institute, 1986). Medical research is, of course, the area where ethical questions are most likely to be difficult, and situations in this context are discussed by Heaney and Dougherty (1988) and Bulpitt (1983). The case study that follows indicates how difficult these questions can be.

CASE STUDY 10

A clinical trial on ECMO

Clinical trials offer some special ethical problems since they involve giving different patients alternative treatments to try to find out which treatment is best. The patients are often very ill and, because the best treatment is not known, some of them may end up receiving rather poor care. It is not ethical to withhold a treatment when there is clear evidence that it is the best of the alternatives available. Hence the researcher is under some pressure to stop a trial as soon as possible, or at least to stop using a treatment as soon as it seems to be worse than other treatments. This has led to the development of a number of designs for sequential clinical trials, which terminate as soon as enough evidence has been found in favour of one treatment (Armitage, 1975), and 'play the winner' designs, which allocate treatments to patients with probabilities that depend on how successful those treatments have been for patients treated earlier.

One study that brings ethical issues into sharp focus was concerned with the use of extracorporeal membrane oxygenation (ECMO) for the treatment of newborn infants with diaphragmatic hernia, an anatomical abnormality that leads to impaired intrauterine growth of at least one lung, and persistent pulmonary hypertension (PPHN), with inadequate oxygenation of this blood. Infants with this condition are at very high risk for the first few days of life, but those that survive this period have a good chance of recovering completely. Essentially, ECMO involves removing blood from the body and artificially oxygenating if before it is returned.

Ware (1989) describes how, in 1986, he and medical colleagues at Boston's Children's Hospital Medical Center and Brigham and Women's Hospital reviewed the literature on the treatment of PPHN using ECMO, and concluded that there was not sufficient evidence available to justify using ECMO on a routine basis. Specifically, they felt uneasy about the rapid acceptance of a new and potentially dangerous technology based on inadequate experience from randomized clinical trials. However, the evidence that was available suggested that ECMO therapy might be much better than the standard treatment for very high risk infants. Hence, Ware and his colleagues were also concerned about the ethics of running a clinical trial with the random allocation of ECMO and

317

the standard treatment if the results for the infants treated first indicated very much higher survival rates with ECMO. Apparently, there was a period of intense debate between the proponents of ECMO, who considered that this provided a breakthrough in the treatment of PPHN, and the sceptics, who were unconvinced by the historical data available, and concerned by the potential side effects of ECMO.

Given this situation, Ware felt that the only type of clinical trial involving the random allocation of treatments that would be ethical was one that controlled the maximum number of deaths that could occur in either the ECMO or the conventionally treated group. This can be achieved by randomly assigning patients to treatment groups until r deaths are observed in one group. At that stage, randomization ceases and all patients are assigned to the other treatment until r deaths occur in that group or the number of survivors is large enough to establish the superiority of the treatment that the patients are finally assigned to.

In the event, this design was used to assess the ECMO treatment, with the maximum number of deaths being four for either the ECMO or the control group. The trial began on 6 February 1986. Patients were randomly assigned to treatments in blocks of four up to the 19th patient. At that stage, 10 patients had received conventional therapy, of which four had died, and nine patients had received ECMO, of which none had died.

Although randomization ceased at that point, the study continued. Those responsible for the recruitment of patients into the study and for the care of the patients were not told immediately that all patients were receiving ECMO, although this soon became apparent. At that stage the investigators met to discuss the need to continue enrolling patients into the study and caring for them in the same way as was done during the randomization phase. It was calculated that in order to have a significant difference between the survival rates for the ECMO and control groups there had to be at least 28 patients surviving ECMO therapy before the fourth death in that group was observed. Therefore the study continued until another 20 patients had received ECMO. At that stage, the results were as shown in Table 10.1.

The principle of 'randomized consent' as proposed by Zelen (1979) was used in the study. According to this principle, a physician does not require patient consent in order to give the conventional therapy for an illness. Hence, only the parents of those patients that were randomized to ECMO were approached

Table 10.1. *The survival of infants given ECMO treatment and the conventional treatment for PPHN (Ware, 1989)*

In phase 1 of the study the patients were randomly allocated to one or other of the treatments in blocks of four. In phase 2 all patients were allocated to ECMO.

	Phase 1		Phase 2	
	ECMO	CT	ECMO	CT
Survived	9	6	19	0
Died	0	4	1	0

CT, conventional treatment; ECMO, extracorporeal membrane oxygenation; PPHN, persistent pulmonary hypertension.

for informed consent. Ware argued that this is a better procedure than one that would have required parents of very ill infants to give their consent to a surgical procedure that might then not be given.

The ECMO clinical trial has created something of a controversy. Eleven biostatisticians were invited to comment on the trial in notes that are appended to Ware's paper. According to some of these biostatisticians, the randomization of patients to conventional medical therapy should never have taken place, and the fact that parents were never told about this was a grave error. On the other hand, other commentators commend Ware for his sensitivity to ethical issues, and one even goes so far as to argue that the randomization of patients to treatments should have been continued after the first 19 patients were enrolled.

In his rejoinder to the comments made by others, Ware identifies five important points concerning his study. The first three relate to questions of ethics, and are discussed below. The other two points are concerned with aspects of the study design and the data analysis that are not directly related to ethical questions. Therefore these will not be pursued further here.

(a) The role of randomization in medical research

Here the basic question is whether clinical trials involving the random allocation of patients to different treatments can be justified in cases where preliminary data indicate that a new treatment is substantially better than the conventional treatment.

The argument in favour of randomized trials is that it is the only way to get really convincing evidence because of shortcomings in data obtained from other sources. The arguments against randomized trials is that they involve purposely giving some patients a treatment that is likely to be less effective than an alternative, and that in fact data obtained in other ways can yield reliable results. At the present time it is not possible to get a general agreement amongst biostatisticians and medical researchers about which of these points of view is correct.

(b) The ethical justification for randomization in the ECMO study

Ware argues that the superiority of ECMO over the standard therapy was very far from being clear when the ECMO study began. A randomized clinical trial was therefore justifiable as a means of clarifying the situation. Here it is important to realize that with hindsight it will often be possible to see that a particular treatment was not the best for some patients who received it. However, the ethical status of a study depends only on the information that was available when the study began.

(c) The principle of randomized consent

An important aspect of the use of randomized consent was that the physicians involved in the ECMO study had decided that it was not appropriate to use the ECMO treatment without further evidence of its efficacy. On this basis, Ware argues that giving the conventional treatment to an infant did not require that the ECMO alternative be discussed with the parents. In fact, it was considered that this would add to the stress of the parents without a corresponding benefit. However, Ware admits that the principle of randomized consent does conflict with the principle of being as open as possible with patients and their families about treatment decisions.

11

Synthesis: carrying out a research study

11.1 Introduction

A research study can be thought of as consisting of five stages:

  (a) Deciding on the objectives of the study
  (b) Planning the collection of the data
  (c) Collecting the data
  (d) Analysing the data
  (e) Writing the research report

In Chapters 1 to 10 the first four of these stages have been discussed in various places, to some extent in isolation from each other. However, in this concluding chapter it is appropriate to review all five stages from the perspective of the research study as a whole. This will be done by discussing each of the stages in turn.

11.2 Deciding on objectives

It should go without saying that it makes no sense to carry out a research study without the objectives being clear both in a general sense and in terms of specific questions to be answered. What is meant here is that it should be possible to describe the purpose of a study by a general statement such as 'the study is intended to assess the attitudes that people have towards abortion on demand', or 'the purpose of the study is to compare the population dynamics of three species of grasshoppers living in a particular area'. A specific question to be answered for the first example might then take the form 'what percentage of the sampled population will answer "yes" to a certain question?', while, for the second example, a specific question might be 'are there significant differences between the survival rates for the different species?'.

Of course, the nature of the specific questions to be asked will depend entirely on the context of a study. But it is important to list these questions at an early stage so as to ensure that the right data are collected to answer them. Furthermore, these questions should be framed in such a way that they are concerned with parameters for well-defined populations, since if this is not done then the standard methods of statistical inference will not be applicable.

When devising specific questions it is worth giving some thought to whether they should be phrased in terms of a test of significance or in terms of estimation. While it can be argued that tests of significance have some role to play in most studies, many statisticians consider nowadays that they tend to be over-used by researchers. Therefore, consideration should be given to replacing some tests of significance by the estimation of population parameters and effects with confidence intervals. One advantage of doing this is that it provides all the information from hypothesis tests, plus an indication of the level of possible sampling errors. Therefore, if a 95% confidence includes the value zero then it is known that the estimated difference is not significantly different from zero at the 5% level. Conversely, a 95% confidence limit that does not include zero indicates a significant difference at the 5% level. At the same time, the width of the interval shows how large estimated effects have to be in order to show significance.

The need to have clear objectives applies equally well to experimental or observational studies. There are plenty of examples of both types of study where it was discovered after the data were collected that some of the important questions could not be answered. In order to avoid this occurring, it is important that researchers should ask themselves how they will react according to the potential outcomes of a study. As the following example shows, it is quite possible to have the situation where a non-significant outcome is meaningful since it indicates the absence of an effect, but a significant outcome has several different possible explanations.

Example 11.1: An inconclusive study

This example is a description of a real study that failed to achieve the required objective. The study was intended to determine whether the use of the available habitat by a fish of species A was affected by the presence of another fish of species B. To this end, three study areas where species A is present and species B is absent were chosen. Another three study areas were also chosen where both species are present. The habitat use of species A in the first three study areas was then compared with the use in the second three areas. Essentially the study design was a static group comparison as discussed in Section 5.5.

To assess habitat use by species A, each of the six study areas was divided into a large number of small quadrats. Some of these quadrats were then randomly sampled from each study area and for each sampled quadrat it was noted whether species A was present, and the characteristics of the quadrat were quantified by making appropriate measurements. From the data obtained it was possible to use logistic regression to produce equations that predict the probability that a quadrat was used by species A as a function of the values of habitat variables in that quadrat. These equations indicated that the probability of species A being present in different types of quadrat depended on whether or not species B was present.

At first sight it appeared that the study had demonstrated that the use of habitat by species A is affected by the presence of species B. Unfortunately, however, it was clear that the distributions of habitat variables in the three areas where species B was present were quite different from what they were in the other three areas. Since it is well-known that the probability of an organism using different types of habitat generally depends on what habitat is available, it follows that one explanation for the results of the study is that species A was changing its use of habitat according to what was available, quite independently of the presence or absence of species B. Hence, the study ended up being inconclusive.

The basic problem was that the presence or absence of species B was strongly confounded with the variables used to characterize habitats (presumably because of habitat selection by species B). It seems likely that this could have been foreseen in advance if the researcher had given some thought to what could be concluded from the different possible outcomes of the study. It would then have become apparent that whereas a non-significant result could be interpreted as giving no evidence of an effect of species B, a significant result would be problematical. Indeed, the researcher would have concluded that the only way to get unambiguous evidence of an effect of the presence of species B would be to use a different study design.

11.3 Planning the collection of data

The data for a research study can be obtained in one of three ways: from records that already exist; by sampling to obtain new data; or by carrying out an experiment. To a large extent, the choice of which of these methods is going to be used will probably be dictated by the circumstances, but in all cases there is likely to be the need to decide on a sampling or experimental design, and on the sample sizes to be used. This is true in many cases even when records that already exist are to be used since it is not practical to use all the available records. Sampling the population of records is then similar to sampling any other population.

Designs for sampling a finite population of identifiable units have been discussed in Chapter 2. In this situation, when there is a choice of the sampling design to be used, the questions that should be addressed are:

(a) Will a simple random sample be all that is needed, or should a more complicated design be used?
(b) If a more complicated design seems appropriate then should this involve stratification, cluster sampling, and/or multistage sampling?
(c) Is systematic sampling a possibility that should be considered?
(d) Is there a suitable supplementary variable that allows the use of regression or ratio estimation?

Experimental designs have been considered in Chapters 5 to 7. The possibilities here range from a simple comparison between a control and a treated group to a complicated multifactor design with blocking to control extraneous sources of variation. With two or more factors it may be worth spending some time thinking about questions such as:

(a) Is there another factor that should be considered as well?
(b) How many levels should be used for each factor, and what should these levels be?
(c) Is a factorial experiment possible, or does this require too many observations?
(d) Is a repeated measures design required?
(e) Should blocking be used to control extraneous sources of variation?
(f) Can the experiment include replicate observations?

11.4 Sample size determination

Once a design has been chosen, either for an observational or an experimental study, the next step is to consider the sample sizes that will be used. Sometimes there will be no choice here since the available data are dictated by the nature of the study design. At other times, the researcher will be able to choose sample sizes fairly freely subject to some resource constraints.

The general principle that should be used either in deciding on appropriate sample sizes or checking whether available sample sizes are adequate, is the one that has been mentioned in Chapter 10 on the basis of ethical considerations in experiments involving human and animal subjects: sample sizes should be large enough to give a high probability of providing clear evidence of any effects that are of practical importance, but should not be unnecessarily large.

The likely result of not giving adequate consideration to sample sizes is that they will be too small, with the result that the researcher will have too much faith in null hypotheses that are not rejected by significance tests, and will estimate unacceptably wide confidence limits for population parameters. The example of clinical trials for cancer treatments was mentioned in Chapter 10. In this case, Armitage (1986) has noted that trials have often been too small to detect plausible differences between the outcomes of different treatments. In the same context, Freiman *et al.* (1978) suggest that perhaps half of all clinical trials have not been large enough to detect a 50% reduction in risk. A similar situation seems to exist in other subject areas as well. For example, in a paper emphasizing the need for power analysis in fisheries in particular and biological research in general, Peterman (1990) describes several studies where important decisions concerning fisheries management have been based on sample sizes that are too small. Also, Manly (1985, p. 400) has noted that the small number of power analyses that have been carried out for studies designed to detect natural selection have indicated that in the past these studies have been too small to detect realistic levels of selection.

The *power* of a statistical test is defined to be the probability of rejecting the null hypothesis when this null hypothesis is not true. For this reason, calculations of sample sizes required to detect effects of a particular magnitude are often called *power analysis*. All research studies should include some initial calculations of the power of statistical tests or the width of confidence intervals (or both of these) that will be obtained with the sample sizes that are planned. This may not be an easy exercise, since crucial information, such as the standard deviation of observations, will often be unknown. A pilot study may help to provide this information, or intelligent guesses may be needed. However, any sample size assessment will generally be better than none.

A useful strategy is to begin by deciding what is the maximum size of study that is possible within the bounds of the resources available. The accuracy that can be expected from a study of this size can then be assessed. If this accuracy is acceptable, but not as good as the researcher would like, then this maximum study size can be used on the grounds that it is the best that can be done. On the other hand, if a study of the maximum size gives an unnecessary level of accuracy then the possibility of a smaller study can be investigated.

The determination of sample sizes for simple random sampling and stratified random sampling for sample surveys has been discussed in Sections 2.5 and 2.7. One of the most useful results in this context is equation (2.9), which says that to estimate a population mean from a simple random sample with a 95% confidence interval of $\bar{x} \pm \delta$, the sample size should be approximately

$$n = N\sigma^2/(N\delta^2/4 + \sigma^2), \qquad (11.1)$$

where N is the population size and σ is the population standard deviation. For an infinite or large population this equation simplifies to

$$n = 4\sigma^2/\delta^2, \qquad (11.2)$$

which is also a conservative result if N is unknown in the sense that it provides an upper limit to the sample size required.

Another useful result is equation (2.11), which says that to obtain a 95% confidence limit for a population proportion of the form $p \pm \delta$, where p is the proportion in a simple random sample, requires that the sample size should be approximately

$$n = N\pi(1 - \pi)/\{N\delta^2/4 + \pi(1 - \pi)\}, \qquad (11.3)$$

where π is the true population proportion, and N is the population size. If N is large, this reduces to

$$n = 4\pi(1 - \pi)/\delta^2, \qquad (11.4)$$

which has the upper limit of

$$n = 1/\delta^2 \qquad (11.5)$$

when $\pi = \frac{1}{2}$.

Studies also often involve the comparison between the means obtained from two or more random samples taken from large or infinite populations. To that end, it can be noted that an approximate 95% confidence interval for the difference between two population means is

$$\bar{X}_1 - \bar{X}_2 \pm 2\sqrt{(\sigma_1^2/n_1 + \sigma_2^2/n_2)}, \qquad (11.6)$$

where $\bar{X}_i$ is the mean of a random sample of size n_i from the ith population, which has standard deviation σ_i. In order that this confidence interval takes the form $\bar{X}_1 + \bar{X}_2 \pm \delta$, it is required that

$$\delta = 2\sqrt{(\sigma_1^2/n_1 + \sigma_2^2/n_2)}.$$

Hence, in the special case when $n = n_1 = n_2$ and $\sigma = \sigma_1 = \sigma_2$ it is necessary to have sample sizes of

$$n = 8\sigma^2/\delta^2. \qquad (11.7)$$

This gives a guide to the sample sizes that are required for the comparison of sample means. The width of the confidence interval is made as small as possible for a given total $n_1 + n_2$ if $n_1 = n_2$, but to a large extent increasing n_1 can compensate for decreasing n_2, and vice versa.

In a similar way, if the differences between two sample proportions p_1 and p_2 is to be used to estimate the difference between the corresponding population proportions π_1 and π_2, then it can be noted that an approximate 95% confidence interval for the difference between the population proportions is

$$p_1 - p_2 \pm 2\sqrt{\{\pi_1(1 - \pi_1)/n_1 + \pi_2(1 - \pi_2)/n_2\}},$$

where n_i is the size of the ith sample. Hence, if this confidence interval is to be of the form $p_1 - p_2 \pm \delta$, for a suitably small value of δ, then it is required that

$$\delta = 2\sqrt{\{\pi_1(1 - \pi_1)/n_1 + \pi_2(1 - \pi_2)/n_2\}}.$$

In that case, if $n = n_1 = n_2$ then the required confidence interval will be obtained providing that

$$n = 4\{\pi_1(1 - \pi_1) + \pi_2(1 - \pi_2)\}/\delta^2.$$

This result is more useful than it might appear at first sight since the terms $\pi_1(1 - \pi_1)$ and $\pi_2(1 - \pi_2)$ are rather insensitive to changes in the values of π_1 and π_2. Hence the required value of n

can be obtained by replacing π_1 and π_2 by their average value $\pi' = \frac{1}{2}(\pi_1 + \pi_2)$. This leads to the required sample size being given by

$$n \approx 8\pi'(1 - \pi')/\delta^2. \qquad (11.8)$$

The largest possible value of n occurs with this equation when $\pi' = \frac{1}{2}$, in which case

$$n \approx 2/\delta^2. \qquad (11.9)$$

Therefore, this is the equation that should be used by the researcher who is uncertain about the magnitude of population proportions.

It must be remembered that equations (11.1) to (11.9) are based on the assumption that sample statistics are approximately normally distributed, and that sample sizes are large enough for the standard errors estimated from samples to be reasonably close to the true standard errors. In essence this means that the sample sizes produced by the equations must be treated with some reservations unless these sizes are at least 20 and, for equations (11.1), (11.2), (11.6) and (11.7), the distribution being sampled is not grossly non-normal. Generally, the larger the sample size, the less important is the normality of the distribution being sampled.

The equations can be used for determining sample sizes either with estimation or hypothesis testing. It just has to be remembered that an effect that is significant at the 5% level is obtained whenever a 95% confidence limit does not include the hypothetical value of a population parameter. For example, suppose that equation (11.2) is used to choose a sample size so as to achieve a 95% confidence interval for a population mean μ of the form $\bar{X} \pm \delta$, for some suitably small value of δ. Then, since $\bar{X}$ will be greater than μ with probability $\frac{1}{2}$, it follows that the confidence interval will include $\mu - \delta$ with probability $\frac{1}{2}$. Thus, $\bar{X}$ will be significantly different from $\mu - \delta$ (on a two-tailed test at the 5% level) with the same probability. A similar argument shows that $\bar{X}$ will be significantly different from $\mu + \delta$ with probability $\frac{1}{2}$. In other words, if the sample size is chosen to produce a 95% confidence interval with a width of $\pm \delta$, then the same sample size will give a probability of at least $\frac{1}{2}$ of $\bar{X}$ being significantly different from any hypothetical mean that is more than δ different from the true population mean. More generally, whenever one of the equations (11.1) to (11.9) is used to determine the sample size that will give a 95% confidence interval with width $\pm \delta$, then this sample size will have a probability of at least $\frac{1}{2}$ of a significant result when the effect being tested is δ or larger.

If desired, sample sizes for tests of significance can be determined in order to achieve any desired probability of detecting an effect of size δ. For example, it might be specified that the probability of detecting a difference between two population means of 100 should be at least 0.95, so that the probability of *type II error* (accepting the null hypothesis when it is false) is $1 - 0.95 = 0.05$.

Graphs and tables are available to achieve aims like this, both for two sample comparisons and for more complicated study designs. Useful references here are Montgomery (1984) and Winer (1971) for designed experiments, Cochran (1977) and Scheaffer *et al.* (1990) for sample surveys, and Machin and Campbell (1987) for clinical trials. Table 10 of Pearson and Hartley (1966) can be used for determining sample sizes for t-tests, and Table 30 of Pearson and Hartley (1972) can be used for determining sample sizes for either t-tests or one factor analysis of variance.

With a complicated study design it may happen that a search of the literature fails to provide any tables or charts for assessing the sample sizes that are needed. In that case as a last resort it is always possible to simulate a large number of sets of data of the type that are expected to arise, and carry out on each of these sets the analysis that is planned for the real data. If these simulations are carried out for appropriate ranges of population parameters and sample sizes then it is possible to determine the minimum sample sizes that are needed to detect the effects that real data are likely to show.

If a pilot study has been carried out or historical data are available, then bootstrapping may provide a convenient alternative to the computer generation of data (Bros and Cowell, 1987), particularly in situations where the distribution of data is very non-normal. Example 11.2 that follows indicates the type of approach that can be used.

It does, of course, sometimes happen that the nature of a study makes it virtually impossible to define the level of effects that should be detected by a test of significance, or the width of desired confidence limits. For example, a sample survey might be being planned with the idea of using the data obtained to estimate a regression relationship between a dependent variable Y and a set of predictor variables X_1 to X_p. Without any data, and no possibility of a pilot survey it is then impossible to know how many cases need to be sampled to get reasonably accurate regression coefficients.

There are some 'rules of thumb' that have been suggested for situations like this, but they are seldom quoted by statisticians because their theoretical basis is obscure. Some of these rules are noted by Crothers (1977) in a discussion of the minimum sample size needed for exploratory social surveys where resource constraints make large samples impractical. He suggests, on the basis of the types of analysis that are likely to be carried out, that a sample of 150 cases is probably adequate in this context.

Finally, before concluding this discussion on sample size determination it must be pointed out that there is often a considerable difference between target sample sizes and the sample sizes actually obtained. There may be many reasons for this, such as the non-response of subjects in social surveys and the failure of recording equipment in an industrial experiment. If the probability of an observation being missing is a function of the value of that observation then a bias will result if this fact is ignored. However, if all observations have the same probability of being missing then this will not be a problem and all that will happen is that the study will not be as powerful as planned. This leads to the obvious recommendation that researchers should, if necessary, make an allowance for missing data when determining target sample sizes.

Example 11.2: Sample size determination for a study on prey consumption by lizards

The following data values are the stomach contents of *Orthoptera*, in milligrams of dry weight, for a sample of 45 eastern short-horned lizards *Phrynosoma douglassi brevirostre* from a certain area:

0 142 0 52 94 0 0 376 50 429 0 0 0 340 0 0 0 0 0 190 0
0 60 0 0 0 0 0 0 10 0 0 8 1042 0 137 7 110 0 965 0 0
110 1006 1524

(Powell and Russell, 1984, 1985; Linton *et al.*, 1989). Suppose, purely for the sake of an example, that a study is being planned to compare the mean consumption of *Orthoptera* by lizards in two other areas, and that the data provided above are the best indication of the type of distribution that is likely to be found for each of these areas, apart from a possible change in the mean. Suppose also that the study requires that the difference in the mean consumption in the two areas should be estimated to within about 250 mg dry weight.

If the requirement for accuracy is interpreted as meaning that a 95% confidence interval for the difference in mean consumption between the two areas should be $\bar{X}_2 - \bar{X}_1 \pm 250$, then equation (11.7) can be used to determine the sizes of the samples to be taken from the two areas. The data shown above have a standard deviation of 334.4. Assuming that this is a good estimate of the population standard deviation, equation (11.7) suggests that the sizes of sample required from the two areas are $n \approx 8 \times (334.4)^2/250^2 = 14.3$, say 14.

Reservations must be held concerning the use of sample sizes as small as 14 since equation (11.7) is based on the assumption that samples are 'large'. In particular, sampling errors in the estimates of the population standard deviation are being ignored. This suggests that it would be more appropriate to use the confidence interval $\bar{X}_2 - \bar{X}_1 \pm t_{5\%,2n-2} \cdot \text{S}\hat{\text{E}}(\bar{X}_2 - \bar{X}_1)$ based on the t-distribution, instead of $\bar{X}_2 - \bar{X}_1 \pm 2 \cdot \text{S}\hat{\text{E}}(\bar{X}_2 - \bar{X}_1)$ based on the normal distribution. The appropriate sample sizes to use in this case can be determined using Table 10 of Pearson and Hartley (1966), as explained in Section 5.8 of that publication. Using the standard deviation of 334.4 found for the pilot data, it can be calculated that if two samples of size 15 are taken then there will be a probability of about 0.5 of detecting a difference as large as 250 in the means of the populations that those samples come from. This implies that a confidence interval for the difference between population means will approximately be the sample mean difference ± 250. Therefore, using the t-distribution to determine sample sizes gives an increase of only one over the sample sizes that are suggested by equation (11.7).

Although sampling errors in estimated standard deviations are accounted for when the t-distribution is used for inferences, there are still grounds for concern about the method for determining sample sizes since the available data indicate that the distribution of the variable being studied is very non-normal. The determination of appropriate sample sizes is therefore better if it uses a method that takes this distribution into account. This can be achieved by carrying out the following bootstrap procedure along the lines suggested by Bros and Cowell (1987):

(a) Choose a lower limit n_L and an upper limit n_U for sample sizes according to the resources available

(b) Take two bootstrap samples of size n_U from the available pilot sample of 45 values, as explained in Section 9.7. That is, take two samples of size n_U with replacement from the 45 values

(c) Use the first n values of sample 1 and the first n values of sample 2 as bootstrap samples of size n, for which sample means $\bar{X}_1$ and $\bar{X}_2$ and sample standard deviations s_1 and s_2 can be calculated. Hence, determine the mean difference $D = \bar{X}_2 - \bar{X}_1$, and the t-statistic $T = D/(s_p\sqrt{2/n})$, where s_p is the usual pooled within-sample standard deviation. Do these calculations for all values of n from n_L to n_U, inclusive

(d) Repeat steps (b) and (c) a large number of times in order to generate the bootstrap distributions of D and T separately for all the sample sizes from n_L to n_U. These distributions can be assumed to approximate the distributions of D and T for samples from two real populations, if those two populations are in fact identical

(e) For each sample size n, find limits for D and T such that 95% of the bootstrap distributions are within these limits

The 95% limits for D that are found at step (e) indicate the likely level of sampling variation in the difference between the two sample means for different sample sizes. The 95% limits for T can be compared with the critical values found in t-distribution tables. If the agreement is good for a particular sample size then this indicates that it will be valid to use the t-distribution for making inferences with samples of this size.

Applying this procedure in the present case indicates that the non-normality in the data need be of no concern. Using 1000 replications of the bootstrap process produced the 95% limits for D and T for sample sizes from 10 to 20 that are shown in Table 11.1. It is apparent that if two samples of size 13 are taken then the sampling error in the difference between the means will be within the range ± 250 with a probability of about 0.95, and that the statistic $T = D/(s_p\sqrt{2/n})$ is, in fact, less variable than is expected from the t-distribution. Therefore, taking samples of this size and calculating a 95% confidence interval as $\bar{X}_2 - \bar{X}_1 \pm t_{5\%,2n-2} \cdot \text{S}\hat{\text{E}}(\bar{X}_2 - \bar{X}_1)$ would seem to be a safe procedure.

The fact that the distribution of T is less variable than expected

332

Table 11.1. *Results of bootstrap sampling of a sample of 45 observations on consumption of Orthoptera by eastern short-horned lizards. (Powell and Russell, 1984, 1985; Linton et al., 1989)*

Sample size	Bootstrap 95% limits for difference between sample means		Bootstrap 95% limits for t-statistics		Critical value from t-table
	Lower	Upper	Lower	Upper	
10	−292	277	−1.83	1.77	2.10
11	−265	260	−1.82	1.82	2.09
12	−260	260	−1.89	1.93	2.07
13	−245	250	−1.94	1.91	2.06
14	−229	232	−1.92	1.86	2.06
15	−221	239	−1.92	1.92	2.05
16	−225	225	−1.86	1.87	2.04
17	−217	214	−1.89	1.77	2.04
18	−207	211	−1.86	1.78	2.03
19	−206	204	−1.83	1.79	2.03
20	−202	195	−1.81	1.83	2.02

from the t-distribution is shown by the fact that 95% of the bootstrap replications gave values within the range -1.94 to $+1.91$, but the t-distribution table predicts that these limits should be -2.06 to $+2.06$ for samples of size 13. A small simulation study indicates that this is a genuine result of sampling a highly non-normal distribution.

Incidentally, it can be noted that the bootstrap sampling indicates the level of sampling variation to be expected for samples drawn from populations with different means since the effect of different means would just be to shift the mean of D by a constant amount, without affecting the distribution in any other way. However, it is obvious that if the two populations being sampled have other differences then the bootstrap distribution of D may not give a good indication of the true distribution of sample mean differences.

11.5 Collecting data

The main points to keep in mind during the process of data collection is the need to do this both accurately and consistently. With a large data set it is easy for errors in recording to occur, and the probability of this will increase considerably if the data have to be transcribed before they can be analysed. Hence, if possible the original records should be made in such a way that they can be punched straight into a computer. It is better still if the original recording is to a computer file.

If several people are involved in taking observations then it is most important that they use the same protocols since observer biases may occur if the people collecting data are allowed to use their own interpretations of instructions and definitions. Detailed written instructions should be provided that cover all the contingencies that can be thought of before recording begins. Preferably, there will be a trial period followed by a review of any difficulties that have arisen, and steps taken to eliminate these.

11.6 Analysing data

It is surprising how many research studies are still carried out without enough thought being given to the analysis of the data. Practising statisticians often complain that many clients come to consult them only when data have been collected in such a way that a satisfactory analysis involves unnecessary complications or is even impossible. In many cases these problems would have been avoided by the client simply thinking in advance about what form the final data would take and how these data would have to be analysed in order to answer the questions posed by the objectives of the study.

It is true, of course, that the data that are collected are sometimes not quite what was expected. However, in a well-planned study some thought will have been given to the types of problem that might occur and how these can be overcome. For example, consideration should be given to how missing data will be handled, and what will be done if the assumptions of the planned analysis are clearly not valid.

11.7 The research report

The research report is probably the only part of a study that will be permanent since after a few years the data are likely either to be lost or difficult to interpret. Therefore, time spent in preparing a clear and comprehensive report is time well spent.

Much can, and has, been written about technical writing, and this is not the place to do more than mention the importance of the topic. Those interested in reading more may find the books by Day (1988), Katz (1985) and Miller and Taylor (1989) to be worth consulting. Gopen and Swan (1990) have recently pointed out the importance of placing information in the order that is expected by readers. They offer seven reader-expectation principles to follow in order to improve technical writing, and argue that readers often find papers and books difficult to understand because these principles are not followed.

References

Abraham, B. (1983). Intervention model analysis. *Encyclopedia of Statistical Sciences* **4**: 207–12.

Achen, C. H. (1986). *The Statistical Analysis of Quasi-Experiments*. University of California Press, Berkeley.

Aitkin, M., Anderson, D., Francis, B. and Hinde, J. (1989). *Statistical Modelling in GLIM*. Clarenden Press, Oxford.

Andersen, P. K. and Vaeth, M. (1988). Survival Analysis. *Encyclopedia of Statistical Sciences* **9**: 119–29.

Armitage, P. (1975). *Sequential Medical Trials*, 2nd Edit. Blackwell, Oxford.

Armitage, P. (1986) Some statistical aspects of clinical trials. In *Pacific Statistical Congress* (eds. I. S. Francis, B. F. J. Manly and F. C. Lam), pp. 5–11. North Holland, The Netherlands.

Barnard, G. A. (1963). Discussion on Professor Bartlett's paper. *Journal of the Royal Statistical Society* **B25**: 294.

Begon, F. J. (1979). *Investigating Animal Abundance*. Edward Arnold, London.

Besag, J. and Diggle, P. J. (1977). Simple Monte Carlo tests for spatial pattern. *Applied Statistics* **26**: 327–33.

Billewicz, W. Z. (1965). The efficiency of matched samples: an empirical investigation. *Biometrics* **21**: 623–44.

Bhattacharyya, M. N. and Layton, A. P. (1979). Effectiveness of seat belt legislation on the Queensland road toll – an Australian case study in intervention analysis. *Journal of the American Statistical Association* **74**: 596–603.

Blower, J. G., Cook, L. M. and Muggleton, J. (1981). *Estimating the Size of Animal Populations*. George Allen and Unwin, London.

BMDP (1989). *SOLO Statistical Package*. BMDP Statistical Software Inc., Los Angeles.

Box, G. E. P. and Cox, D. R. (1964). An analysis of transformations. *Journal of the Royal Statistical Society* **B26**: 211–52.

Box, G. E. P. and Tiao, G. C. (1975). Intervention analysis with applications to economic and environmental problems. *Journal of the American Statistical Association* **70**: 70–9.

Bros, W. E. and Cowell, B. C. (1987). A technique for optimizing sample size (replication). *Journal of Experimental and Marine Biology and Ecology* **114**: 63–71.

Bulpitt, C. J. (1983). *Randomized Controlled Clinical Trials*. Martinus Nijhoff, The Hague.

Bumpus, H. C. (1898). The elimination of the unfit as illustrated by the introduced sparrow, *Passer domesticus*. *Biological Lectures, Marine Biology Laboratory, Woods Hole*, 11th Lecture, pp. 209–26.

Burk, D. (1980). *Cancer mortality linked with artificial fluoridation in Birmingham, England*. Paper presented at the 4th International Symposium on the Prevention and Detection of Cancer, Wembley, UK, July 1980.

Burnham, K. P., Anderson, D. R. and Laake, J. L. (1980). Estimation of density from line transect sampling of biological populations. *Wildlife Monographs* 72.

Cain, A. J. and Sheppard, P. M. (1950). Natural selection in *Cepaea*. *Genetics* 39: 89–116.

Campbell, D. T. and Stanley, J. C. (1963). *Experimental and Quasi-Experimental Designs for Research*. Houghton Mifflin, Boston.

Carpenter, S. R., Frost, T. M., Heisey, D. and Kratz, T. K. (1989). Randomized intervention analysis and the interpretation of whole ecosystem experiments. *Ecology* 70: 1142–52.

Chatfield, C. and Collins, A. J. (1980). *Introduction to Multivariate Analysis*. Chapman and Hall, London.

Cochran, W. G. (1977). *Sampling Techniques*. Wiley, New York.

Cochran, W. G. (1983). *Planning and Analysis of Observational Studies*. Wiley, New York.

Cochran, W. G. and Cox, G. M. (1957). *Experimental Designs*, 2nd Edit. Wiley, New York.

Coleman, J. S. (1966). *Equality of Educational Opportunity*. Government Printing Office, Washington, DC.

Cook, T. D. and Campbell, D. T. (1979). *Quasi-Experimentation: Design and Analysis Issues for Field Settings*. Houghton-Mifflin, Boston.

Cook-Mozaffari, P., Bulusu, L. and Doll, R. (1981). Fluoridation of water supplies and cancer mortality. I. A search for an effect in the U.K. on risk of death from cancer. *Journal of Epidemiology and Community Health* 35: 227–32.

Cook-Mozaffari, P. and Doll, R. (1981). Fluoridation of water supplies and cancer mortality. II. Mortality trends after fluoridation. *Journal of Epidemiology and Community Health* 35: 233–8.

Cormack, R. M. (1968). The statistics of capture–recapture methods. *Annual Review of Oceanography and Marine Biology* 6: 455–506.

Cox, D. R. (1969). Some sampling problems in technology. In *New Developments in Survey Sampling* (eds. N. L. Johnson and H. Smith), pp. 506–27. Wiley, New York.

Cox, D. R. and Oakes, D. (1984). *Analysis of Survival Data*. Chapman and Hall, London.

Crosbie, J. and Sharpley, C. F. (1989). *DMITSA, A Statistical Program for Analysing Data from Interrupted Time Series*. Faculty of Education, Monash University, Victoria, Australia.

Crothers, C. (1977). Sample size selection for exploratory social surveys.

New Zealand Statistician **12** (1): 10–16.

Day, R. A. (1988). *How to Write and Publish a Scientific Paper*. Oryx Press, Phoenix, Arizona.

Deddens, J. A. and Koch, G. G. (1988). Survival analysis, grouped data. *Encyclopedia of Statistical Sciences* **9**: 129–34.

DiCiccio, T. J. and Romano, J. P. (1988). A review of bootstrap confidence intervals. *Journal of the Royal Statistical Society* **B50**: 338–54.

Diggle, P. J. (1983). *Statistical Analysis of Spatial Point Processes*. Academic Press, London.

Diggle, P. J. and Milne, R. K. (1983). Bivariate Cox processes: some models for bivariate spatial point patterns. *Journal of the Royal Statistical Society* **B45**: 11–21.

Douglas, J. W. B. (1960). 'Premature' children at primary schools. *British Medical Journal* **1**: 1008–13.

Durbin, J. and Watson, G. S. (1951). Testing for serial correlation in least squares regression. *Biometrika* **38**: 159–78.

Dwass, M. (1957). Modified randomization tests for non-parametric hypotheses. *Annals of Mathematical Statistics* **28**: 181–7.

Eberhardt, L. L. (1978). Transect methods for population studies. *Journal of Wildlife Management* **42**: 1–31.

Eberhardt, L. L. and Thomas, J. M. (1991). Designing environmental field studies. *Ecological Monographs* **61**: 53–73.

Edgington, E. S. (1987). *Randomization Tests*, 2nd Edit. Marcel Dekker, New York.

Efron, B. (1979). Bootstrap methods: another look at the jackknife. *Annals of Statistics* **7**: 1–26.

Everitt, B. S. (1977). *The Analysis of Contingency Tables*. Chapman and Hall, London.

Fisher, R. A. (1925). *Statistical Methods for Research Workers*, 1st Edit. Oliver and Boyd, Edinburgh.

Fisher, R. A. (1935). *The Design of Experiments*, 1st Edit. Oliver and Boyd, Edinburgh.

Fisher, R. A. (1936). The coefficient of racial likeness and the future of craniometry. *Journal of the Royal Anthropological Institute* **66**: 57–63.

Freiman, J. A. Chalmers, T. C., Smith, H. and Kuebler, R. R. (1978). The importance of beta, the type II error, and the sample size in the design and interpretation of the randomized control trial. *New England Journal of Medicine* **299**: 690–4.

Genstat 5 Committee (1987). *GENSTAT 5 Reference Manual*. Clarenden Press, Oxford.

Gibbons, J. D. (1982). Distribution free methods. *Encyclopedia of Statistical Sciences* **2**: 400–8.

Gibbons, J. D. (1986). Randomness, tests of. *Encyclopedia of Statistical Sciences* **7**: 555–62.

Gilbert, R. O. (1987). *Statistical Methods for Environmental Pollution*

REFERENCES

Monitoring. Van Nostrand Reinhold, New York.

Gopen, G. D., and Swan, J. A. (1990). The science of scientific writing. *Science* **78**: 550–8.

Gray, H. L. and Schucany, W. R. (1972). *The Generalized Jackknife Statistic*. Marcel Dekker, New York.

Green, E. L. (1973). Location analysis of prehistoric Maya sites in northern British Honduras. *American Antiquity* **38**: 279–93.

Greenhouse, S. W. and Geisser, S. (1959). On methods in the analysis of profile data. *Psychometrika* **24**: 94–112.

Harris, R. J. (1985). *A Primer of Multivariate Statistics*, 2nd Edit. Academic Press, Orlando.

Harte, D. (1986). Statistical methods in road safety. In *Pacific Statistical Congress, proceedings* (eds. I. S. Francis, B. F. J. Manly and F. C. Lam) pp. 312–4. North-Holland, Amsterdam.

Hayne, D. W. (1949). Two methods for estimating populations from trapping records. *Journal of Mammalogy* **30**: 399–411.

Healy, M. J. R. (1988). *GLIM: An Introduction*. Clarenden Press, Oxford.

Heaney, R. P. and Dougherty, C. J. (1988). *Research for Health Professionals*. Iowa State University Press, Ames.

Higham, C. F. W., Kijngam, A. and Manly, B. F. J. (1982). Site location and site hierarchy in prehistoric Thailand. *Proceedings of the Prehistoric Society* **48**: 1–27.

Hinkley, D. V. (1983). Jackknife methods. *Encyclopedia of Statistical Sciences* **4**: 280–7.

Hochberg, Y. and Tamhane, A. C. (1987). *Multiple Comparison Procedures*. Wiley, New York.

Hodder, I. and Orton, C. (1976). *Spatial Analysis in Archaeology*. Cambridge University Press, Cambridge.

Hodge, S. D. and Moore, P. G. (1972). Data uncertainties and least squares regression. *Applied Statistics* **21**: 185–95.

Holland, P. W. and Rubin, D. B. (1986). Research designs and causal inference: on Lord's paradox. In *Survey Research Designs: Towards a Better Understanding of Their Costs and Benefits* (eds. R. W. Pearson and R. F. Boruch), pp. 7–37. Springer-Verlag Lecture Notes in Statistics **38**, Berlin.

Hurlbert, S. H. (1984). Pseudoreplication and the design of ecological field experiments. *Ecological Monographs* **54**: 187–211.

Hutchings, M. J. (1978). Standing crop and pattern in pure stands of *Mercurialis perennis* and *Rubus fruiticosus* in mixed deciduous woodland. *Oikos* **31**: 351–7.

Inhelder, B. and Piaget, J. (1958). *The Growth of Logical Thinking from Childhood to Adolescence*. Basic Books, New York.

International Statistical Institute (1986). Declaration on professional ethics. *International Statistical Review* **54**: 227–42.

Jolly, G. M. (1965). Explicit estimates from capture–recapture data with death and immigration – stochastic model. *Biometrika* **52**: 225–47.

Judge, G. G., Hill, R. C., Griffiths, W. E., Lutkepohl, H. and Lee, T. (1988). *Introduction to the Theory and Practice of Econometrics*. Wiley, New York.

Katz, M. J. (1985). *Elements of a Scientific Paper*. Yale University Press, New Haven.

Koch, G. G., Elashoff, J. D. and Amara, I. A. (1988). Repeated measurements – design and analysis. *Encyclopedia of Statistical Sciences* **8**: 46–73.

Knoke, D. and Burke, P. J. (1980). *Log-Linear Models*. Sage Publications, Beverly Hills.

Ku, H. H. and Kullback, S. (1974). Log-linear models in contingency table analysis. *American Statistician* **28**: 115–22.

Laing, R. M. (1987). *The Lockstitch Seam: a Model of the Geometric Structure and Tensile Behaviour*. Ph.D. Thesis, University of Otago.

Laing, R. M. and Pearshouse, C. (1987). Micro software development aids elucidating tensile behaviour of the lockstitch seam. *Textile Research Journal* **57**: 256–64.

Lemeshow, S. (1985). Nonresponse (in sample surveys). *Encyclopedia of Statistical Sciences* **6**: 333–6.

Lindsey, J. K. (1989). *The Analysis of Categorical Data Using Glim*. Springer-Verlag, Berlin.

Linton, L. R., Edgington, E. S. and Davies, R. W. (1989). A view of niche overlap amenable to statistical analysis. *Canadian Journal of Zoology* **67**: 55–60.

Lord, F. M. (1967). A paradox in the interpretation of group comparisons. *Psychological Bulletin* **68**: 304–5.

Lord, F. M. (1968). Statistical adjustments when comparing preexisting groups. *Psychological Bulletin* **72**: 336–7.

Lord, F. M. (1973). Lord's paradox. In *The Encyclopedia of Educational Evaluation* (eds. S. B. Anderson, S. Bell, and R. T. Murphy), pp. 232–6. Jossey-Bass, San Francisco.

Machin, D. and Campbell, M. J. (1987). *Statistical Tables for the Design of Clinical Trials*. Blackwell, Oxford.

Madansky, A. (1988). *Prescriptions for Working Statisticians*. Springer-Verlag, New York.

Madenjian, C. P., Jude, D. J. and Tesar, F. J. (1986). Intervention analysis of power plant impact on fish populations. *Canadian Journal of Fisheries and Aquatic Science* **43**: 819–29.

Mahon, R. (1980). Accuracy of catch-effort methods for estimating fish density and biomass in streams. *Environmental Biology of Fishes* **54**: 343–60.

Manly, B. F. J. (1985). *The Statistics of Natural Selection on Animal Populations*. Chapman and Hall, London.

REFERENCES

Manly, B. F. J. (1986). *Multivariate Statistical Methods: a Primer*. Chapman and Hall, London.

Manly, B. F. J. (1991). *Randomization and Monte Carlo Methods in Biology*. Chapman and Hall, London.

Manly, B. F. J. and McAlevey, L. (1987). A randomization alternative to the Bonferroni inequality with multiple F tests. In *Proceedings of the Second International Tampere Conference in Statistics* (eds. T. Pukkila and S. Puntanen), pp. 567–73. Department of Mathematical Sciences, University of Tampere, Finland.

Manly, B. F. J., McAlevey, L. and Stevens, D. (1986). A randomization procedure for comparing group means on multiple measurements. *British Journal of Mathematical and Statistical Psychology* **39**: 183–9.

Manly, B. F. J. and Shannon, A. G. (1974). An analogical replication of a Piagetian experiment on New Guineans. *Malaysian Journal of Education* **11**: 77–82.

Marquardt, D. W. and Snee, R. D. (1975). Ridge regression in practice. *American Statistician* **29**: 3–20.

Marx, B. D. and Smith, E. P. (1990). Weighted multicollinearity in logistic regression: diagnostics and biased estimation techniques with an example from lake acidification. *Canadian Journal of Fisheries and Aquatic Science* **47**: 1128–35.

McCullagh, P. and Nelder, J. A. (1989). *Generalized Linear Models*, 2nd Edit. Chapman and Hall, London.

McDonald, L. L. and Manly, B. F. J. (1989). Calibration of biased sampling procedures. In *Estimation and Analysis of Insect Populations* (eds. L. L. McDonald, B. F. J. Manly, J. Lockwood and J. Logan), pp. 467–83. Springer-Verlag, Berlin.

McKechnie, S. W., Ehrlich, P. R. and White, R. R. (1975). Population genetics of *Euphydryas* butterflies. I. Genetic variation and the neutrality hypothesis. *Genetics* **81**: 571–94.

McNemar, Q. (1955). *Psychological Statistics*. Wiley, New York.

Mead, R. (1988). *The Design of Experiments: Statistical Principles for Practical Applications*. Cambridge University Press, Cambridge.

Menkins, G. E. and Anderson, S. H. (1988). Estimation of small mammal population size. *Ecology* **69**: 1952–9.

Miller, J. I. and Taylor, B. J. (1989). *The Thesis Writer's Handbook*. Alcove Publishing Company, Oregon.

Miller, R. G. (1974). The jackknife – a review. *Biometrika* **61**: 1–15.

Miller, R. (1985). Multiple comparisons. *Encyclopedia of Statistical Sciences* **5**: 679–89.

Mohr, L. B. (1988). *Impact Analysis for Program Evaluation*. Dorsey Press, Chicago.

Montgomery, D. C. (1984). *Design and Analysis of Experiments*, 2nd Edit. Wiley, New York.

Nelder, J. A. and Wedderburn, R. W. M. (1972). Generalized linear models. *Journal of the Royal Statistical Society* A135: 370–84.

Neter, J., Wasserman, W. and Kutner, M. H. (1983). *Applied Linear Regression Models*. Irwin, Homewood, Illinois.

Noreen, E. W. (1989). *Computer Intensive Methods for Testing Hypotheses: an Introduction*. Wiley, New York.

Oldham, P. D. and Newell, D. J. (1977). Fluoridation of water supplies and cancer – a possible association? *Applied Statistics* 26: 125–35.

Otis, D. L., Burnham, K. P., White, G. C. and Anderson, D. R. (1978). Statistical inference from capture data on closed animal populations. *Wildlife Monographs*: 62.

Parr, W. C. and Schucany, W. R. (1980). The jackknife: a review. *International Statistical Review* 48: 73–8.

Payne, C. D. (ed.) (1987). *The GLIM System, Release 3.77*, Numerical Algorithms Group Ltd, Oxford.

Pearson, E. S. and Hartley, H. O. (1966). *Biometrika Tables for Statisticians*, Volume 1. Cambridge University Press, Cambridge.

Pearson, E. S. and Hartley, H. O. (1972). *Biometrika Tables for Statisticians*, Volume 2. Cambridge University Press, Cambridge.

Peterman, R. M. (1990). Statistical power analysis can improve fisheries research and management. *Canadian Journal of Fisheries and Aquatic Science* 47: 2–15.

Piantadosi, S., Byar, D. P. and Green,, S. B. (1988). The ecological fallacy. *American Journal of Epidemiology* 127: 893–904.

Pitman, E. J. G. (1937a). Significance tests that can be applied to samples from any distribution. *Journal of the Royal Statistical Society* B4: 119–30.

Pitman, E. J. G. (1937b). Significance tests that can be applied to samples from any distribution. II. The correlation coefficient test. *Journal of the Royal Statistical Society* B4: 225–32.

Pitman, E. J. G. (1937c). Significance tests that can be applied to samples from any distribution. III. The analysis of variance test. *Biometrika* 29: 322–35.

Pollock, K. H., Nichols, J. D., Brownie, C. and Hines, J. E. (1990). Statistical inference for capture–recapture experiments. *Wildlife Monographs* 107.

Powell, G. L. and Russell, A. P. (1984). The diet of the eastern short-horned lizard (*Phrynosoma douglassi brevirostre*) in Alberta and its relationship to sexual size dimorphism. *Canadian Journal of Zoology* 62: 428–40.

Powell, G. L. and Russell, A. P. (1985). Growth and sexual size dimorphism in Alberta populations of the eastern short-horned lizard, *Phrynosoma douglassi brevirostre*. *Canadian Journal of Zoology* 63: 139–54.

Quenouille, M. H. (1956). Notes on bias in estimation. *Biometrika* 43: 353–60.

REFERENCES

Rampino, M. R. and Stothers, R. B. (1984a). Terrestrial mass extinctions, cometary impacts and the sun's motion perpendicular to the galactic plane. *Nature* **308**: 709–12.

Rampino, M. R. and Stothers, R. B. (1984b). Geological rhythms and cometary impacts. *Science* **226**: 1427–31.

Ratkowsky, D. A. (1983). *Nonlinear Regression Modelling*. Marcel Dekker, New York.

Raup, D. M. and Sepkoski, J. J. (1984). Periodicity of extinctions in the geologic past. *Proceedings of the National Academy of Sciences* **81**: 801–5.

Rayner, J. C. W. and Best, D. J. (1989). *Smooth Tests of Goodness of Fit*. Oxford University Press, New York.

Rindskopf, D. (1987). A compact BASIC program for log-linear models. In *Computing Science and Statistics: Proceedings of the 19th Symposium on the Interface* (eds. R. M. Heiberger and M. T. Martin), pp. 381–6. American Statistical Association, Alexandria, Virginia.

Ripley, B. D. (1981). *Spatial Statistics*. Wiley, New York.

Riska, B. (1985). Group size factors and geographical variation of morphometric correlation. *Evolution* **39**: 792–803.

Robinson, W. S. (1950). Ecological correlations and the behaviour of individuals. *American Sociological Review* **15**: 351–7.

Rogers, A. (1974). *Statistical Analysis of Spatial Dispersion*. Pion, London.

Rosenbaum, P. R. (1989). The role of known effects in observational studies. *Biometrics* **45**: 557–69.

Savin, N. E. and White, K. J. (1977). The Durbin–Watson test for serial correlation with extreme sample sizes or many regressors. *Econometrica* **45**: 1989–96.

Scheaffer, R. L., Mendenhall, W. and Ott, L. (1990). *Elementary Survey Sampling*. 4th Edit. PWS-KENT, Boston.

Schuman, H. and Presser, S. (1981). *Questions and Answers in Attitude Surveys*. Academic Press, New York.

Seber, G. A. F. (1965). A note on the multiple-recapture census. *Biometrika* **52**: 249–59.

Seber, G. A. F. (1982a). Capture–recapture methods. *Encyclopedia of Statistical Sciences* **1**: 367–74.

Seber, G. A. F. (1982b). *Estimation of Animal Abundance and Related Parameters*, 2nd Edit. Griffin, London.

Seber, G. A. F. (1986). A review of estimating animal abundance. *Biometrics* **42**: 267–92.

Sharpley, C. F. (1986). Fallibility in the visual assessment of behavioural interventions: time series statistics to analyse time series data. *Behavioural Change* **3**: 26–33.

Sharpley, C. F. (1987). Time series analysis of behavioural data: an update. *Behavioural Change* **4**: 40–5.

Sharpley, C. F. and Alavosius, M. P. (1988). Autocorrelation in behavioural data: an alternative perspective. *Behavioural Assessment* **10**:

243–51.

Simpson, G. G., Roe, A. and Lewontin, R. C. (1960). *Quantitative Zoology*. Harcourt, Brace and World, New York.

Snedecor, G. W. and Cochran, W. G. (1980). *Statistical Methods*, 7th Edit. Iowa State University Press, Ames.

Snee, R. D. (1977). Validation of regression models: methods and examples. *Technometrics* **19**: 415–28.

Solow, A. R. (1989). Bootstrapping sparsely sampled spatial point patterns. *Ecology* **70**: 379–82.

Southwood, T. R. E. (1978). *Ecological Methods with Particular Reference to Insect Populations*, 2nd Edit. Chapman and Hall, London.

Stewart-Oaten, A., Murdoch, W. W. and Parker, K. R. (1986). Environmental impact assessment: 'pseudo-replication' in time? *Ecology* **67**: 929–40.

Stothers, R. (1979). Solar activity cycle during classical antiquity. *Astronomy and Astrophysics* **77**: 121–7.

Strand, L. (1972). *A model for stand growth*. IUFRO Third Conference Advisory Group of Statisticians. INRA, Paris, pp. 207–16.

'Student' (1931). The Lanarkshire milk experiment. *Biometrika* **23**: 389–406.

Sudman, S. and Bradburn, N. M. (1982). *Asking Questions: A Practical Guide to Questionnaire Design*. Jossey-Bass, San Francisco.

Taylor, J. (1931). Milk tests in Lanarkshire schools. *Nature* **127**: 466.

Tortora, S. D. (1985). Nonsampling errors in surveys. *Encyclopedia of Statistical Sciences* **6**: 336–40.

Tukey, J. W. (1958). Bias and confidence in not quite large samples (Abstract). *Annals of Mathematical Statistics* **29**: 614.

Upton, G. J. G. (1978). *The Analysis of Cross-Tabulated Data*. Wiley, New York.

Ware, J. H. (1989). Investigating therapies of potentially great benefit: ECMO. *Statistical Sciences* **4**: 298–340.

White, G. C., Anderson, D. R., Burnham, K. P. and Otis, D. L. (1982). *Capture–Recapture and Removal Methods for Sampling Closed Populations*. Los Alamos National Laboratory Report LA 8787-NERP, Los Alamos, New Mexico.

Winer, B. (1971). *Statistical Principles in Experimental Design*, 2nd Edit. McGraw-Hill, New York.

Yiamouyiannis, J. and Burk, D. (1977). Fluoridation and cancer: age-dependence of cancer mortality related to artificial fluoridation. *Fluoride* **10**: 102–25.

Younger, M. S. (1985). *A First Course in Linear Regression*. Duxbury Press, Boston.

Zelen, M. (1979). A new design for randomized clinical trials. *New England Journal of Medicine* **300**: 1242–5.

Zippin, C. (1956). An evaluation of the removal method of estimating animal populations. *Biometrics* **12**: 163–89.

Author index

AUTHOR INDEX

AUTHOR INDEX

Subject index

SUBJECT INDEX

for randomness of spatial points 58, 69, 72–5, 79, 85–6, 295–8
McNemar's test for correlated proportions 242–4
Monte Carlo, *see under* Monte Carlo methods
on regression residuals 107–8, 174
T^2 266
Time series, *see also under* experimental designs
autoregressive model 172
graphical analysis 168, 169, 175–6, 177
modelling 168, 175, 177
regression analysis 168, 170–171, 173–174, 175–176, 177

Transformation
arc-sine 199
general power (Box–Cox) 234
inverse tanh 300
logarithmic 106, 115, 199, 200, 229, 234
reciprocal 88, 99, 234
square root 199, 201, 234
with analysis of variance 199–201, 234
with regression 88, 99, 106

Variance to mean ratio 75–7, 79, 83–4

World standard population 186

Yates' correction 241–2